Inside the Common Core Classroom

Practical ELA Strategies for Grades K–2

Lesley Mandel Morrow

Rutgers, The State University of New Jersey

Erin Kramer

Amy Monaco

PEARSON

Boston • Columbus • Indianapolis • New York • San Francisco • Upper Saddle River
Amsterdam • Cape Town • Dubai • London • Madrid • Milan • Munich • Paris • Montréal • Toronto
Delhi • Mexico City • São Paulo • Sydney • Hong Kong • Seoul • Singapore • Taipei • Tokyo

Vice President and Editorial Director: Jeffery Johnston
Acquisitions Editor: Meredith Fossel
Editorial Assistant: Maria Feliberty
Executive Marketing Manager: Krista Clark
Program Manager: Karen Mason
Project Manager: Cynthia DeRocco
Editorial Production Service: Electronic Publishing Services Inc., NYC
Manufacturing Buyer: Deidra Skahill
Electronic Composition: Jouve
Interior Design: Electronic Publishing Services Inc., NYC
Photo Researcher: Jorgensen Fernandez
Cover Designer: Central Covers

Credits and acknowledgments borrowed from other sources and reproduced, with permission, in this textbook appear on the appropriate page within text or on page 200.

Cover Image Credit: © Monkey Business Images / Shutterstock

Note: Every effort has been made to provide accurate and current Internet information in this book. However, the Internet and information on it are constantly changing, so it is inevitable that some of the Internet addresses listed in this textbook will change.

Library of Congress Cataloging-in-Publication Data

Morrow, Lesley M.
  Inside the common core classroom : practical ELA strategies for grades K–2 / Lesley M. Morrow, Erin Kramer, Amy Monaco.
    pages cm
  Includes bibliographical references and index.
  ISBN 978-0-13-336299-2
 1. Language arts (Elementary)—United States.   2. Education, Elementary—Standards—United States.   3. Language arts—Correlation with content subjects—United States.   4. Curriculum planning. I. Title.
  LB1576.M796   2014
  375'.001—dc23
                                                                          2013038900

10 9 8 7 6 5 4 3 2 1

ISBN 10: 0-13-336299-X
ISBN 13: 978-0-13-336299-2

Dedications

Lesley Mandel Morrow

- *To my students from long ago and my students today, who have taught me so much about teaching.*

Erin Kramer

- *For Mom, my first and most important teacher.*

Amy Monaco

- *For my mom, Joanne, who filled my childhood with books, and for my husband, Matt, who is my favorite everything.*

Contents

Preface

WELCOME TO THE AGE OF THE COMMON CORE! Thank you for joining us in our quest to teach students to meet the Common Core English Language Arts (ELA) Standards.

This volume, *Inside the Common Core Classroom: Practical ELA Strategies for Grades K–2*, is part of Pearson's *College and Career Readiness Series*. The books in this series have been written for in-service teachers to support their implementation of the Common Core State Standards for English language arts in K–12 classrooms. The four volumes in the series address the standards in grades K–2, 3–5, 6–8, and 9–12, respectively.

The purpose of the series is to help teachers create connections between the Common Core and their school curriculums. Each book provides in-depth information about the standards at a particular grade-level band and offers examples of a variety of teaching ideas to support students' meeting the expectations of the ELA Standards.

About This Book

This book addresses the early childhood grades, kindergarten through grade 2, and the elements in the CCSS that are most important for these grades. The standards discussed, and the order in which they appear in this book, reflect what is important for students in early childhood.

Chapter 1 examines the development of skills in speaking, listening, and language. In fact, speaking/listening and language represent two different areas of the CCSS, but they fit well together. Oral language development is crucial for young children, and building vocabulary and learning the social skills of language lay the foundation for later skill development. Literacy begins with language.

Chapter 2 focuses on the development of foundational skills. This area of the CCSS is a major focus in the early childhood grades but less so in all of the later grades. Children need to learn phonemic awareness and phonics quickly in K–2 so they can become automatic, fluent readers. A good deal of time is spent on foundational skills in these grades, and students are expected to achieve these skills by the end of second grade. Reaching this benchmark allows the focus of literacy instruction to shift to reading comprehension and writing.

Reading comprehension of literature and of informational text are the topics of Chapters 3 and 4, respectively. Although children in K–2 are not yet automatic, fluent readers, the CCSS suggest that they can and should engage in thinking about the meaning of text, the author's purpose in writing, and how one book compares to other similar books that have been read to them or they have read themselves. Reading does not involve a set of isolated skills; rather, it involves constant engagement in a range of skills from early on.

Chapter 5 is about developing skills in writing. The CCSS give writing an important role in literacy development—as it deserves. Writing goes hand in hand with reading. Children study a variety of texts and use the styles of these texts as models for their own writing. The topics students are asked to write about are text related, as well. The CCSS reinforce in children the constant need to give evidence for understanding the texts they read, whether they respond in discussion or writing.

Another hallmark of the CCSS is the integration of literacy instruction into the content areas. Language arts and literacy skills are vital to learning in the content areas. An important way to integrate literacy instruction into the content areas is through the use of thematic units.

Chapter 6 discusses the use of themes, which are usually developed in social studies or science and explore topics such as the weather and plants. In the context of a theme, reading and writing are more than just isolated skills. Rather, they prove relevant tools for use in accomplishing real-life tasks.

Finally, Chapter 7 turns to the importance of using the CCSS throughout the school day by describing activities in a first-grade classroom in which young children are engaged in literacy activities across the curriculum. It must be the goal of early childhood teachers to have children be fluent readers by the end of third grade. We know that if the children are not reading at grade level by then, it will be difficult for them to achieve grade level later. This last chapter has a very important message for teachers in the primary grades: You must teach reading all day long. In addition to providing explicit instruction, use art, music, science, social studies, and the other content areas to help you teach reading. Children are highly motivated to read when they are reading for a meaningful purpose.

Acknowledgments

We would like to thank Barbara Strickland, Cynthia DeRocco, Kathryn Boice, and Meredith Fossel of Pearson Education as well as Katie Watterson at Electronic Publishing Services.

We would also like to thank the reviewers for this first edition: Helen Comba, School District of the Chathams (Chatham, NJ) and Kenneth Kunz, Bloomfield College.

Introduction

Donna Ogle

THE COMMON CORE STATE STANDARDS (CCSS) provide a challenging set of expectations that public schools must meet to ensure that all students can be successful in meeting the literacy demands of the twenty-first century. The CCSS also make clear that developing literacy is a shared responsibility and challenge educators to think and work together to meet these expectations. As part of the extended reach of the CCSS, the English Language Arts (ELA) standards include literacy in science, social studies, and technical subjects as integral to this process. These standards underscore the reality that skills in reading, writing, and oral language are needed across the content areas. The ELA CCSS invite teachers to work together within and across grade levels and content areas to ensure that students will meet these expectations.

Erin Kramer

Across the United States, the national, state, and local organizations that have taken this challenge seriously are in the process of analyzing current curricula and adjusting the foci of instruction and expected student outcomes according to these new needs and demands. The two national assessment consortia—the Partnership for Assessment of Readiness for College and Career (PARCC, n.d.) and SMARTER Balance (n.d.)—are in the process of designing new assessment systems, which will be administered for the first time during the 2014–2015 school year. These consortia have suggested how school curricula should be organized to encompass the broad-reaching outcomes elaborated in the CCSS. Taking the CCSS seriously means making some significant adjustments in how our schools have focused on literacy and the kinds of literacy-related opportunities they provide. Our students deserve this support. They want to be successful both within and beyond schooling, and we want them to have this success.

Defining the Need for the Change

THE CCSS DESCRIBE IN GRADE-BY-GRADE DETAIL the wide range of competencies that literacy entails and that teachers need to develop in their students. The starting point for this effort is central to the standards' importance: What is required of students to be college and career ready?

Several research reports over the last decade have alerted interested educators to the decline in difficulty of many school texts and to the challenge faced by students with low reading proficiency when they take college-level tests. In fact, Appendix A of the CCSS cites a 2006 ACT report, *Reading Between the Lines,* to illustrate this two-part problem (NGA & CCSSO, 2010b, Appendix A, p. 2). Recognizing this problem led the developers of the CCSS to collect texts being used by students in freshmen-level college/university courses and by individuals entering the workforce after high school. These texts were compared with high school texts and the types and difficulty levels of assigned student work.

In this analysis, the CCSS developers identified a significant gap between the work required of upper-level high school students and the expectations for success in college and career. (See Appendix A of the CCSS for elaboration on this issue [NGA & CCSSO, 2010b].) The CCSS were then developed with this end point in mind: to determine the level of language arts development needed at each grade level for students to be prepared for these greater literacy demands and thus ready for college and career.

After the CCSS had been written, they were reviewed by college faculty who teach freshman- and sophomore-level courses, who gave the standards high marks. Interestingly, in addition to the need for students to read informational texts critically and to write effective analytical essays (not personal reflection pieces), these faculty rated the oral communication skills identified in the CCSS as particularly important.

The fact that perspectives from higher education and the workforce were included in developing the CCSS is important. The standards make this connection very clear: Students need to be college and career ready.

The CCSS are significant in another way, too. Since the first round of standards was developed in the late 1990s, individual states have crafted their own standards and measured achievement with their own state-specific assessments. The only comparison of achievement across states has been made by the National Assessment of Educational Progress (NAEP), and these evaluations have regularly revealed huge state-by-state differences in literacy achievement. Now, with the CCSS, we have, for the first time, a set of standards that has been adopted by most states across the country.

This high level of adoption will help all educators evaluate their success and feel confident that their students are receiving a high-quality education that will serve them beyond public school. Both the standards and the assessments being developed can help all educators engage in a shared conversation and commitment to excellence. Rather than relying on the current patchwork of state standards, the CCSS bring together a common set of standards and permit the development of more common assessments.

Expectations for Literacy Achievement

AS THE UNITED STATES MOVES FORWARD WITH THE NEW STANDARDS, all educators need to be involved and take seriously new expectations for the future. The CCSS raise the bar for student literacy achievement in several ways:

- Reading comprehension is at the heart of the new standards. To be college and career ready, students must understand challenging texts and attend to authors' ideas and ways of presenting information. In the CCSS Reading standards, three clusters identify these foci: Key Ideas and Details, Craft and Structure, and Integration of Knowledge and Ideas. For both literature and informational texts, readers are expected to engage in careful reading of the ideas presented, to recall main ideas and details, to recognize the organization of information and author's craft, and to synthesize and critically respond to what they have read.

- This expectation for greater understanding is heightened by the expectation that students will read texts at a more accelerated level of difficulty than currently designated for grade levels by readability formulas and reading anthologies. For twelfth-grade texts, the expected level will be about 200 Lexile points higher than the current level.

- The CCSS also devote greater attention to reading informational text, so it receives equal coverage as reading fictional literature. Most elementary programs and secondary language arts courses have been developed primarily around fictional/narrative literature. The CCSS create a broader framework for literacy development that includes the content areas, especially social studies, science, and technical subjects. With two sets of standards for reading—one for literature and one for informational text—this shift in foci to informational texts and to the importance of using reading to build knowledge is clear. At the secondary level, the CCSS differentiate expectations for literacy development in social studies, science, and technical subjects. The curriculum design from PARCC (n.d.), which establishes four basic modules, includes a balance of informational and literary texts across the modules.

- The CCSS emphasize not only the understanding of individual texts but also the importance of reading across texts to look for different authors' purposes and the evidence authors provide in support of their ideas. Students who read only one text on a topic or theme have little opportunity to learn about how authors can vary in terms of purpose and presentation of ideas. The CCSS clearly advocate that students should read several texts on the same topic or theme. In addition, completing quarterly research projects provides individuals with opportunities to search for information across multiple texts and media sources and to use that information critically in their reporting.

- The shift in how information is communicated in the twenty-first century is also recognized in the CCSS. We live in a visual society: All sorts of images try to inform us and persuade us. The ability to use visual and graphic information thoughtfully is expected of students. In fact, visual images can be powerful motivators to engage students in thoughtful analyses of how ideas are communicated to us and influence us. Across the content areas, readers are also expected to use electronic sources in building their knowledge in presenting information and completing research projects.

- There is also a shift in focus in the writing standards from writing personal narratives to writing expository and argumentative texts. Students need to be able to use evidence to support their arguments, as well as to recognize possible alternative points of view. In addition, writing is now being used as a way of measuring students' reading comprehension. Students need to think about the meanings of the texts they read, how authors present and support ideas, and what counter-arguments and evidence are provided.

- Although speaking and listening have always been part of the language arts, the CCSS recognize the importance of these communication tools. This priority is evident in the Speaking and Listening Standards and also embedded in the expectations that students discuss what they read at every grade level and learn to report to classmates what they learn from individual research projects. The preliminary assessment design from PARCC (n.d.) includes a school-based assessment of oral skills midway through the year. Even though these skills are difficult to measure using large-scale assessments, they are important. The value of speaking and listening skills has been well established by the university and workplace communities.

- The CCSS also include expectations for vocabulary. Specifically, students should learn and use standard forms of English and appropriate general academic and domain-specific vocabulary in both writing and oral language. Vocabulary and word-learning strategies need to be developed concurrently with the knowledge and content literacy standards, especially as related to the domain-specific terms students need to know to understand the content of science, social studies, and technical subjects.

Implementing the CCSS

IMPLEMENTING THE CCSS REPRESENTS A SIGNIFICANT CHALLENGE TO TEACHERS and schools. To address the difficulty of this task, many states have put together teams to guide their thinking about what is already being done and what needs to be adjusted in the current curriculum to meet expectations for literacy in the twenty-first century. Other educational organizations have also made significant efforts to help in the development of curriculum and instructional frameworks—for example, the Lucas Foundation, Annenberg Foundation, Alliance for Effective Education, AchieveNY, Gates Foundation, International Reading Association, and National Council of Teachers of English.

Publishers have responded, as well, by reorienting materials to reflect the broader expectation for responding to texts and by including more academic writing and attention to content. An interesting publisher's initiative has brought together teacher teams from school districts and used their materials to reorganize the content and rewrite the questions in the published programs to align more closely with the CCSS.

The major goal of all of these efforts is to better prepare students for college and careers. Doing so requires addressing the range of texts students read, the depth of thinking they do, and the styles of writing they perform. Given these new and challenging expectations, professionals across the educational system need to collaborate in helping students from preschool through grade 12 develop the competencies, commitment, and confidence needed for life beyond high school.

Rethinking the Complexity of the Texts Students Read

The issue of text complexity is central to the CCSS and one that deserves study by teachers and school teams. Students need to engage in more challenging texts at each grade level, at least beyond the primary grades, and they need to read more informational texts, which are rich in content.

The authors of the CCSS have tried to move away from a single, numerically derived formula for determining the appropriate reading levels of texts of all kinds. According to the CCSS, three criteria should be considered when determining the level of any text:

1. **Qualitative evaluation of the text:** levels of meaning, structure, language conventionality and clarity, and knowledge demands

2. **Quantitative evaluation of the text:** readability measures and other scores of text complexity

3. **Matching the reader to the text and the task:** reader variables (e.g., motivation, knowledge, and experiences) and task variables (e.g., the purpose and complexity of the task assigned and the questions posed) (NGA & CCSSO, 2010b, p. 4).

Appendix B of the CCSS (NGA & CCSSO, 2010c) provides lists of illustrative books that have been "leveled." The purpose of these lists is not to imply that these books should be used in the schools, but rather to identify books that are familiar to the educational community. However, teachers who want simply to select books from these lists need to remember the third criterion: matching the reader to the text and the task.

Given the variety of interests, experiences, and needs of students across the United States, many teachers will want to use contemporary, high-interest materials to motivate students to think and reflect deeply about important issues. Moreover, instead of permitting students to read only books at their designated levels (based on Lexiles or Fountas & Pinnell scores), teachers will ask students in the intermediate grades and higher to read several books or articles on the same topic, beginning with a comfortable-level book/article and then using the knowledge they have developed to read more difficult texts on the same topic.

Using this strategy is certainly one way to help students increase their reading power. The CCSS guidelines also provide models of how teachers can engage groups of students in close readings of anchor texts or targeted short texts. When teachers regularly model an analytical and questioning approach to reading, students will likely follow the same approach. It is also important that students engage with a large quantity of texts, finding their own favorite authors and experiencing the joy of being real readers.

Organizing Instruction into Content-Rich Units

The range and complexity of literacy standards included in the CCSS has prompted many organizations (e.g., PARCC and SMARTER Balance), as well as school districts and state education departments (e.g., Wisconsin Department of Public Instruction), to reorganize their literacy priorities to align with the CCSS by designing units with content-related themes and topics. Using this approach, instruction in literacy is combined with instruction in social studies and science. Many school districts have asked teams of teachers to develop one unit as a starting point with plans to expand this effort over time.

A clear message from the developers of the CCSS is that students need to be engaged in learning content in social studies, science, and technical subjects at a deeper level than is now often the case. In the CCSS guidelines, the final section about the elementary standards is entitled "Staying on Topic Within a Grade and Across Grades: How to Build Knowledge Systematically in English Language Arts K–5" (NGA & CCSSO, 2010a, p. 33). Included in this section is a matrix illustrating how students should encounter the same topic (in this example, the human body) at increasingly deeper levels across all of the grades. This shift in combining attention to content knowledge with literacy development is one of the hallmarks of the CCSS.

While combining these purposes makes good sense, it means that schools must expand efforts at integrating reading and writing with content area instruction. Classroom and school libraries should contain ample amounts of informational books and magazines at a variety of levels of complexity so that all students have access to the materials needed to develop deep knowledge. As the CCSS authors explain in the section "Staying on Topic Within a Grade and Across Grades":

> Building knowledge systematically in English language arts is like giving children various pieces of a puzzle in each grade that, over time, will form one big picture. At a curricular or instructional level, texts—within and across grade levels—need to be selected around topics or themes that systematically develop the knowledge base of students. Within a grade level, there should be an adequate number of titles on a single topic that would allow children to study that topic for a sustained period. The knowledge children have learned about particular topics in early grade levels should then be expanded and developed in subsequent grade levels to ensure an increasingly deeper understanding of these topics. Children in the upper elementary grades will generally be expected to read these texts independently and reflect on them in writing. However, children in the early grades (particularly K–2) should participate in rich, structured conversations with an adult in response to the written texts that are read aloud, orally comparing and contrasting as well as analyzing and synthesizing, in the manner called for by the *Standards*. (NGA & CCSSO, 2010a, p.33)

At the secondary level, there is an even greater expectation for students to develop the strategies necessary for reading the varied texts and materials that contain the key content of disciplinary study. Reading primary source documents in history and science is a central part of students' literacy engagement. Also, the texts used in math and science require students to analyze a variety of visual displays, including equations, tables, diagrams, and graphs. As noted in the Carnegie Report *Writing to Read* (Graham & Hebert, 2010), for students to comprehend and produce these types of texts, they must be immersed in the language and thinking processes of these disciplines and they must be supported by an expert guide: their teacher.

Given the expectation for students to develop the competence needed to comprehend the wide variety of texts that is required for success in and beyond schooling, it is clear that the responsibility for literacy development cannot reside solely with English language arts teachers. Meeting this expectation requires both the development of foundational knowledge that makes deep learning possible and the skills needed to read a wide variety of text types and formats across the disciplines. The CCSS challenge all content area teachers to accept their part in developing the literacy skills, dispositions, discipline-specific discourse, and academic vocabulary requisite for students to become independent learners. The more often that elementary and secondary reading/literacy coaches team up with their content area colleagues, the more likely that CCSS goals will be met by providing interesting and positive instructional experiences for students.

The thematic-unit framework provides students with the opportunity to read several texts on the same theme or topic and build their background knowledge of a specific topic. Spending more time on a specific topic also helps students to deepen their knowledge of the content and become familiar with the academic and domain-specific vocabulary central to that learning. In addition, by reading across several texts, students can develop their understanding of the ways different authors select materials to include in particular texts and then organize that information, as well as the value of reading deeply to build clear understanding of complex ideas.

Having these commitments to reading makes students' written and oral communications much stronger. Students know what they are explaining and have options to represent their ideas, including visual, graphic, and oral formats. This ability to develop one's own understanding based on research and then to present one's ideas is woven into the four research projects students are expected to do each year. In addition, the CCSS directive to engage in a deeper study of topics encourages teachers to vary the kinds of learning experiences they provide for their students—differentiating texts/materials, activities, products, and assessments (Tomlinson's framework).

Engaging in Schoolwide Collaboration for Change

The challenges and cross-content literacy expectations of the CCSS can be achieved within a long-range timeframe and with the understanding that they will develop over the course of students' schooling. Realizing these requisites for achievement can unite teachers. The CCSS underscore the importance of involving teams of educators representing all grade levels, special services (e.g., English language learning, special education, library and media), and content areas in studying the CCSS, analyzing their implications, and designing ways to implement them over time.

Discussing the CCSS across grade levels is a good way to start. Providing visual displays that trace the same standard across different grades will help teachers to understand the structure and rationale that underlie the CCSS. An example follows using Standard 2 of the elementary Anchor Standards for Reading, which appears in the cluster Key Ideas and Details:

Standard 2: Determine central ideas or themes of a text and analyze their development; summarize the key supporting details and ideas.

Table I.1 shows the grade-level expectations for Standard 2 for reading both literature and informational text for kindergarten through fifth grade, allowing examination of the expectations across grades.

TABLE I.1 ● *Anchor Standards for Reading, Key Ideas and Details, Standard 2:* K–Grade 5

Kindergarten	First Grade	Second Grade
Literature 2. With prompting and support, retell familiar stories, including key details	**Literature** 2. Retell stories, including key details, and demonstrate understanding of their central message or lesson	**Literature** 2. Recount stories, including fables and folktales from diverse cultures, and determine their central message, lesson, or moral.
Informational Text 2. With prompting and support, identify the main topic and retell key details of a text.	**Informational Text** 2. Identify the main topic and retell key details of a text.	**Informational Text** 2. Identify the main topic of a multiparagraph text as well as the focus of specific paragraphs within the text.

Third Grade	Fourth Grade	Fifth Grade
Literature 2. Recount stories, including fables, folktales, and myths from diverse cultures; determine the central message, lesson, or moral and explain how it is conveyed through key details in the text	**Literature** 2. Determine a theme of a story, drama, or poem from details in the text; summarize the text.	**Literature** 2. Determine a theme of a story, drama, or poem from details in the text, including how characters in a story or drama respond to challenges or how the speaker in a poem reflects upon a topic; summarize the text.
Informational Text 2. Determine the main idea of a text; recount the key details and explain how they support the main idea.	**Informational Text** 2. Determine the main idea of a text and explain how it is supported by key details; summarize the text.	**Informational Text** 2. Determine two or more main ideas of a text and explain how they are supported by key details; summarize the text.

Source: NGA & CCSSO (2010).

Clearly, within Standard 2, there is a gradual progression of difficulty from kindergarten through fifth grade. At each grade level, there is the same basic expectation—that students learn to retell stories and identify main ideas—but the level of the expectation varies. In kindergarten, the teacher is clearly involved with the students, providing prompting and support. By first grade, students are expected to retell independently, and by second grade, they are expected to do so for a wider range of materials. By fifth grade, students are expected to apply this skill with drama, and in reading informational text, they are expected to identify two main ideas.

While the spiraling nature of these expectations may seem somewhat arbitrary, looking across grade levels and text types should indicate the sense of shared effort that is needed among teachers. In addition, it should provide a starting point for conversations about what students are able to do and what they need to learn to ensure ongoing development in reading comprehension. No one grade level of teachers is responsible for students' mastery of any standard, but across the grades, teachers should guide students in using reading skills in increasingly challenging and varied materials. Teachers should think together to find ways to help students apply their abilities to retell stories and identify main ideas/supporting details in the texts they read each year.

Just as it is important for teams of teachers to look at the standards' expectations for skill development across the grades, it is important for them to read across the areas within the CCSS. In contrast to the orientation in some districts and schools, in which teaching focuses on one standard at a time, the areas within the CCSS are interrelated and build on each other. Not only are standards provided for both literature and informational text, but in addition, many key expectations are scattered across the reading, writing, and language standards. For example, a cluster called Integration of Knowledge and Ideas is included in the standards for Reading Literature, Reading Informational Text, Writing, and Speaking and Listening. The cluster Integration of Knowledge and Ideas appears in the two groups of Reading standards. However, the research standards are an important place where integration occurs and where students are held accountable for using this ability.

The Speaking and Listening Standards address the importance of students creating visual and media displays—both skills that are often overlooked in contemporary literacy instruction in the elementary grades. In the past, visual and media literacy seem to have been the purview of secondary instruction, but in the CCSS, they are introduced in the early elementary grades. Highlighting this aspect of integration will likely prompt some important reflection among teachers: Just how are students encouraged to interpret visuals and to use media displays to augment their presentations?

Some important instructional areas that teachers are accustomed to seeing as parts of reading development are embedded elsewhere in the CCSS. Vocabulary, for example, does not have a separate set of standards, as do reading literature and writing, yet developing vocabulary skills is very important and is addressed in several sections of the CCSS. Teacher teams might begin by studying the Language Standards section, Vocabulary Acquisition and Use, with its focus on learning academic and domain-specific vocabulary, and then locate other places in the standards where vocabulary skills are addressed.

In addition, teacher teams need to consider carefully the expectation to include science, social studies, and technical subjects that is part of their responsibility in implementing these new more content-focused standards. Some states, such as Wisconsin, have developed their own extensions of the CCSS (Wisconsin Department of Public Instruction, n.d.), and these models can provide valuable resources as school teams examine their curriculum options and make decisions about how to move forward.

Figure I.1 provides several illustrations of how the standards in various sections and clusters are connected. In each example, the Anchor Standard is provided first, followed by the grade-level expectations for one or more grades (as noted in parentheses at the end of each description).

Assessment in the CCSS

IN RECOGNIZING THE DEPTH OF THE CCSS and the high level of expectations for students' literacy development, teachers need to monitor the pace of their instruction carefully, challenging students on a regular basis but not overwhelming them. Similarly, assessment must be ongoing without overwhelming instruction.

Assessment should be formative, thus helping teachers modify their instruction. The best formative assessment is rooted in instruction and depends on teachers being adept at gathering information from students' classroom engagement and work. Throughout this series of books,

FIGURE I.1 ● Examples of Connections Across the CCSS

Anchor Standards for Reading

Integration of Knowledge and Ideas

Standard 7: Integrate and evaluate content presented in diverse media and formats, including visually and quantitatively, as well as in words.

- *Literature:* Analyze how visual and multimedia elements contribute to the meaning, tone, or beauty of a text (e.g., graphic novel, multimedia presentation of fiction, folktale, myth, poem) (grade 5).
- *Informational Text:* Explain how specific images (e.g., a diagram showing how a machine works) contribute to and clarify a text (grade 2).

Anchor Standards for Writing

Research to Build and Present Knowledge

Standard 8: Gather relevant information from multiple print and digital sources, assess the credibility and accuracy of each source, and integrate the information while avoiding plagiarism.

Text Types and Purposes

Standard 2: Write informative/explanatory texts to examine a topic and convey ideas and information clearly and accurately through the effective selection, organization, and analysis of content.

a. Introduce a topic clearly, provide a general observation and focus, and group related information logically; include formatting (e.g., headings), illustrations, and multimedia when useful to aiding comprehension (grade 5).

Anchor Standards for Speaking and Listening

Presentation of Knowledge and Ideas

Standard 5: Make strategic use of digital media and visual displays of data to express information and enhance understanding of presentations.

- Create audio recordings of stories or poems; add drawings or other visual displays to stories or recounts of experiences when appropriate to clarify ideas, thoughts, and feelings (grade 2).

Source: NGA & CCSSO, 2010.

the authors provide examples of ways to assess students' readiness and learning of key content and strategies. Assessment is an area in which teacher/administrative discussions and decisions are critically important.

In addition, the requirements of the CCSS include large-scale comparative assessments to ensure that schools across the country have the same expectations of students. These assessments involve students in responding to a variety of texts and in formulating some of their responses in writing. In fact, one of the most important changes in assessment prompted by the CCSS is the use of students' written responses to measure their reading comprehension. Achieving this deeper look at students' comprehension is complicated by several pragmatic issues, such as the time and cost involved in scoring students' writing. Regardless, this approach is certainly a major part of the assessment systems being designed. Assessment systems for research (using technology) and speaking and listening are also still being developed, so these are other areas in which teachers and informal classroom assessments will continue to be important.

Using These Books to Enhance Study of the CCSS

THIS SERIES OF TEACHER RESOURCE BOOKS WAS created in response to the invitation issued by the CCSS for literacy educators to refocus the instruction they provide to help prepare students for college and career. These books are intended to support teachers, administrators, and teacher teams as they look across grade levels while designing CCSS-responsive instruction.

As noted earlier, the CCSS expect teachers to think broadly about the impact of their instruction and the foundation they lay for students' future literacy development. For many teachers, meeting this expectation will be a challenge, and these books can provide guidance in several areas: adjusting instruction, adding reading and writing of informational text, creating content-rich instructional units, and assessing students in different ways.

In writing the four books in this series, the authors have been conscious of the importance of helping teachers build across grade levels. These books can be used together to support a rich discussion and analysis. When possible, the authors have included the same major chapters on comprehension, writing, vocabulary, language, and other areas of the CCSS. Teachers at different grade levels can read about the particular expectations for their levels and consider appropriate examples and instructional suggestions. Then, in discussions with teachers of other grade levels, they can learn from others and think through how to create the most supportive instructional sequence and organization using themes and content units. The books are very practical and include activities and frameworks that teachers can use to help students become competent in using literacy for pleasure and for learning.

These books are not intended to be used alone; rather, teachers should read them while studying the CCSS. To begin, all teachers should download the CCSS and appendices so they are accessible and can be referred to regularly (see URLs for these materials in the References). In addition, the standards and related tools are available on several useful apps from organizations such as Mastery Connect and Learning Unlimited (again, see the References). It is also helpful to bookmark the websites for PARCC (n.d.) and SMARTER Balanced (n.d.) and then check with them periodically. In fact, so many resource sites are coming online that it is worth checking from time to time to see what might be worth reviewing. School districts, educational organizations, and state departments of education are developing instructional units and often make them available (or at least provide some of the structural components).

Much within the CCSS themselves also deserves careful analysis, study, and discussion among teachers of all grades. These efforts should lead to an identification of what is already in the curriculum and where instruction is currently aligned versus misaligned with the CCSS. Teachers must bear in mind that with the central focus on understanding texts, assessments need to be refocused, too. Specifically, schools should ask students to respond in writing to the content of the stories and articles they read so that a baseline can be developed to guide instructional decisions and the time allotted to each aspect of engagement with texts. Many states and districts have developed pilot assessments to ascertain how well their students do on tasks similar to those proposed by the two large consortia: PARCC and SMARTER Balanced. All teachers will find it useful to review the development of the assessments periodically and to compare them to the tools they use to assess their own students.

In designing this series of books, we have attempted to focus on the most important aspects of the CCSS and to provide a set of instructional strategies and tools that will help teachers adjust their instruction as needed to address these standards. Most of these strategies and tools have been tested by teachers and research studies and can therefore be used reliably, and others are variations of good instructional practices that reflect particular emphases of the CCSS. Some of these strategies and tools may seem familiar to teachers and have perhaps already been incorporated into their instructional routines. Regardless, these measures now take on added importance, because they can help align instruction with the expectations of the CCSS and the requirements of the assessments currently being developed.

It is important for teachers to develop a few strong instructional routines that allow them to observe and monitor students' growth over time. These routines should underscore the components of good reading comprehension, thereby helping students adopt them as regular reading practices. It is also important for teachers to keep students central in planning. Students should be able to see the purpose in whatever they are asked to do, and they should be involved in the assessment of their learning needs and achievements. Moreover, students' particular interests and experiences should be honored in classroom activities and other forms of engagement.

The CCSS provide an opportunity for teachers and districts to rethink the priorities, emphases, and assessments that are currently in place and to review how students are already engaged. The CCSS also challenge schools to look at the materials being used and the collaboration taking place across disciplines in the development of students' literacy. As stated in the beginning of this Introduction, the CCSS present both an opportunity and a challenge. It is up to educators to respond thoughtfully and with vision and commitment to all students.

REFERENCES

American College Testing (ACT). (2006). *Reading between the lines: What the ACT reveals about college readiness in reading.* Iowa City, IA: Author.

Graham, S., & Hebert, M. (2010). *Writing to read: Evidence for how writing can improve reading. A Carnegie Corporation Time to Act Report.* Washington, DC: Alliance for Excellent Education. Retrieved from http://carnegie.org/fileadmin/Media/Publications/WritingToRead_01.pdf.

Learning Unlimited. (n.d.). Learning Unlimited Common Core resources. *Learning Unlimited.* Retrieved from www.learningunlimitedllc.com/common-core.

Mastery Connect. (n.d.). Goodies. *Mastery Connect.* Retrieved from www.masteryconnect.com/learn-more/goodies.html.

National Assessment Governing Board. (2008). Reading framework for the 2009 National Assessment of Educational Progress. Washington, DC: U.S. Government Printing Office.

National Governors Association Center for Best Practices & Council of Chief State School Officers (NGA & CCSSO). (2010a). *Common Core State Standards.* Washington, DC: Authors. Retrieved from www.corestandards.org/assets/CCSSI_ELA%20Standards.pdf.

National Governors Association Center for Best Practices & Council of Chief State School Officers (NGA & CCSSO). (2010b). Appendix A, *Common Core State Standards.* Washington, DC: Authors. Retrieved from www.corestandards.org/assets/Appendix_A.pdf.

National Governors Association Center for Best Practices & Council of Chief State School Officers (NGA & CCSSO). (2010c). Appendix B, *Common Core State Standards.* Washington, DC: Authors. Retrieved from www.corestandards.org/assets/Appendix_B.pdf.

Partnership for Assessment of Readiness for College and Careers (PARCC). (n.d.). *PARCC.* Retrieved from www.parcconline.org.

SMARTER Balanced Assessment Consortium. (n.d.). Common Core State Standards Tools & Resources. *SMARTER Balanced.* Retrieved from www.smarterbalanced.org/k-12-education/common-core-state-standards-tools-resources.

Wisconsin Department of Public Instruction. (n.d.) Common Core State Standards. *Wisconsin Department of Public Instruction.* Retrieved from http://standards.dpi.wi.gov/stn_ccss.

chapter 1

Speaking, Listening, and Language Development

WE BEGIN WITH A DISCUSSION OF LISTENING, SPEAKING, and language development. In this section, we combine two of the CCSS Anchor Standards, since many of the standards in these categories are similar in K–2 and some don't apply at these grade levels. The Common Core State Standards for Speaking and Listening are addressed along with the standards for Language. The next area is Foundational Skills, followed by a chapter on comprehension of narrative literature, which addresses the Reading Standards for Literature, a chapter on comprehension of informational literature, which addresses the Reading Standards for Informational Text, and finally, Writing.

Erin Kramer

Speaking, Listening, and Language Development

THIS SECTION COMBINES DISCUSSION OF THE SPEAKING AND Listening standards with the Vocabulary Acquisition and Use category in the Language standards. In early childhood, we help children to acquire initial literacy skills. In this chapter, we discuss the acquisition of expressive and receptive language, or speaking and listening, which are a part of the beginnings of literacy.

In early childhood, listening and speaking establish the foundation not only for literacy development, but also for academic success (Dickinson & Tabors, 2001; Roskos, Tabors, & Leinhart, 2009). A child's proficiency in speaking and listening is demonstrated by his or her ability to learn many new vocabulary words each week, to apply the correct syntax (i.e., grammar), and to understand social aspects of language use (e.g., when it is appropriate to speak, what is appropriate to say in a certain situation). Research has shown that a child's success in literacy can be predicted at the age of 3 based on the number of words in his or her speaking vocabulary. It is also known that children from high socioeconomic status (SES) backgrounds have twice as many words in their vocabularies at 3 years old than children from so-called at-risk backgrounds (Hart & Risley, 1995). Throughout the early childhood years, children must learn vocabulary and syntax in order to have coherent conversations.

Standard 1 of the Speaking and Listening standards addresses the conventions that govern how conversations are co-constructed by communication partners. Collaboration is an important element of communication for children to learn because it allows them to participate in conversations. Having a conversation involves a number of skills, such as initiating or establishing a topic, maintaining focus and making relevant contributions to the topic, and ultimately, terminating a topic. Individuals in a conversation need to be both collaborative and cooperative, with participants communicating relevant and clear information to one another.

Children have to learn rules related to direct and indirect speech and the roles that speakers and listeners are expected to take in different contexts. *Direct speech* is a direct request or direction to do something, such as "Get me my shoes." *Indirect speech* is a request or direction intended to result in the same action but made in a polite way—for example, "My shoes are where you are standing. Will you please bring them over to me?"

Children must also understand that a speaker's role in a conversation determines what vocabulary words are used and how information is presented. For example, a child must learn that casual, familiar language can be used with peers at recess (e.g., "Hey, how you doin'?") but not with a teacher (e.g., "Good morning, Ms. Hill. How are you?").

Conversational rules take time to learn. Young children, particularly those in pre-K and kindergarten, are not yet able to use the rules of conversation. Children learn them within conversational contexts from adults who have the responsibility of modeling the rules, conventions, and roles of conversational partners. Predictable contexts and routines provide children with opportunities to practice their emerging conversational skills. In these contexts, teachers may scaffold children's developing speaking attempts. It is important to recognize that young children make more coherent contributions to a conversation when they are talking about an activity in which they are currently participating or a topic for which they have prior information or experience.

A conversation consists of both speaking and listening. Children need to learn how to construct conversations so their discussions become increasingly more complex. Children need to stay on topic, avoiding the common practice of beginning with one idea and then introducing other new ideas within a short period of time (Gillam & Reutzel, 2013).

The complexity of children's language must also develop. Therefore, in addition to acquiring many new vocabulary words each week, children must expand their understanding of language structure, moving from simple sentences to those that contain adjectives, adverbs, prepositional phrases, and dependent clauses (Biemiller, 2006; Fernald & Weisleder, 2011; Harris, Golinkoff, & Hirsh-Pasek, 2011). Similarly, students in first and second grade need to develop listening skills to be able to understand complex text that is read to them (Blair, 2002).

Research has shown that children are most likely to learn the words and language patterns that they hear the most (Christie, Enz, & Vukelich, 2007; Dickinson & Tabors, 2001; Hart & Risley, 1995). Therefore, we must expose them to the same words frequently while also introducing new words. The use of grade-level word lists will help children learn vocabulary through explicit instruction, and children will also learn words that are embedded during instruction in all of the content areas (Dickinson & Tabors, 2001).

The K–Grade 2 Common Core State Standards for Speaking and Listening are divided into two categories. The first category is Comprehension and Collaboration, and the second category is Presentation of Knowledge and Ideas.

The category Presentation of Knowledge and Ideas includes the skills students need to talk about people, places, ideas, feelings, and events in their lives. Children in K through grade 2 are expected to be able to tell stories, provide descriptions, give explanations, and ask and answer questions that require clarification or more information. The skills in this category include not only those needed to deliver an oral presentation in the form of a read-aloud and to participate in a play but also those needed to utilize drawings, photos, videos, and multimedia tools as visual aids.

The category Presentation of Knowledge and Ideas includes many skills for children to learn. For example, children need to understand what topics are appropriate to present or talk about in the classroom, on the playground, and in conversations with adults. Discussions with children should focus on developing their practical knowledge about language use. Children with practical knowledge of appropriate language know not only when to say what but also how much to say and to whom (Gillam & Reutzel, 2013). Children must be able to ask and answer questions about the oral language they hear to confirm that they understand and to get clarification if needed. Some comprehension questions asked of children relate to explicit information stated in oral discourse or written text, and other questions require children to make inferences. In both instances, children must listen carefully to new information and then remember it. Children also need to retrieve information from their background knowledge to answer questions when asked.

As you read the standards for each grade, you will notice their spiraling nature. Students are expected to demonstrate capacity in increasingly more complex linguistic, cognitive, and practical skills over time.

Putting the Speaking and Listening Standards into Practice

In this section, we illustrate the types of experiences young students should have in kindergarten and the primary grades to learn and achieve the six ELA CCSS for Speaking and Listening. We do this by providing classroom vignettes, which depict strategies that demonstrate the application of the identified standard.

Standards for Speaking and Listening

Table 1.1 provides the first Comprehension and Collaboration standard from the CCSS for Speaking and Listening, which focuses on strategies for participating in collaborative conversations.

TABLE 1.1 ● *Speaking and Listening Standard 1 for K–Grade 2: Comprehension and Collaboration*

Kindergarten	Grade 1	Grade 2
Participate in collaborative conversations with diverse partners about kindergarten topics and texts with peers and adults in small and larger groups.	Participate in collaborative conversations about grade 1 topics and texts with peers and adults in small and larger groups.	Participate in collaborative conversations with diverse partners about grade 2 topics and texts with peers and adults in small and larger groups.

Source: NGA & CCSSO (2010).

Speaking and Listening Standard 1   Participate in collaborative conversations with diverse partners about *kindergarten topics and texts* with peers and adults in small and larger groups (kindergarten).

    a. Follow agreed-upon rules for discussions (e.g., listening to others and taking turns speaking about the topics and texts under discussion).

    b. Continue a conversation through multiple exchanges.

In the Common Core Classroom

Collaborative Conversations: Kindergarten

Last week, the kindergartners in Ms. Tasir's class read the story *I Went Walking* (Williams, 1996). This simple, rhythmic book describes the animals one boy sees as he goes for a walk. For homework, each student was asked to go for a walk outside with a parent, grandparent, older sibling, or caregiver to pick up one item to share during morning meeting this week.

    Ms. Tasir plays the class song, which signals the children to clean up and gather on the carpet for morning meeting. Four students will share today. During sharing time, students know to look at the person that is talking. Only one person—the person who is sharing—is allowed to speak. After sharing, the person selects three people who are raising their hands to make comments or ask questions. These are the agreed upon rules the class has developed for Speaking and Listening Standard 1.

    Students begin morning meeting by greeting each other in their usual way. The teacher starts the greeting by getting the attention of the child to her right, making eye contact, smiling, and saying hello. Once the greeting has gone all of the way around the circle, the teacher invites the first student to begin sharing.

    Ms. Tasir: Last week, we read *I Went Walking*. Each of you went for a walk for homework and picked up something you found to share. Today, we will have the first four people share what they brought in. Please remember to ask your questions and comments only after the person who is sharing has described what he or she brought. George, you are first.

    George: I went walking and I saw this red leaf.

    Ms. Tasir: Wow, what a pointy leaf! Did you see others like it?

    George: I saw a lot of other pointy leaves, but none were as red as this one!

    Ms. Tasir: Questions and comments?

Casalyn: I like your red leaf. I got leaves in my yard. We pile them up and jump in them!

George: Oh, yeah! I do that, too. But you gotta take your glasses off first 'cause they can break.

Dee: What colors did you see?

George: All the colors.

Ms. Tasir: I think Dee means what colors of leaves did you see?

George: Well, there are green ones on the trees but yellow and red on the ground.

Bobby: You stole mine. I got a leaf, too.

Ms. Tasir: Yes, it's neat that you both brought leaves. When you go, maybe you can tell how your leaf is different from George's.

The next three students share their items, as well. Ms. Tasir guides the conversation and helps the students stay on topic. The fact that the students are each sharing a similar yet unique experience has helped them develop talk into a collaborative conversation, instead of the presentation-style talk of a typical Show and Tell. Ms. Tasir notes this observation and makes plans to incorporate more activities like this one into share time.

Tips for the Teacher

ROUTINE ACTIVITIES SUCH AS morning meeting provide structured opportunities for students to participate in collaborative conversations on a regular basis. Teachers must thoughtfully plan times to incorporate practice with Speaking and Listening Standard 1 into their daily schedules. We also recommend holding conversations about texts in whole- and small-group settings and providing discussion time after a shared experience (e.g., field trips, visits by special guests, and classroom events).

Table 1.2 provides the second Comprehension and Collaboration standard from the CCSS for Speaking and Listening, which focuses on strategies for understanding the key ideas and details of an oral or multimedia presentation.

TABLE 1.2 • *Speaking and Listening Standard 2 for K–Grade 2: Comprehension and Collaboration*

Kindergarten	Grade 1	Grade 2
Confirm understanding of a text read aloud or information presented orally or through other media by asking and answering questions about key details and requesting clarification if something is not understood.	Ask and answer questions about key details in a text read aloud or information presented orally or through other media.	Recount or describe key ideas or details from a text read aloud or information presented orally or through other media.

Source: NGA & CCSSO (2010).

Speaking and Listening Standard 2   Recount or describe key ideas or details from a text read aloud or information presented orally or through other media (second grade).

In the Common Core Classroom

Recounting Key Ideas and Details: Second Grade

The second-graders in Ms. Kopor's class sit in a circle with sheets of song lyrics in their hands. Today, they will listen to the song "Rock 'n Roll for Mother Earth," written and performed by John Farrell (2010a). This opening activity will kick off a unit on healthy environmental practices.

Ms. Kopor prompts her students to listen for the ideas about how to take care of the earth. Students follow along on their sheets of lyrics as they enjoy the music. After listening, they take turns discussing the key ideas from the song, Speaking and Listening Standard 2.

> **Ms. Kopor:** This song gave us some big ideas about how to take care of the earth. What is something you heard in the song that goes with that theme?
>
> **Kelly:** It said to keep the water clean.
>
> **Ms. Kopor:** Good, Kelly. What do you know about keeping the water clean from your own life?
>
> **Kelly:** Well, I remember looking at a photograph of a factory that was dumping stuff into the water. Then the water was not healthy.
>
> **Ms. Kopor:** Thank you for sharing, Kelly. What other details did we hear in the song?
>
> **Juan:** Help clean up the air. You can walk to a friend's house if it's not so far. You can bike, too.
>
> **Ms. Kopor:** I like the detail you added Juan. Who else wants to tell us something from the song?
>
> **Lilly:** We work to clean up litter and recycle. I always put my bottles and cans in the green bin.
>
> **Tawnique:** I went on a litter pick-up with my troop.
>
> **Ms. Kopor:** That's wonderful, Tawnique. Here's another line I remember: "Let's preserve her treasures." What do we think that means?
>
> **Triel:** The treasure of the earth is, like, its nature. The birds and the trees and stuff. It's all the things that make it beautiful. So we have to keep them healthy.

Ms. Kopor can tell that the students not only have a solid understanding of the song but also have significant background knowledge to build on in this unit. Students discussed the most important details and related it to their prior knowledge.

Plans for the Teacher

Materials Needed to Get Started

Song, sheets of lyrics, music player

Content of Lesson

Select an age-appropriate song that matches a theme being studied in your classroom, such as "Rock 'n Roll for Mother Earth" (Farrell, 2010b). Download the lyrics or create a lyrics sheet if they are not available. To begin, gather students in a whole-group meeting area. Introduce the activity with a statement that tells students what to listen for (e.g., "Listen for the ideas that tell about how to take care of the earth."). Play the song as students follow along on their sheets of lyrics. After students listen, invite them to discuss the key ideas or details they identified as they listened.

Differentiation

Students can be given highlighters to use when identifying key ideas and details on the lyrics sheets. This will help aid students' memory, focus their attention, and increase their participation.

Assessment

Listen to the students and check for accuracy of ideas. Take notes for later use, if necessary.

Table 1.3 provides the final Comprehension and Collaboration standard from the CCSS for Speaking and Listening, which focuses on asking and answering questions about information presented orally.

TABLE 1.3 ● *Speaking and Listening Standard 3 for K–Grade 2: Presentation of Knowledge and Ideas*

Kindergarten	Grade 1	Grade 2
Ask and answer questions in order to seek help, get information, or clarify something that is not understood.	Ask and answer questions about what a speaker says in order to gather additional information or clarify something that is not understood.	Ask and answer questions about what a speaker says in order to clarify comprehension, gather additional information, or deepen understanding of a topic or issue.

Source: NGA & CCSSO (2010).

Speaking and Listening Standard 3   Ask and answer questions about what a speaker says in order to gather additional information or clarify something that is not understood (first grade).

In the Common Core Classroom

Asking Clarifying Questions: First Grade

For the first few weeks of school, Mr. Vantripe's first-graders learn about their school community. They take a tour of the school and meet some of the school workers. For the students' first homework assignment, they will view and comment on a slideshow with photographs of the people who work in their school. Mr. Vantripe created his slideshow using VoiceThread, which is a unique digital tool that allows users to make comments in three formats: text, audio, and video. For this assignment, Mr. Vantripe's young learners will use the audio comment feature to ask a question to gain further information or clarify a point: Speaking and Listening Standard 3.

The conversation grows throughout the week as more students complete the assignment. Mr. Vantripe even joins in to answer some of the questions and guide his students' comments. The transcript of audio comments that follows shows part of the final version of this conversation.

Mr. Vantripe: This is Ms. Yolan. She is the principal.

Student 1: What does the principal do?

Student 2: How old is she?

Mr. Vantripe: Ms. Yolan is only 32. That's pretty young for a principal! She helps run the school. She makes sure all of the students are safe, and she runs meetings with the teachers.

Student 8: How does she make sure we're safe?

Mr. Vantripe: Remember that the school rules are written to keep us safe and help us learn. Ms. Yolan checks that all students follow the school rules. If people are not following the rules, she'll talk to them about it and help them fix their mistakes.

Mr. Vantripe: This is Ms. Washington. She is the school nurse. She gives out bandages and medicine.

Student 4: Does she give shots?

Student 12: I like her. She's nice.

Mr. Vantripe: Student 12, can you change your comment into a question?

Student 12: Do you like her?

Mr. Vantripe: Ms. Washington is very nice. I like her a lot. She helps teachers when they're not feeling well, too! She does not give out shots. You need to see your doctor to get a shot.

Mr. Vantripe: This is Mr. Joe, our custodian. He cleans.

Student 3: What is he cleaning?

Student 9: When does he clean?

Mr. Vantripe: Mr. Joe cleans a lot of different places. He cleans the floors after school. He cleans the lunchroom after lunch. If there's a big spill during the day, he cleans that, too.

These first-graders did a phenomenal job asking questions to gain further information. They finish up this lesson by watching the slideshow together as a class and making a list of the question words they used.

Tips for the Teacher

USING QUESTIONS TO GAIN further information and clarify ideas is an important part of effective communication. Explicit instruction within an authentic and engaging learning situation—like the one Mr. Vantripe sets up in his classroom— is what young learners need to help them master Speaking and Listening Standard 2.

Table 1.4 provides the first Presentation of Knowledge and Ideas standard from the CCSS for Speaking and Listening, which focuses on strategies for presenting information orally.

TABLE 1.4 ● *Speaking and Listening Standard 4 for K–Grade 2: Presentation of Knowledge and Ideas*

Kindergarten	Grade 1	Grade 2
Describe familiar people, places, things, and events, and with prompting and support, provide additional detail.	Describe people, places, things, and events with relevant details, expressing ideas and feelings clearly.	Tell a story or recount an experience with appropriate facts and relevant, descriptive details, speaking audibly in coherent sentences.

Source: NGA & CCSSO (2010).

Speaking and Listening Standard 4   Tell a story or recount an experience with appropriate facts and relevant, descriptive details, speaking audibly in coherent sentences. (second grade)

In the Common Core Classroom

Telling Stories and Recounting Experiences: Second Grade

Ms. Holder is reading *Math Rashes and Other Classroom Tales* (Evans, 2002) with a group of second-grade students who read above grade level. This collection of short stories is ideal for small-group reading instruction, because each chapter contains a complete story that can be read in one sitting. Today, students read a chapter titled "The Spelling Worm" and used sticky notes to write down text-based connections. Now, they discuss their notes and share stories with the group for Speaking and Listening Standard 4. They begin their discussion with a brief student summary. It is Jovi's turn to lead.

Jovi: This chapter is about Kate. She has trouble spelling and writing complete sentences. Her mealworm is magical, just like stuff in the other chapters, and he helps her by spelling words. In the end, she learns to use her dictionary. Erin, tell us what you wrote down.

Erin: *(Reading from her sticky note)* Kindergarten caterpillar. Oh, remember in kindergarten, when we got a caterpillar to take care of? We hatched it and it became a butterfly, and then we let it go outside.

Korey: We did that, too! We named him Butter. There was red stuff all over his cage, but Ms. Schoppy said it wasn't blood.

Ms. Holder: What part of the story made you think about the caterpillars you hatched in kindergarten?

Erin: Well, in this chapter, Kate has a mealworm, which is like a caterpillar, and they're hatching them for science class. That's what we did with the caterpillars.

Ms. Holder: Good text-to-self connection, Erin. Can you pick someone else to share who made a different connection?

Lou: In this story, Bob spells the words for Kate. We have our own tools to use, too. They're not magical. When I need a word, I look at the word wall. I'll search around, and if I don't find it then, I check my spelling dictionary. Then I raise my hand and see if you'll spell it for me if it's not there. I was writing a story about the Giants' game yesterday, remember? You spelled *Giants* for me under the letter *G.*

The conversation continues until each student has had a chance to share at least one story. Students naturally recount their stories as they describe the connections they make to the book.

Plans for the Teacher

Materials Needed to Get Started

Texts for each student, sticky notes

Content of Lesson

First, select a text with which your students are likely to make connections. Books about children in familiar situations lend themselves well to this activity. To begin this lesson, provide directions for writing text-based connections down on sticky notes and model the process, if necessary. After students have read the selection and marked down their thoughts on sticky notes, invite them to share their stories.

Differentiation

Scaffold students' storytelling by prompting them or asking clarifying questions.

Assessment

Listen to the students and take notes on the clarity and presentation of their ideas.

Table 1.5 provides the second Presentation of Knowledge and Ideas standard from the CCSS for Speaking and Listening, which focuses on strategies for using visual aids to assist in presenting information orally.

TABLE 1.5 ● *Speaking and Listening Standard 5 for K–Grade 2:* **Presentation of Knowledge and Ideas**

Kindergarten	Grade 1	Grade 2
Add drawings or other visual displays to descriptions as desired to provide additional detail.	Add drawings or other visual displays to descriptions when appropriate to clarify ideas, thoughts, and feelings.	Create audio recordings of stories or poems; add drawing or other visual displays to stories or recounts of experiences when appropriate to clarify ideas, thoughts, and feelings.

Source: NGA & CCSSO (2010).

> *Speaking and Listening Standard 5* Add drawings or other visual displays to descriptions when appropriate to clarify ideas, thoughts, and feelings (first grade).

In the Common Core Classroom
Presenting with Visual Displays: First Grade

In the first week of school, Mr. Davidson read the story *Clifford Takes a Trip* (Bridwell, 1966) and presented a big, red stuffed animal of Clifford to the students as their class pet. That weekend, Mr. Davidson brought Clifford home and took photographs of what they did together as an example for the students. The following Monday, Mr. Davidson showed the pictures to the students and described Clifford's trip to his house. The photographs served as a visual, which first-graders need to be able to use to meet Speaking and Listening Standard 5. After the presentation, the photographs were placed in an album in the classroom library.

Each week, a different child takes home Clifford and then tells about the dog's newest trip on the following Monday. This Monday, it is Flora's turn to share.

Flora: Over the weekend, I took Clifford to my soccer game. He had to sit on the side when I played. Here is Clifford in Georgie's stroller. He has to sit on the side, too, because he's just a baby! And then we went for ice cream. Mom didn't get Clifford one. We shared. See?

Mr. Davidson: It looks like you had a lot of fun with Clifford, Flora. Questions and comments?

Kelsea: What kind of ice cream did you get?

Flora: I got cookie dough. *(Pointing to the photograph)* See the chunks?

Kelsea: Oh yeah, I knew that. It's my favorite!

Flora: Yeah, me, too. I always get cookie dough.

Ike: I like your soccer shirt. Green's my favorite color.

Flora: Thanks.

Odon: Georgie looks happy with Clifford. It was nice you shared.

Flora: Yeah, Georgie did a good job watching Clifford when I was playing.

The visual provided by the photographs really help Flora's classmates understand what she did over the weekend. They spark conversation and provide extra information that Flora's words alone cannot convey.

Tips for the Teacher

FOR STUDENTS WHO HAVE trouble with oral language, a visual aid, such as a photograph or a drawing, can provide a means for them to gain entry into a successful oral language experience. The CCSS require our students to become proficient with the use of visual displays as a method of clarifying their ideas (NGA & CCSSO, 2010). In a Common Core classroom, students use these visuals at various times during the language arts block (e.g., draw and write journals) and within the content areas. The teacher first models the process and then scaffolds instruction for the students. The teacher assists during students' presentations by pointing out specific aspects and posing questions. Throughout the elementary years, students should demonstrate an increasing level of proficiency with the use of visual displays.

Table 1.6 provides the final Presentation of Knowledge and Ideas standard from the CCSS for Speaking and Listening, which focuses on strategies for enhancing clarity when presenting information orally.

TABLE 1.6 ● *Speaking and Listening Standard 6 for K–Grade 2:* Presentation of Knowledge and Ideas

Kindergarten	Grade 1	Grade 2
Speak audibly and express thoughts, feelings, and ideas clearly.	Produce complete sentences when appropriate to task and situation.	Produce complete sentences when appropriate to task and situation in order to provide requested detail or clarification.

Source: NGA & CCSSO (2010).

Speaking and Listening Standard 6   Speak audibly and express thoughts, feelings, and ideas clearly (kindergarten).

In the Common Core Classroom

Using an Appropriate Speaking Voice: Kindergarten

Ms. Samfield sits with a reading group as they add the finishing touches to their journal entries. Today, they are responding to the text *Getting Dressed* (Brown, n.d.) by drawing and writing about what they did to get ready for school.

When the students are ready to present their writing to the group, Ms. Samfield begins by reviewing the sharing procedures.

Ms. Samfield: What should we look like and sound like when our friends are sharing?

Children: Quiet! Eyes on the speaker!

Ms. Samfield: Good! What voice do we use when it is our turn to go?

Children: A big voice!

Ms. Samfield: Do we shout?

Children: No!

Ms. Samfield: Okay, you sound ready. Trinity, tell us what you did in your journal.

Trinity: It's my favorite sweater. It's red.

Ms. Samfield: And what does your sentence say, dear?

Trinity: *(Reads quietly)* I put on my sweater.

Ms. Samfield: What a lovely sweater it is! Can you read the sentence again so everyone can hear you? Nice, big voice now!

Trinity: *(Louder)* I put on my sweater.

Ms. Samfield: Good job, Trinity! I like how she used the words from the story to help with the sentence. Tucker, your turn.

Tucker: I put on my boots.

Ms. Samfield: Wow! You used the words from the story to help you write, too. You were also ready with a nice, big voice for us. Could you hear Tucker? Yes, me, too. Go ahead, Bobby.

Bobby: I did brushing my teeth. Is that wrong? Here I am brushing my teeth with my racecar toothbrush. I didn't do the words in the book.

Ms. Samfield: No, that's right Bobby. It's something you do to get ready. You did a really nice job. I like that you told us a detail about your toothbrush. It's a racecar! Can you read us your sentence?

Bobby: I brush my teeth with my racecar toothbrush in the morning before I come to school.

Ms. Samfield: Wow! Your sentence had great detail! Can you pass me your journal? I would like to write that below your sentence in case you want me to read it back to you later on.

Ms. Samfield writes Bobby's sentence below his own writing, which is an emergent form of writing that consists mainly of strings of consonants. While all students were successful with minimal prompting, Ms. Samfield notes that Bobby was the most confident speaker. He spoke clearly and was easily understood.

Tips for the Teacher

SPEAKING AND LISTENING STANDARD 6 focuses on developing the ability to adapt speech to satisfy the listener. In the early elementary years, audible speech and clarity of ideas are the focus of instruction, and the production of complete sentences is the goal by second grade. As in this vignette, many young students need plenty of practice with speaking in front of a group of people. Developing a "big voice" can be accomplished by providing plenty of time for oral language activities within the classroom. Students need time to be both the speaker and the listener to understand that clear speech is essential for effective communication.

Defining the Standards for Vocabulary Instruction

VOCABULARY ACQUISITION AND USE IS A CATEGORY IN the Language standards. We have combined this category with the Speaking and Listening standard and will discuss them together here.

These standards focus on children's capacity to learn vocabulary independently. According to the standards, children can learn words independently if they (1) use contextual information from the general topic of the conversation or text; (2) use information about parts of words, such as prefixes, suffixes, and roots; and (3) use resources such as the dictionary, glossary, and various technologies. Helping children to learn the meanings of words on their own, or becoming word conscious (Stahl & Nagy, 2006), is important, because it is impossible for teachers to teach students the meanings of all of the words they need to know.

What Strategies Help Children Acquire Vocabulary?

The standards do not tell us how we should teach vocabulary; rather, they discuss outcomes for children. We know that young children need to acquire many new words daily. By the age of 6, a child should have acquired 14,000 words, which means learning about 2,500 words a year (Hart & Risley, 1995), to help them with literacy development.

Graves (2000) created researched-based categories for vocabulary instruction (Baumann & Kame'enui, 2004; Stahl & Nagy, 2006), and his categories represent a comprehensive vocabulary program (Baumann, Blachowicz, Manyak, Graves, & Olejnik, 2009–2012). The components that Graves (2006) described are: "(1) providing rich and varied language experiences; (2) teaching individual words; (3) teaching word-learning strategies; and (4) fostering word consciousness" (p. 5). Each of these components is discussed in the following list and referred to in the actual standards:

1. **Provide rich and varied language experiences.** Children who are immersed in a literacy-rich environment are likely to develop expressive and receptive vocabulary (Hart & Risley, 1995). Likewise, children acquire words through the rich vocabulary in printed texts—both narrative and expository—by listening to parents and teachers read aloud (Bus, van Ijzendoorn, & Pellegrini, 1995; Elley, 1989). Students also acquire vocabulary through independent reading (Cunningham, 2005; Swanborn & de Glopper, 1999). The standards state that children need to acquire a rich and varied vocabulary. This can happen by involving children in many language experiences, such as independent reading and being read to. Thus, the CCSS support providing a literacy-rich environment with many language experiences for children, through conversations, read-alouds, or independent reading (NGA & CCSSO, 2010).

2. **Teach individual words.** Each grade level has a list of vocabulary words to be learned. According to research, we should teach these words by having children learn their definitions, using the words in context, and having repeated experiences with the words (Nagy & Scott, 2000). Standards that align with Graves's (2000, 2006) evidenced-based framework for learning vocabulary can be found in the CCSS when they address providing multiple exposures to words and teaching individual words. These standards can be found in the CCSS categories Informational Text: Craft and Structure and Vocabulary Acquisition and Use.

3. **Teach word-learning strategies.** In early childhood, children are helped to understand the meanings of words by using context clues from sentences that contain unknown words. With older children, learning new words involves morphemic analysis, which consists of determining the meaning of a word by looking at its root, prefixes, and suffixes. Support for this strategy is provided by the work of researchers and stated as an outcome in the CCSS (Baumann, Edwards, Boland, Olejnik, & Kame'enui, 2003; Buikema & Graves, 1993). With children in pre-K through grade 2, minimal work is done with morphemes, because the children are not developmentally ready for it.

4. **Foster word consciousness.** Several studies have documented the characteristics of children who are word conscious (Scott, Vevea, & Flinspach, 2010). Children are word conscious when they know when to use particular words that are colorful or interesting in their oral or written language. Similarly, children are word conscious when they ask definitions for words that they do not understand (Blachowicz, Fisher, Ogle, & Watts-Taffe, 2006).

Table 1.7 provides the Vocabulary Acquisition and Use standard from the CCSS, which focuses on strategies for learning words independently.

TABLE 1.7 • *Vocabulary Acquisition and Use Standard 4: Focus on Strategies for Independence: K–2*

Kindergarten	Grade 1	Grade 2
Determine or clarify the meaning of unknown and multiple-meaning words and phrases based on *kindergarten reading and content*.	Determine or clarify the meaning of unknown and multiple-meaning words and phrases based on *grade 1 reading and content*, choosing flexibly from an array of strategies.	Determine or clarify the meaning of unknown and multiple-meaning words and phrases based on *grade 2 reading and content*, choosing flexibly from an array of strategies.
a. Identify new meanings for familiar words and apply them accurately (e.g., knowing *duck* is a bird and learning the verb *to duck*). b. Use the most frequently occurring inflections and affixes (e.g., *-ed, -s, re-, un-, pre-, -ful, -less*) as a clue to the meaning of an unknown word.	a. Use sentence-level context as a clue to the meaning of a word or phrase. b. Use frequently occurring affixes as a clue to the meaning of a word. c. Identify frequently occurring root words (e.g., *look*) and their inflectional forms (e.g., *looks, looked, looking*).	a. Use sentence-level context as a clue to the meaning of a word or phrase. b. Determine the meaning of the new word formed when a known prefix is added to a known word (e.g., *happy/unhappy, tell/retell*). c. Use a known root word as a clue to the meaning of an unknown word with the same root (e.g., *addition, additional*). d. Use knowledge of the meaning of individual words to predict the meaning of compound words (e.g., *birdhouse, lighthouse, housefly; bookshelf, notebook, bookmark*). e. Use glossaries and beginning dictionaries, both print and digital, to determine or clarify the meaning of words and phrases.

Source: NGA & CCSSO (2010).

Standards for Vocabulary Acquisition and Use

Following is a vignette that illustrates classroom practices that demonstrate children determining or clarifying the meanings of unknown and multiple-meaning words and phrases independently.

Language Standard 4   Determine or clarify the meaning of unknown and multiple-meaning words and phrases based on *grade 2 reading and content,* choosing flexibly from an array of strategies (second grade).

In the Common Core Classroom

Unknown and Multiple Meaning Words: Second Grade

Ms. Hewfox has set up an Amazing Animals theme in her second-grade classroom, providing many exciting learning opportunities for the students. They will be visited by a dog from the local animal shelter that does tricks, engage in research on the animal of their choice, and read many true and fictional stories about animals. For today's lesson, Ms. Hewfox has selected an informational text, *Odd Animal Helpers* (Reyes, 2011), to read aloud to the class.

Ms. Hewfox connects the class iPad to the projector and displays the text on the interactive whiteboard for all of the students to see. Before reading, she reviews vocabulary from the text, prompting students to use a variety of strategies to determine the meanings of the words and phrases (Language Standard 4).

> **Ms. Hewfox:** This book is about animals that work together. The author uses the words *symbiotic relationship* to describe the way two animals help each other out. On page 3, the author tells us what *symbiotic relationship* means right in that sentence. Sometimes, an author tells readers what a word means, just like in this sentence, if it is a really important word to understand. Other times, you have to use other strategies to help you understand. Let's go to page 11. Can you read the small, yellow word? It's a two-syllable word. Attack the first syllable and then the second: *mu-cus.* Okay, so we could read it, but do we understand what the word means? Let's read the sentence it is in.

The students read together.

> **Ms. Hewfox:** I think there's a clue word in that sentence that gives us a hint to what mucus might be. What is the clue word?
>
> **Eva:** Slimy.
>
> **Ms. Hewfox:** Good. Mucus is something that is slimy that covers the clownfish. What part of our bodies might be considered slimy?
>
> **Wallace:** *(Giggling)* Inside our noses!
>
> **Ms. Hewfox:** That's right. We might have mucus in our noses or in our mouths. Let's check the glossary's definition of mucus.

Ms. Hewfox and the students flip to the glossary and read the definition together before they move on to the next vocabulary word.

Ms. Hewfox: On the same page we have another word: *lure*. Let's read the sentence and see if we can replace it with another word that might make sense to help us understand the meaning of the sentence.

Rob: How about *trick*?

Ms. Hewfox: Okay, *trick* will work in that sentence. To *lure* is when you get someone to follow you. So the clownfish is tricking the bigger fish by getting them to follow them into the anemone. Let us look at page 12 now. What is this big, long word? Where do you think we need to split the syllables? *Trans-port-ed.* Does that sound like another word you've heard before?

Flo: *Transportation?*

Ms. Hewfox: Yes, the two words are related. They are both from the base word *transport*. If *transportation* is something you take to get around, like a bus or a car, what does *transported* mean?

Flo: Something was moved?

Ms. Hewfox: Right! We can use related words to help us understand vocabulary, too. Good, now let's read to find out about these amazing animals that work so well together. If you come to a word you don't understand, give me a signal and we'll see if we can use a strategy to figure it out.

The class listens as Ms. Hewfox reads the text aloud. They pause to review the meanings of the words *hover* and *agile* during reading. After reading, the students begin to take a greater responsibility for determining the meanings of unknown words during small-group and independent reading. They will continue using unknown word strategies throughout the year.

Plans for the Teacher

Materials Needed to Get Started

Informational text with challenging vocabulary

Content of Lesson

Read the text and determine its appropriateness based on the level of challenge the vocabulary will provide your students. The perfect book will have a handful of unknown words without overwhelming students with new vocabulary. As you preview the book, write down the words and phrases that will most likely be challenging to your students. Note the strategy that will best work for determining the meaning of each word or phrase.

To begin the lesson, preview the vocabulary with the group. Start by modeling the process using think-alouds, and eventually allow students to take over by prompting them to use the appropriate strategy. Read the text together and pause to review a few of the previewed words and to determine the meanings of other vocabulary words that present a challenge. Provide time for similar activities in small-group and independent reading settings.

Differentiation

For beginning readers, focus on one strategy at a time before asking readers to use a combination of strategies.

Assessment

Listen to students' responses and take notes, if necessary. Further assess students and provide additional instruction during small-group or independent reading time.

The second set of Vocabulary Acquisition and Use standards focus on children's understanding of the connections and relationships in word meanings. These standards are identified in Table 1.8.

TABLE 1.8 ● *Vocabulary Acquisition and Use Standard 5: Focus Word Relationships: K–2*

Kindergarten	Grade 1	Grade 2
With guidance and support from adults, explore word relationships and nuances in word meanings.	With guidance and support from adults, demonstrate understanding of word relationships and nuances in word meanings.	Demonstrate understanding of word relationships and nuances in word meanings.
a. Sort common objects into categories (e.g., shapes, foods) to gain a sense of the concepts the categories represent.	a. Sort words into categories (e.g., colors, clothing) to gain a sense of the concepts the categories represent.	a. Identify real-life connections between words and their use (e.g., describe foods that are *spicy* or *juicy*).
b. Demonstrate understanding of frequently occurring verbs and adjectives by relating them to their opposites (antonyms).	b. Define words by category and by one or more key attributes (e.g., a *duck* is a bird that swims; a *tiger* is a large cat with stripes).	b. Distinguish shades of meaning among closely related verbs (e.g., *toss, throw, hurl*) and closely related adjectives (e.g., *thin, slender, skinny, scrawny*).
c. Identify real-life connections between words and their use (e.g., note places at school that are *colorful*).	c. Identify real-life connections between words and their use (e.g., note places at home that are *cozy*).	
d. Distinguish shades of meaning among verbs describing the same general action (e.g., *walk, march, strut, prance*) by acting out meanings.	d. Distinguish shades of meaning among verbs differing in manner (e.g., *look, peek, glance, stare, scowl*) and adjectives differing in intensity (e.g., *large, gigantic*) by defining or choosing them or by acting out the meanings.	

Source: NGA & CCSSO (2010).

The vignette that follows will help illustrate how to implement strategies for the acquisition of vocabulary with a focus on word relationship strands.

Language Standard 5   With guidance and support from adults, demonstrate understanding of word relationships and nuances in word meanings (first grade).

In the Common Core Classroom

Understanding Word Relationships and Nuances: First Grade

Ms. Billino's first-graders are studying sensory language, which they refer to as "words for the five senses." They are collecting and sorting words that activate the senses. In the last book they read, *Noisy Breakfast* (Blonder, 1994), students found many words, which they discussed and added to the "Hearing" poster. They then made real-life connections by identifying other objects that make the same sound (e.g., snack bags *pop*, sinks *drip*).

Today, students will follow similar procedures as they read an informational text entitled *I Am Snow* (Marzollo, 1998). As students perform this sorting activity, they discover word relationships for Language Standard 5.

> **Ms. Billino:** Let's listen to see if we can find more words for the five senses. Please raise your hand when you hear something for our posters.
>
> *The class listens as Ms. Billino reads the first page.*
>
> **Ryan:** *Drip.*
>
> **Ms. Billino:** Good! That sounds familiar. I think we have that one already. What list should I check to see if we already have that word?
>
> **Ryan:** *Hearing.*
>
> **Ms. Billino:** Okay, let's check. *(Reading)* "Crack, drop, rattle, pop, sizzle, drip." Yes, there it is! *Drip* is on the "Hearing" poster. Way to go!
>
> *Ms. Billino continues reading.*
>
> **Erica:** *Bounce.*
>
> **Ms. Billino:** *Bounce.* Right, now let's go through each sense. Where does it belong? Smell? No. Taste? No! Touch? Maybe. Can you feel a bounce?
>
> **Erica:** Yes.
>
> **Ms. Billino:** Hearing? Maybe. What sound does a bounce make?
>
> **Erica:** Boing!
>
> **Ms. Billino:** Okay, let's say it's not for hearing then. If it said "Boing," I'd put it for hearing. Sight? Maybe. Can you see a bounce?
>
> **Erica:** Yes.
>
> **Ms. Billino:** So we need to choose between touch and sight. What makes the most sense for how the word is used in this book? Is it something you feel or see?
>
> **Erica:** See.
>
> **Ms. Billino:** I agree. Let's put it on the "Sight" poster.
>
> *Ms. Billino reads a couple more pages before another student raises his hand.*
>
> **Ian:** *Wet* and *sticky.* They are for the "Touch" poster!

Ms. Billino: Good. What else is wet?

Ian: My dog's nose!

Ms. Billino: That's true! What else is sticky?

Ian: Glue and marshmallow treats!

Ms. Billino reads one more page.

Janis: Dry and *fluffy*.

Ms. Billino: What sense do they belong with?

Janis: Touch.

Ms. Billino: Good. What else do you know that's fluffy?

Janis: My poodle!

Ms. Billino: Good. Anyone else?

Georgie: Whipped cream!

Ms. Billino: Okay, let's keep listening.

Ms. Billino reads the rest of the book. Students find one more word on the last page.

Victoria: Drip.

Ms. Billino: I think we have that one, too! What poster should we check?

Victoria: It was in *Noisy Breakfast!* It's on the "Hearing" poster.

Ms. Billino: Wow! Great job. We have a lot of words we found! I love words, don't you?

Ms. Billino's students are not only learning about word relationships, but they are also starting to become word conscious. Soon, these students will find sensory language in their independent reading without their teacher's prompt. Whenever they discover a word that matches one of the five senses, they write it on a sticky note and add it to a poster. Using sticky notes allows Ms. Billino to check the words and adjust them, if necessary. Once she has checked a word, she writes it on a poster.

Tips for the Teacher

SORTING WORDS HELPS STUDENTS construct a deeper understanding of the categories to which the words belong. In Ms. Billino's class, we see students developing knowledge of sensory language. For these students, sounds can now be described with the words *crack, drop, rattle, pop, sizzle,* and *drip*. With every new word that gets added to a poster, the children further their understanding of what it means for a word to be a "sound word." Vocabulary Acquisition and Use Standard 5 requires students to demonstrate their knowledge of word relationships and nuances in meaning. To develop this knowledge, we must provide playful activities (e.g., sorts, acting games, and word hunts) to increase students' interest in words and develop word consciousness.

The last Vocabulary Acquisition and Use standard emphasizes how children can learn vocabulary from multiple sources. The standard presented in Table 1.9 is about children's ability to express and use vocabulary. Being able to write and express particular words suggests that a child has internalized those words.

TABLE 1.9 ● *Vocabulary Acquisition and Use Standard 6:* Expressive Vocabulary: K–2

Kindergarten	Grade 1	Grade 2
Use words and phrases acquired through conversations, reading and being read to, and responding to texts.	Use words and phrases acquired through conversations, reading and being read to, and responding to texts, including using frequently occurring conjunctions to signal simple relationships (e.g., *because*).	Use words and phrases acquired through conversations, reading and being read to, and responding to texts, including using adjectives and adverbs to describe (e.g., *When other kids are happy that makes me happy.*).

Source: NGA & CCSSO (2010).

Language Standard 6   Use words and phrases acquired through conversations, reading and being read to, and responding to texts (kindergarten).

In the Common Core Classroom

Using Vocabulary: Kindergarten

The kindergartners are learning about making choices. They know that it can sometimes be hard to decide what a good choice is and what a bad choice is. For this theme, Ms. Jenkies has found a great book about making a really tough decision: *Hey, Little Ant* (Hoose & Hoose, 1998). In this book, a boy is about to crush an ant when the ant speaks up and begs to be let go. At the end, the reader gets to decide what should be done, which makes this an excellent book for a discussion.

Before reading this book, the class previews the target vocabulary words: *squish, crumb, speck, crook,* and *giant.* The students and teacher mime some of the words and discuss others. Then, Ms. Jenkies gives a short introduction connecting this book to the class's Making Choices theme.

When it is time to read, Ms. Jenkies sings the text to the children to the tune provided in the book. Many students hum along and bob their heads, fully engrossed in the reading. After the last line of the book is sung the authors' question hangs in their air, waiting to be answered—to squish or not to squish? The discussion begins as many students raise their hands for a turn to speak. They naturally use the target vocabulary in their discussion for Language Standard 6.

Yonique: He shouldn't squish that ant.

Ms. Jenkies: Why do you think that he shouldn't squish the ant, Yonique?

Yonique: He's gonna kill it! He's a giant and the ant's a little speck. Think of the family!

Ms. Jenkies: Yonique has a good point. If he steps on the ant, he'll squish it. It will be dead and the ant's family will miss it. Who wants to add to that?

Annalee: It's not nice. She's gotta give the crumb to her family.

Walter: But Ant's a crook. Ant stole that crumb. Squish it!

Annalee: It's just a speck. They didn't want it anyway. It was on the *floor!* No eating off the floor.

Ms. Jenkies: Okay, we have more to think about now. Annalee added that the ant has to feed the crumb to its family. It's only a little speck that the people don't want anyway—probably because it fell on the floor. But Walter thinks that she's a crook because she stole the food. It wasn't hers to take. Who else wants to say what should be done?

Bo: Well, I won't squish the ant. I don't want a giant to squish me!

Ms. Jenkies: So you would treat the ant the way you would want to be treated.

Bo: Yeah, being mean is not a good decision. They are different. That's okay!

Ms. Jenkies: Yes, Bo reminds us that it's okay to be friends with people who are different from you. Being mean is never a good decision. Who else would squish the ant?

Robin: Real ants get in your food. They all come, not just *one* ant and *one* crumb. Gross!

Ms. Jenkies: Yes, Robin has a point. In real life, a whole colony of ants might come and crawl in your food. It's not usually just one ant taking one crumb. Having insects in your food is pretty disgusting. Okay, I think we've heard a lot of good points to help us make a final decision. Let's take a vote. Raise your hand if you would not squish the ant. Raise your hand if you would squish the ant.

The children vote and Ms. Jenkies writes down the result on a piece of chart paper to conclude the lesson.

Throughout the week, the class will enjoy listening to this story again and again, eventually singing along. Working in centers, the students will complete journal entries to show what they would do. The vocabulary cards Ms. Jenkies made to illustrate the target words are posted in the writing center for the children to reference during this activity. Finally, the students share their journal entries in small groups during guided reading, giving them yet another opportunity to use the vocabulary they learned from listening and responding to this text.

Tips for the Teacher

FOR STUDENTS TO BE able to internalize new vocabulary, they need multiple experiences with words. Ms. Jenkies provides these experiences for her students. Suggested activities include the use of repeated readings, illustrated vocabulary cards and displays, discussions surrounding a topic or theme, and reader's response journals.

When planning lessons for Vocabulary Acquisition and Use Standard 6, consider selecting children's literature that elicits emotional reactions from the students, as *Hey, Little Ant* (Hoose & Hoose, 19998) does in this lesson. Other high-interest texts, including informational texts, may also be well suited for this type of lesson, because they will help generate rich discussions and encourage students to use vocabulary from the text.

Conventions and Knowledge of Language

Ideas are considered the most important aspect of communication, but unless we express our ideas according to the conventions of spoken language, other people may have difficulty understanding us. In fact, after how we look, how we speak is the next strongest impression that we make on others. Individuals who don't follow the conventions of language when they speak are less likely to be understood than those who do. Moreover, these individuals will likely have difficulty getting a college education and building a career. People who speak in incomplete sentences and pronounce words incorrectly are viewed as lacking the skills necessary for success in college and career.

Young children struggle to learn the conventions of language along with the social aspects of language use. When they begin school, they have a range of experiences with and knowledge of language. Some may be English language learners, and others may use African American Vernacular English, which has its own grammar. As teachers, we must respect students' language differences, but also help them to learn standard English (Delpit, 1995). Children need to understand the appropriate uses of formal and informal English. Vernacular expressions are appropriate for casual conversations with friends, siblings, and peers, whereas formal English is appropriate for communicating with teachers in college and with colleagues and employers in the workplace.

Given the differences between the language used at home and in the classroom, children need to know how to switch between formal and informal English to be successful in school. Children in grade 2 are capable of switching from formal to informal and back again. Thus, second-grade teachers need to engage children in explicit discussions and explorations of differences between formal and informal language through reading or being read to and listening to others. These discussions will help children to understand the different language registers and that the "correctness" of language depends on a variety of factors, such as communication context, audience, purpose, and desired impact on the listener or reader.

Teaching formal grammar seems to have little value on improving it. Grammar is made up of rules that determine word order, word use, sentence structure, word choice, sentence type, story structure, and sentence and paragraph form. Research by the National Council of Teachers of English (NCTE, 2008) showed that teaching grammar using a formal drill/skill approach did not improve written or oral language. In fact, in some cases, using this approach was detrimental to those students who were proficient in oral language and writing (Linden & Whimbey, 1990; Noyce & Christie, 1983). Similar to writing skills, speaking skills are also likely to improve when children have the opportunity to speak often in meaningful contexts and have good models of standard English from their teachers (Andrews et al., 2006).

Knowledge of language and its grammar is best learned through context-based instruction that focuses on sentence construction (Graves, 1983; Saddler & Graham, 2005). Providing functional contexts for embedding instruction that targets key grammatical concepts seems to be the best strategy (e.g., Blaauw-Hara, 2006; Fearn & Farnan, 2007). Table 1.10 identifies the standards for grammar and usage and knowledge of language.

TABLE 1.10 ● *Conventions of Standard English Standard 1 for Grades K–2: Focus on Grammar and Usage and Knowledge of Language*

Kindergarten	Grade 1	Grade 2
Demonstrate command of the conventions of standard English grammar and usage when writing or speaking. a. Print many upper- and lowercase letters. b. Use frequently occurring nouns and verbs. c. Form regular plural nouns orally by adding /s/ or /es/ (e.g., *dog, dogs; wish, wishes*). d. Understand and use question words (interrogatives) (e.g., *who, what, where, when, why, how*). e. Use the most frequently occurring prepositions (e.g., *to, from, in, out, on, off, for, of, by, with*). f. Produce and expand complete sentences in shared language activities.	Demonstrate command of the conventions of standard English grammar and usage when writing or speaking. a. Print all upper- and lowercase letters. b. Use common, proper, and possessive nouns. c. Use singular and plural nouns with matching verbs in basic sentences (e.g., *He hops; We hop*). d. Use personal, possessive, and indefinite pronouns (e.g., *I, me, my; they, them, their; anyone, everything*). e. Use verbs to convey a sense of past, present, and future (e.g., *Yesterday I walked home; Today I walk home; Tomorrow I will walk home*). f. Use frequently occurring adjectives. g. Use frequently occurring conjunctions (e.g., *and, but, or, so, because*). h. Use determiners (e.g., *articles, demonstratives*). i. Use frequently occurring prepositions (e.g., *during, beyond, toward*). j. Produce and expand complete simple and compound declarative, interrogative, imperative, and exclamatory sentences in response to prompts.	Demonstrate command of the conventions of standard English grammar and usage when writing or speaking. a. Use collective nouns (e.g., *group*). b. Form and use frequently occurring irregular plural nouns (e.g., *feet, children, teeth, mice, fish*). c. Use reflexive pronouns (e.g., *myself, ourselves*). d. Form and use the past tense of frequently occurring irregular verbs (e.g., *sat, hid, told*). e. Use adjectives and adverbs, and choose between them depending on what is to be modified. f. Produce, expand, and rearrange complete simple and compound sentences (e.g., *The boy watched the movie; The little boy watched the movie; The action movie was watched by the little boy*).

Source: NGA & CCSSO (2010).

Language Standard 1   Demonstrate command of the conventions of Standard English grammar and usage when writing or speaking (kindergarten).

In the Common Core Classroom

Using Conventions: Kindergarten

Ms. Kaliki knows that parents love seeing photographs of their children at school, and kindergarten parents perhaps enjoy seeing them most of all. Seeing photographs not only brings smiles to parents' faces, but it also keeps them informed of the activities their children engage in during school.

Ms. Kaliki has decided to create a VoiceThread slideshow with her kindergartners at the end of every month. Each monthly slideshow will be made up of photographs taken by the teacher or a parent volunteer that capture some of the activities students have engaged in throughout the month. Involving the children in the creation of the slideshow provides an authentic context to practice forming complete sentences, identifying common nouns and verbs, pluralizing nouns, and practicing other conventions of spoken language for Language Standard 1.

Today, Ms. Kaliki's class is creating its fifth VoiceThread to describe the activities that have taken place in the month of January. Ms. Kaliki has already selected the photographs to be included and uploaded them onto the VoiceThread. She has made sure that there is at least one photograph of each child.

Ms. Kaliki: Here's a picture of Harry! What do you have in your hand Harry?

Harry: A book.

Ms. Kaliki: What are you doing with the book?

Harry: Reading.

Ms. Kaliki: What should we say for the sentence?

Ms. Kaliki gives Harry the microphone and presses the "Record" button.

Harry: I read a book.

Ms. Kaliki: That's a good start. I think our parents might be interested in knowing a little bit more about the book. What do you remember about this book, Harry?

Harry: He sleeps in the winter and misses the party. Booohooohoooo!

Ms. Kaliki: That's right. This month we learned about animals in the winter. You are talking about *Bear Snores On,* by Karma Wilson, one of the books I read to you for that theme. What do you want to say after "I read a book"?

Ms. Kaliki presses the "Record More" button.

Harry: *Bear Snores On.* We did animals in the winter.

Ms. Kaliki: Here is a picture of Emmy. Emmy, who are you pretending to be?

Emmy: I'm a chipmunk.

Ms. Kaliki: What are you doing?

Emmy: I'm crawling in the tunnel to sleep.

Ms. Kaliki: Good. That's perfect. Are you ready for the microphone?

Emmy: What did I say?

Ms. Kaliki: I'm a chipmunk. I'm crawling in the tunnel to sleep.

Emmy repeats what Ms. Kaliki said. Ms. Kaliki adds a second comment to tell parents that the class transformed their dramatic play area into caves and tunnels for this month.

Ms. Kaliki: Here's a picture of Zelia. Zelia, what is on the table in front of you?

Zelia: My journal.

Ms. Kaliki: What are you writing about in your journal?

Zelia: The bird flies south.

Ms. Kaliki: Okay, what can we say for the VoiceThread?

Zelia: I write, "The bird flies south."

Ms. Kaliki: Great. Let's record.

Ms. Kaliki records Zelia.

Ms. Kaliki: Here's a picture of Joseph. What are you making?

Joseph: A mitten.

Ms. Kaliki: You have two there. What do we say if you have two? "Joseph has two m—"?

Ivan: Mittens.

Joseph: I made mittens.

Ms. Kaliki: Can you add to that? I made mittens out of . . .

Ms. Kaliki presses "Record."

Joseph: I made mittens out of cotton balls.

Ms. Kaliki: Good. Here's another picture just like Joseph's. Maria, can you change Joseph's sentence to say what you made mittens out of? Say, "I made mittens out of . . ."

Maria: I made mittens out of feathers.

The class continues to identify the activities in the pictures and record complete sentences to create their VoiceThread. Every once in a while, the teacher pauses to add more information to the slide. When the class is finished Ms. Kaliki embeds the VoiceThread into her classroom website and notifies the parents. While viewing, many parents record or type comments to their children, which become a permanent part of the slideshow.

Plans for the Teacher

Materials Needed to Get Started

VoiceThread, microphone, photographs of students

Content of Lesson

Take photographs of the students engaging in classroom activities throughout the month. Upload the photos to the VoiceThread site (http://ed.voicethread.com) by clicking the "Create" tab and following the simple steps provided. For this lesson, have students take turns describing what they are doing in the photographs. Guide their use of language conventions, and encourage them to expand on their sentences. Locate the "Comment" button on the slideshow and record the students' speech when they are ready.

Differentiation

Vary the amount of scaffolding you offer each student. Prompt the student with guiding questions or rephrase his or her speech, if necessary.

Assessment

Keep a checklist of the conventions students are expected to be able to master in your grade level. Use the checklist to track your students' progress.

The last Language standard is presented in Table 1.11.

TABLE 1.11 ● *Knowledge of Language Standard 3 for Grades K–2*

Kindergarten	Grade 1	Grade 2
(Begins in grade 2)	(Begins in grade 2)	Use knowledge of language and its conventions when writing, speaking, reading, and listening.
		a. Compare formal and informal uses of English.

Source: NGA & CCSSO (2010).

Language Standard 3   Use knowledge of language and its conventions when writing, speaking, reading, or listening (second grade).

a. Compare formal and informal uses of English.

In the Common Core Classroom
Formal vs. Informal English: Second Grade

This month, Ms. Kramer's class has become extremely excited about the book *Jonathan James and the Whatif Monster* (Nelson-Schmidt, 2012). The class has read the book, acted it out, wrote other stories in response, and thoroughly enjoyed the eBook version using the app Demibooks Storytime. Now, Ms. Kramer has a huge surprise for her students: They are going to Skype with the author! Ms. Kramer uses this opportunity to review with her students the importance of using conventions when speaking and writing. As students prepare for the Skype session, they craft questions for the author that reflect their understanding that certain situations call for the use of formal English, as described in Language Standard 3.

>*Ms. Kramer:* I have a really big surprise for you today. We are going to get to talk with one of your favorite authors on Skype next week. She wrote a book about a monster that puts doubts in your mind . . .
>
>*Class:* Michelle Nelson-Schmidt?!

Ms. Kramer: Yes! I want to get ready for this very important day. Let's each come up with some questions we would like to ask her. When we write our questions, how do we want to sound? Would it be appropriate to talk to Ms. Michelle the same way we talk to our very good friends, or do we want to use formal English?

Class: We want to use formal English! She's very important.

Ms. Kramer: Oh yes, definitely. So, can someone give us a silly example of what *not* to say?

Darien: Hey, how ya' doin'? How's your mom?

Ms. Kramer: *(Laughs)* Good, because we don't really know her mom, right? How else could we say "How ya' doin'?"

Darien: Good morning. How are you today?"

Ms. Kramer: Okay, Darien. Thanks. So, what questions do we want to know about? Let's write a few together before you go off and write questions with a buddy.

Tina: How long does it take to write one book?

Ms. Kramer: Okay, let me write that down. How does that question sound? Did Tina use formal English? Yes, I believe she did, too.

Rigo: So, I want to know if she's got, like, things she's afraid to do, you know?

Ms. Kramer: Okay, Rigo. Can you help me put that into a question that uses formal English?

Rigo: Are you afraid to do some things, like Jonathan James when the Whatif Monster is whispering in his ear?

Ms. Kramer: Excellent, Rigo. Let's take one more question. Then you'll finish in pairs.

Elisa: What's it like being so famous? Does your hand fall off from signing so many autographs?

Ms. Kramer: Okay. Can we say that a little differently? What do you mean when you say "hand fall off"?

Elisa: Well, that's when your hand is really tired and you don't want to write anymore.

Ms. Kramer: So, can I write, "Does your hand ever get so tired from signing autographs that you don't want to write any more?"

Elisa: Yes, that works.

Ms. Kramer: Okay, now work with your buddy to write down some questions together.

Students work in pairs to complete the task. At the end of their work session, the students share their questions, and then the questions are added to the list of questions to ask Michelle Nelson-Schmidt. A few questions are reworded, as Ms. Kramer emphasizes the need to use formal English.

Tips for the Teacher

HELPING STUDENTS MEET LANGUAGE Standard 3 can be challenging. For some students, formal English comes naturally, but for the others, it can feel like learning a new language. Ms. Kramer provides an enticing reason for her students to phrase their questions using formal English. Providing your students with an authentic audience is one way to motivate them to grapple with language conventions.

Listening and Speaking Throughout the Day

SOME OF THE LISTENING AND SPEAKING STANDARDS SEEM difficult for young children; however, it is important to deal with the standards in ways that are instructionally appropriate. The Vocabulary Acquisition and Use standard can be enhanced by integrating the language arts in the content areas with themes that bring new words into the discussion. Language use will be much richer when a well-developed theme runs throughout science, math, social studies, art, music, and play.

For instance, suppose the theme is about the five senses. Students will use sensory words about seeing, hearing, touching, tasting, and smelling, and all of these words will require the use of description. When making a cake, students will discuss the recipe, ingredients, and utensils needed, techniques such as kneading and mixing, and so on. While the cake bakes in the oven, students will describe the pleasant aroma that fills the room. After the cake comes out of the oven, students will discuss how it changed forms: from batter to a cake. Frosting and decorating the cake will provide students with additional topics for detailed descriptions. Finally, upon eating the cake, students will describe how it looks, smells, tastes, and even feels in terms of texture. Integrating a theme throughout the content areas provides an ideal context for expanding students' vocabulary.

Summary and Conclusions

THE ELA CCSS FOR LISTENING AND SPEAKING ARE divided into two categories: (1) Comprehension and Collaboration and (2) Presentation of Knowledge and Ideas. Each category includes three standards for a total of six ELA CCSS Listening and Speaking standards in kindergarten through grade 2 (NGA & CCSSO, 2010).

In this chapter, we discussed the research evidence base that supports the inclusion of the Listening and Speaking Anchor Standards in kindergarten through grade 2 as a part of the ELA CCSS to support the later development of reading and writing skills. We asserted that speaking and listening provide the very cognitive and linguistic foundations of early reading and writing development in schooling (Watts-Taffe & Breit-Smith, 2013). It follows that neglecting the development of oral language abilities, including speaking and listening, will likely limit or undermine young students' acquisition of early reading and writing skills.

ACTIVITIES

1. Design a web of clues that children can refer to during multiple activities to help them remember to provide sufficient detail in their descriptions of objects, concepts, and illustrations.

2. To encourage children to use interesting words in their descriptions, provide a box of surprise items. The child puts his or her hand in the box and pulls out whatever item he or she touches first. The child then describes the item, speaking in sentences and using at least five adjectives—for example, "I pulled out a stuffed animal that is a teddy bear. He is brown and white, he is furry and soft, and he has black eyes."

3. Ask kindergarten children to augment their stories, poems, and descriptions by creating illustrations, diagrams, and other graphics.

4. To facilitate children's use of complete sentences, have a Show and Tell about the topic of instruction. For instance, when children come up to talk about the plants they have been

growing, they must do so in complete sentences. If a child is having trouble, model how the presentation should be done—for example, "I planted this seed, and now little green buds are showing."

5. Set up a digital recorder. Have the children retell and record a story that you recently read to the class. The recorder will type up the story, which you can then print out for students to read and evaluate.

REFERENCES

Andrews, R., Torgeson, C., Beverton, S., Freeman, A., Locke, T., Low, G., Robinson, A., & Zhu, D. (2006). The effect of grammar teaching on writing development. *British Educational Research Journal, 32,* 39–55.

Baumann, J. F., Blachowicz, C. L. Z., Manyak, P. C., Graves, M. F., & Olejnik, S. (2009–2012). *Development of a multi-faceted, comprehensive, vocabulary instructional program for the upper-elementary grades* (R305A090163). Washington, DC: U.S. Department of Education, Institute of Education Sciences, National Center for Education Research, Reading and Writing Program.

Baumann, J. F., Edwards, E. C., Boland, E., Olejnik, S., & Kame'enui, E. W. (2003). Vocabulary tricks: Effects of instruction in morphology and context on fifth-grade students' ability to derive and infer word meanings. *American Educational Research Journal, 40,* 447–494.

Baumann, J. F., & Kame'enui, E. J. (Eds.). (2004). *Vocabulary instruction: Research to practice.* New York, NY: Guilford Press.

Biemiller, A. (2006). Vocabulary development and instruction: A prerequisite for school learning. In D. K. Dickinson & S. B. Neuman (Eds.), *Handbook of early literacy* (Vol. 2, pp. 41–51). New York, NY: Guilford Press.

Blaauw-Hara, M. (2006). Why our students need instruction in grammar, and how we should go about it. *Teaching English in the Two-Year College, 34,* 165–178.

Blachowicz, C. L. Z. & Fisher, P. J. (2002). Best practices in vocabulary instruction: What effective teachers do. In L. M. Morrow, L. Gambrell, & M. Pressley (Eds.), *Best practices in literacy instruction* (2nd ed., pp. 87–110). New York, NY: Guilford Press.

Blachowicz, C. L. Z., Fisher, P. J. L., Ogle, D., & Watts-Taffe, S. (2006). Vocabulary: Questions from the classroom. *Reading Research Quarterly, 41,* 524–539.

Blair, C. (2002). School readiness: Integrating cognition and emotion in a neurobiological conceptualization of child functioning at school entry. *American Psychologist, 57,* 111–127.

Buikema, J. L., & Graves, M. F. (1993). Teaching students to use context cues to infer word meanings. *Journal of Reading, 36,* 450–457.

Bus, A. G., van Ijzendoorn, M. H., & Pellegrini, A. D. (1995). Joint book reading makes for success in learning to read: A meta-analysis in intergenerational transmission of literacy. *Review of Educational Research, 65,* 1–21.

Christie, J. F., Enz, B. J., & Vukelich, C. (2007). *Teaching language and literacy: Preschool through the elementary grades.* Boston, MA: Allyn & Bacon.

Cunningham, P. (2005). *Phonics they use: Words for reading and writing.* Boston, MA: Allyn & Bacon.

Delpit, L. (1995) *Other people's children: Cultural conflict in the classroom.* New York, NY: New Press.

Dickinson, D. K., & Tabors, P. O. (Eds.). (2001). *Young children learning at home and school: Beginning literacy with language.* Baltimore, MD: Paul H. Brookes.

Elley, W. B. (1989). Vocabulary acquisition from listening to stories. *Reading Research Quarterly, 24,* 174–187.

Fearn, L., & Farnan, N. (2007). When is a verb? Using functional grammar to teach writing. *Journal of Basic Writing, 26,* 63-87.

Fernald, A., & Weisleder, A. (2011). Early language experience is vital to developing fluency. In S. B. Neuman & D. K. Dickinson (Eds.), *The handbook of early literacy research* (Vol. 3, pp. 3–19). New York, NY: Guilford Press.

Gillam, S., & Reutzel, D. R. (In press, 2013). Common core state standards (CCSS): New directions for enhancing young children's oral language development. In L. M. Morrow, T. Shanahan, & K. Wixson (Eds.), *Common core state standards:* Impact on literacy instruction. New York, NY: Guilford Press.

Graves, D. H. (1983). *Writing: Teachers and children at work.* Exeter, NH: Heinemann.

Graves, M. F. (2000). A vocabulary program to complement and bolster a middle-grade comprehension program. In B. M. Taylor, M. F. Graves, & P. van den Broek (Eds.), *Reading for meaning: Fostering comprehension in the middle grades* (pp. 116–135). Newark, DE: International Reading Association.

Graves, M. F. (2006). *The vocabulary book: Learning and instruction.* New York, NY: Teachers College Press.

Harris, J., Golinkoff, R. M., & Hirsh-Pasek, K. (2011). Lesson from the crib for the classroom: How many children really learn vocabulary. In S. B. Neuman & D. K. Dickinson (Eds.), *The handbook of early literacy research* (Vol. 3, pp. 49–65). New York, NY: Guilford Press.

Hart, B., & Risley, T. R. (1995). *Meaningful differences in the everyday experience of young American children.* Baltimore, MD: Paul H. Brookes.

Linden, M. J. & Whimbey, A. (1990). *Why Johnny can't write.* Hillsdale, NJ: Lawrence Erlbaum Associates.

Nagy, W. E., & Scott, J. A. (2000). Vocabulary processes. In M. L. Kamil, P. B. Mosenthal, P. D. Pearson, & R. Barr (Eds.), *Handbook of reading research* (Vol. 3, pp. 269–284). Mahwah, NJ: Lawrence Erlbaum Associates.

National Council of Teachers of English (NCTE). (2008). Writing now: A policy research brief produced by the National Council of Teachers of English. Urbana, IL: Author.

National Governors Association Center for Best Practices & Council of Chief State School Officers (NGA & CCSSO). (2010). *Common core state standards.* Washington, DC: Authors. Retrieved from www.corestandards.org/assets/CCSSI_ELA%20Standards.pdf

Noyce, R., & Christie, J. (1983). Effects of an integrated approach to grammar instruction on third graders' reading and writing. *Elementary School Journal, 84,* 63–69.

Roskos, K., Tabors, P. O., & Leinhart, L. A. (2009). *Oral language and early literacy in preschool: Talking, reading, and writing.* Newark, DE: International Reading Association.

Saddler, B., & Graham, S. (2005). The effects of peer-assisted sentence-combining instruction on the writing performance of more and less skilled young writers. *Journal of Educational Psychology, 97,* 43–54.

Scott, J. A., Vevea, J., & Flinspach, S. (2010, December). Vocabulary growth in fourth-grade classrooms: A quantitative analysis. In K. Moloney (Chair), *The VINE Project: A three-year study of word consciousness in fourth-grade classrooms.* Symposium conducted at the meeting of the National Reading Conference, Fort Worth, TX.

Stahl, S. A., & Nagy, W. E. (2006). *Teaching word meanings.* Mahwah, NJ: Erlbaum.

Swanborn, M. S. L., & de Glopper, K. (1999). Incidental word learning while reading: A meta-analysis. *Review of Educational Research, 69,* 261–285.

Watts-Taffe, S., & Breit-Smith, A. (2013). Language standards. In L. M. Morrow, T. Shanahan, & K. Wixson (Eds.), *Teaching with the common core standards for English language arts: PreK–2.* New York, NY: Guilford Press.

CHILDREN'S LITERATURE CITED

Blonder, E. (1994). *Noisy breakfast.* New York, NY: Scholastic.

Bridwell, N. (1966). *Clifford takes a trip.* New York, NY: Scholastic.

Brown, F. (n.d.). *Getting dressed.* Reading A–Z. Retrieved from http://www.readinga-z.com/book.php?id=28

Evans, D. (2002). *Math rashes and other classroom tales.* New York, NY: Scholastic.

Farrell, J. (2010a). Rock 'n roll for Mother Earth. *John Farrell's original songs from How about you?* and *The sons and the daughters* [MP3 files]. Edmeston, NY: Hope River Music.

Farrell, J. (2010b). Rock 'n roll for mother earth [Song lyrics]. Retrieved from http://www.johnfarrell.net/samples.htm

Hoose, P. M., & Hoose, H. (1998). *Hey, little ant.* Berkeley, CA: Tricycle Press.

Marzollo, J. (1998). *I am snow.* New York, NY: Scholastic.

Nelson-Schmidt, M. (2012). *Jonathan James and the Whatif monster.* La Jolla, CA: Kane Miller.

Reyes, G. (2011). *Odd animal helpers.* New York, NY: Scholastic.

Williams, S. (1996). *I went walking.* San Diego, CA: Red Wagon Books/Harcourt.

Wilson, K. (2002). *Bear snores on.* New York, NY: Margaret K. McElderry Books.

Foundational Skills Development

FOUNDATIONAL SKILLS, OR WORD STUDY, IS THE SINGLE area in the English Language Arts (ELA) Common Core State Standards (CCSS) that is not significantly different in terms of what and how we have taught in the past. Fewer skills are listed, which is a positive change, as students are able to more fully comprehend the skills outlined per grade level. The skills are placed primarily in kindergarten and grades 1 and 2 and explicit instruction is recommended, but when the opportunity arises, teachers are also encouraged to illustrate skills being taught in the context of connected text. "The CCSS recognize that foundational skills help students become independent readers. The ultimate goal in reading, however, is to comprehend texts in many disciplines" (NGA & CCSSO, 2010, p. 15). Having a strong understanding of these foundational skills will help a child to achieve this goal.

Darrin Henry/Fotolia

Foundational Skills Development

THE FOUNDATIONAL SKILLS STANDARDS HELP STUDENTS TO UNDERSTAND concepts of print, the alphabetic principle, and other basic conventions of the English writing system. Research has demonstrated that children become fluent readers, capable of comprehending what they read, when they can do the following:

- Decode automatically.
- Understand that letters have sounds that, when put together appropriately, can make words.
- Blend and segment letters to make words.

Foundational skills should be taught in a systematic, explicit manner but also be embedded in the reading and writing in which students are engaged. This approach reflects the CCSS emphasis on "an integrated model of literacy" (NGA & CCSSO, 2010, p. 4). According to the CCSS, a particular child should be taught only those skills he or she needs; therefore, differentiated instruction is recommended as an instructional approach.

Children who struggle with reading often need more instruction in foundational skills. Word study includes not only phonics and decoding but also involves building a sight vocabulary, learning to read pictures to help to figure out words, and using the context of a sentence to help to determine the meanings of words. These skills are as important as decoding.

Students in pre-K through grade 2 often progress through three stages of spelling development: emergent, letter-name alphabetic, and within-word pattern. Most children in preschool and kindergarten are in the *emergent* literacy stage. Emergent learners draw, scribble, and eventually incorporate features of print into their writing. While they do not read conventionally, they "pretend read" using the illustrations and their knowledge of a story to tell it as they hold the book (Sulzby, 1985).

The second stage of spelling development is the *letter-name alphabetic* stage. As learners continue to engage in explicit instruction and meaningful reading and writing activities, they learn about letters and develop a critical understanding of the *alphabetic principle,* which includes the concepts that phonemes, or individual sounds, correspond to letters and that the text on a page is arranged from left to right. This awareness is the onset of beginning reading in the conventional sense, into which many children move during the kindergarten year.

Next, children begin to systematically explore *within-word patterns* (Bear, Invernizzi, Templeton, & Johnston, 2012). When young children write, they try to match sounds to the letters they know. When children begin to include the features of long-vowel spelling in their writing, it suggests they are moving beyond the process of thinking about printed words, which is an important benchmark. They are becoming conventional readers who can chunk two or three letters together and know how that group of letters corresponds to sound.

Research Concerning the Acquisition of Literacy

Becoming literate is a process that begins at birth and continues throughout life. Children differ in their rates of literacy achievement, and they must not be pressured into accomplishing tasks or be placed on a predetermined schedule. Researchers have found that children learn that print can be functional as a first step in reading and writing (McGee & Morrow, 2005). The first words that a child says, reads, and writes are those that have meaning, purpose, and function in his or her life, such as family names, food labels, road signs, and names of fast-food restaurants.

After understanding the functions of print, the child becomes interested in the forms of print. Details about names, sounds, and configurations of letters and words now serve the child's learning more than a simple understanding of how print functions.

Next, the child learns the conventions of print. This process involves recognition that we read and write from left to right, that punctuation serves a purpose in reading and writing, and that spaces demarcate letters and words. Although recognizing the functions of print dominates the first stages of reading and writing development, children acquire an interest in and notions about the forms and conventions of print at the same time but to a lesser degree.

Researchers warn that children do not systematically progress from one developmental stage to the next in early reading and writing. They can take one step forward one day and move one step backward the next day. For example, you might test a child's knowledge of the alphabet and find that he or she can identify 15 letters, but the next day, you might find that he or she can identify only 12 letters. Factors such as focus and retention of material influence the progression of early learners.

There are three developmental levels in word recognition. Children first identify words through context, then using letter–sound cues, and finally relying on sounding out words (Cunningham, 2009; McCormick & Mason, 1981). Children's initial questions and comments during story readings are related to the pictures and the meanings of the stories. As children gain experience with story readings, their questions and comments begin to concern the names of letters, the reading of individual words, and attempts to sound out words (Cunningham, 2013; McAfee & Leong, 1997; Neuman & Roskos, 1998). The functions of print dominate early responses, and the forms of print become more important in later responses.

For some children, early reading and writing is embedded in real-life experience. Many families do things together that involve meaningful literacy. They write each other notes, lists, holiday greetings, and directions. Many children, however, do not have these opportunities and therefore may not have developed the same skills at the same age (Allington, 2009; Kuhn et al., 2006). Children are likely to become involved in literacy activities if they view reading and writing as functional, purposeful, and useful.

Studies of early reading and writing behaviors clearly illustrate that young children first acquire information about reading and writing through their functional uses (Cook-Cottone, 2004; McGee & Morrow, 2005). The following items represent only a sample of the functional literacy information with which children come in contact every day: grocery lists; directions on toys, packages, household equipment, and medicine containers; recipes; telephone messages; school-related notices; religious materials; menus; environmental print inside and outside the home; mail; magazines; newspapers; storybook readings; TV channels; telephone numbers; conversations among family members; letters; and their names. Young children are also aware of emails, text messages, and video game directions, and they are interested in literacy and technology. Children are familiar with these forms of literacy, participate in them, pretend to use them at play, and understand their purposes.

Parents, child-care providers, and preschool and kindergarten teachers need to provide experiences with reading similar to the experiences children have already had. To that end, it is crucial that teachers provide both explicit and embedded instruction in the foundational skills outlined in the CCSS. The following sections will discuss each of the skills included in the CCSS and provide instructional practices that teachers can utilize to provide their students with the foundational skills necessary to reach higher levels of literacy acquisition.

Emphasis of the CCSS Foundational Skills

Early and effective teaching of foundational skills will enable children to engage, experience, and independently read more complex texts over time—a central goal of the CCSS. In the early literacy period, in which children are learning how to figure out words, they need to work with text on a daily basis to become successful at decoding. The complex texts that students encounter during the early literacy stage include books teachers read aloud to them, rather than books they are able to read themselves.

Although the foundational skills are not ultimately the most important literacy skills to be learned, in pre-K through second grade, meeting the goals of the Foundational Skills standard is quite important for students to be able to progress to the next stages of working with comprehension and complex texts. In the past, foundational skills were commonly prioritized before comprehension skills in early literacy. However, within the Reading standards, the CCSS place Literature and Informational Text before Foundational Skills.

We might assume this was done to show that ultimately, the comprehension of text is the most important aspect of literacy instruction. However, we cannot forget that without the foundational skills, students will find it difficult to become fluent readers who can comprehend what they read.

Putting the Foundational Skills Standards into Practice

THE CATEGORIES OF FOUNDATIONAL SKILLS IDENTIFIED IN THE CCSS are Print Concepts, Phonological Awareness, Phonics and Word Recognition, and Fluency. In the following sections, we will discuss each category of skills and suggest some possible ways to teach these skills to young children across the early stages of literacy development.

Print Concepts

Table 2.1 provides the standards for children's early understanding of print concepts (grades K–1), and related pre-K standards are noted below.

TABLE 2.1 ● *Print Concept Standards for Grades K–1*

Kindergarten	Grade 1
Demonstrate understanding of the organization and basic features of print.	Demonstrate understanding of the organization and basic features of print.
a. Follow words from left to right, top to bottom, and page by page.	a. Recognize the distinguishing features of a sentence (e.g., first word, capitalization, ending punctuation).
b. Recognize that spoken words are represented in written language by specific sequences of letters.	
c. Understand that words are separated by spaces in print.	
d. Recognize and name all upper- and lowercase letters of the alphabet.	

Source: NGA & CCSSO (2010).

Related Pre-K Standards

- Recognize that alphabet letters are a special category of visual graphics that can be individually named.
- Recognize that print is what is read in stories.
- Understand that different forms are used for different functions of print (e.g., a list for groceries).
- Identify 10 letters in the alphabet, especially those in own name (Snow, Burns, & Griffin, 1998, p. 61).

Some of the print concepts are fairly new to early literacy instruction. Only within the last 30 years have we realized that learning to read from left to right on the page is a skill that needs to be taught. This is, however, a critical skill for students to learn, because in some other languages, reading is done from top to bottom or right to left.

Recognizing that words are presented in written language in sequences of letters and that words are separated by spaces are concepts we need to teach when a child is only 4 or 5 years old. The alphabet is a topic that we have always recognized as a print concept that necessitates direct instruction; however, it is also true that children can learn to read without knowing letter names. In first grade, the concepts about print that should be taught are recognizing the features of a sentence, such as capitalization at the beginning and punctuation at the end.

In this section of the chapter, we will provide examples of types of experiences that will aid students in developing proficiency with print concepts. The following classroom vignettes and lesson ideas illustrate and describe strategies related to each identified standard.

Print Concepts

Foundational Skills Standard 1   Demonstrate understanding of the organization and basic features of print (first grade).

a. Recognize the distinguishing features of a sentence (e.g., first word, capitalization, ending punctuation).

In the Common Core Classroom

Features of Print: First Grade

The first-graders in Ms. Mayfield's class have gathered on the carpet for shared reading time. Ms. Mayfield stands at the easel with the big book *Who Hops?* displayed (Davis, 1998). She introduced the book the previous day, and it will serve as the shared reading book for the week.

>*Ms. Mayfield:* Who can read for us the title of the shared reading book for this week?
>*Katherine:* It's called *Who Hops?*
>*Ms. Mayfield:* Great reading. And can someone remember the author?

Tyler: Katie . . . Dav . . . Katie Davis?

Ms. Mayfield: You're absolutely correct. I read this book aloud to you yesterday, and today I will reread it. But please join in reading with me if you can remember some of the words.

Ms. Mayfield begins to read the book aloud without interruption, and several students join in with her. Others giggle at the silly parts of the story, such as when the author says that cows can moo and give milk but that they don't hop!

Ms. Mayfield: Great reading, everyone. Today, we're going to take a closer look at some of the pages in our book, and we'll be looking at different parts of sentences. How do you know when you see a sentence?

Olivia: There's a capital at the beginning and a period at the end.

Ms. Mayfield: Great ideas, Olivia. Can anyone add to that?

Gabriel: It's not always a period. Sometimes it's a question mark if it's a question sentence.

Trisha: Or the other one! An exclamation point!

Ms. Mayfield: You are all correct. Let's look at this page.

Ms. Mayfield opens the book to a page that contains a sentence beginning with the word Who.

Ms. Mayfield: Can anyone come up and point to the first word in this sentence?

A student comes up and points to the word who.

Ms. Mayfield: What do you notice about this word?

Alyson: It has a *w*?

Ms. Mayfield: That's right, but can you say more about that? What's special about the w?

Alyson: Oh, I know! It has a capital letter in the beginning.

Ms. Mayfield: Right! Why does this word begin with a capital letter?

Alyson: Because it's the first word in the sentence. So that's where the sentence starts.

Ms. Mayfield: Smart thinking! Can someone come up and find the punctuation in this sentence?

A student comes up and points to the question mark.

Ms. Mayfield: Great work. What do we call this type of punctuation?

Emery: It's a question mark. And that means the sentence is over.

Ms. Mayfield: You're absolutely right. Everyone, it's smart to remember that every sentence begins with a capital letter and ends with punctuation. Let's try this out with partners.

Ms. Mayfield passes out smaller copies of Who Hops? *to all sets of partners.*

Ms. Mayfield: Working with your partner, try to find the beginning and end of each sentence in this book. Your hint is to look for capital letters and punctuation. I'll be around to listen in to your thinking.

Ms. Mayfield walks around as students engaged in this activity. She notices that two students are having difficulty identifying the types of punctuation and decides to meet with them later that day to review this concept.

Plans for the Teacher
Materials Needed to Get Started

A big book for shared reading and smaller copies (or photocopied pages) for students

Content of Lesson

To engage students in a similar lesson, begin by having them sit on the carpet or in the classroom meeting area and then display a big book so they all have a clear view of the print. Model the goal of this standard, recognizing the distinguishing features of a sentence, and provide students with the opportunity to practice in a whole-class setting.

Differentiation

Teachers may need to scaffold students' responses in a whole-class discussion to ensure not only that individuals can recognize capitalization and punctuation but also to confirm that they have an understanding of why these print features are present in a text.

Assessment

By providing partners with copies or photocopies of a text, teachers can quickly observe whether students are able to meet this objective and then plan for further small-group or individual instruction.

Foundational Skills Standard 1   Demonstrate understanding of the organization and basic features of print (kindergarten).

 d. Recognize and name all upper- and lowercase letters of the alphabet.

Features of Print: Kindergarten   Systematic teaching of the alphabet is necessary. Teachers frequently ask what letters they should teach first and how often they should teach a new letter. One of the most common practices is to teach the alphabet from beginning to end one letter a week. If the letter of the week is *B*, teachers can do many different activities. The letter should be introduced and written in both upper- and lowercase. The children can do a worksheet that asks them to circle the upper- and lowercase Bs on the page. At another time, the class can bake butter cookies in the shape of the letter B, and similar activities can follow.

This letter-of-the-week approach has been criticized when each letter is presented in isolation from meaning and it takes 26 weeks to introduce all of the letters. Some have suggested teaching a letter a day or two or three letters a week. That way, the alphabet is introduced quickly and teachers can go back and review each letter again (Levin et al., 2006). Reutzel carried out a study teaching kindergarten children the alphabet using the letter-of-the-week approach with one group and the letter-of-the-day approach with another group. Those in the letter-of-the-day group improved significantly in letter recognition compared to those in the letter-of-the-week group. Students' improvement was attributed to the constant review of letters throughout the year, after the letters had been introduced in an initial lesson (Reutzel & Cooter, 2009).

Many teachers help children identify the letters by beginning with the letters in their own names; this can be considered an effective way to begin teaching the alphabet. Another suggested approach when teaching a thematic unit is to select a few letters to feature that are used in the context of the theme. For example, in a unit on transportation, feature *b* for *boat, t* for *train, p* for *plane,* and *c* for *car*. It is crucial to assess children individually by using flashcards to determine which letters they do and do not know, and focus instruction on gaps in knowledge.

We know that students learn more quickly when we teach familiar letters first and identify letter sounds that are pronounced similarly to letter names, such as *b, p,* and *d*. Letters that occur frequently in print are also learned more easily, such as *r, t,* and *n*. Letter learning is reinforced and learned at a deeper and more lasting level when children write letters concurrently with learning letter names. Letters that do not "say their sounds"—such as *y, w,* and *h*—and those that do not appear frequently—such as *q, x,* and *z*—are often more difficult for students to learn and should be taught after the more easily learned letters. Also, letters that look similar can be confused by children, such as *m, n,* and *w*; *p, b, d,* and *q*; *l, n,* and *h*; *r, w, m, x, k,* and *y*; and *t* and *f* (McGee, 2007; Treiman & Kessler 2003). Letters that are more difficult to learn may need an increased amount of instruction.

Different researchers suggest different orders for teaching the letters. Some propose beginning with the most frequently used letters, while others feel strongly about children learning the letters of their names first. Some prefer the meaningful thematic approach; for instance, if students are learning about winter, the teacher would teach *w, s,* and *c* for *winter, snow,* and *cold*.

Ultimately, it is best to use multiple approaches to alphabet instruction. The majority of children will need multiple exposures to the same letter to truly retain this information (Justice & Piasta, 2011).

Phonological Awareness

Phonological awareness is a skill that requires children to break down speech to identify and manipulate its pieces and parts, beginning with large units of sound (syllables) and moving to smaller speech units (onsets and rimes) and finally to the smallest units of sound (phonemes) (Ziegler & Goswami, 2005). The importance of phonological awareness in early literacy development was recognized after the report of the National Reading Panel (2000) was issued. Table 2.2 highlights the standards for phonological awareness (grades K–1), and related pre-K standards are noted below.

TABLE 2.2 • *Phonological Awareness Standards for Grades K–1*

Kindergarten	Grade 1
Demonstrate understanding of spoken words, syllables, and sounds (phonemes). a. Recognize and produce rhyming words. b. Count, pronounce, blend, and segment syllables in spoken words. c. Blend and segment onsets and rimes of single-syllable spoken words. d. Isolate and pronounce the initial, medial vowel, and final sounds (phonemes) in three-phoneme (consonant-vowel-consonant, or CVC) words. (This does not include CVCs ending with /l/, /r/, or /x/.) e. Add or substitute individual sounds (phonemes) in simple, one-syllable words to make new words.	Demonstrate understanding of spoken words, syllables, and sounds (phonemes). a. Distinguish long from short vowel sounds in spoken single-syllable words. b. Orally produce single-syllable words by blending sounds (phonemes), including consonant blends. c. Isolate and pronounce initial, medial vowel, and final sounds (phonemes) in spoken single-syllable words. d. Segment spoken single-syllable words.

Source: NGA & CCSSO (2010).

Related Pre-K Standard

● Pays attention to separable and repeating sounds in language (e.g., *Peter, Peter, Pumpkin Eater, Peter Eater* [Snow, Burns, Griffin, 1998, p. 61]).

Early literacy instruction in phonological awareness and phonemic awareness ultimately serves to help students become independent readers. Teaching these skills to children should be done concurrently with other strategies for learning to read, such as acquiring sight words and learning how to use context clues and picture clues. Children need to have a holistic view of books and reading, as well as more abstract skills, as they learn to decode unknown words.

Phonological awareness is the ability to recognize the sound structure of language. It involves identifying and manipulating larger parts of spoken language, such as whole words, syllables, and word chunks (e.g., *-at, -an*). Segmenting, blending, and substituting one sound for another are important skills for young learners to develop.

Phonological awareness can be viewed as an umbrella term, and phonemic awareness is a skill that falls under that umbrella. *Phonemic awareness* refers to children's ability to recognize, identify, and manipulate phonemes—the smallest units of sound. Phonemic awareness, like phonological awareness, is an oral language activity. However, children's skills in both areas develop in concert with alphabet knowledge, each reinforcing the other; thus, teachers must teach them concurrently—both explicitly and in the context of reading and writing activities. In addition, phonemic awareness and phonological awareness are considered precursors to understanding phonics, and students must first develop these skills to be able to to learn phonics skills.

Even though phonemic awareness and phonological awareness underlie students' success in learning to read, they are only single elements of a comprehensive reading program. The concurrent use of several word study skills is necessary to develop proficient readers (Reutzel & Cooter, 2009). According to the report of the National Reading Panel (2000), a total of 18 hours' instruction in phonemic and phonological awareness is needed during the kindergarten year for a child to learn these skills. In a 180-day school year, that is about 6 minutes per day.

FIGURE 2.1 ● Scope and Sequence for Instruction in Phonemic Awareness

Phoneme isolation	What's the first sound in *boat*?
Phoneme identification	What is the same sound in *cow, cat,* and *cute*?
Phoneme categorization	Which word doesn't belong in this group: *run, ring, rope, tub*?
Phoneme blending	What is this word: /p/-/ă/-/t/?
Phoneme segmentation	How many sounds are in the word *tin*? Stretch the sounds: /t/ - /ĭ/ - /n/. How many sounds are in the word *pin*?
Phoneme deletion	What is the word *keep* without the /k/?
Phoneme addition	Add /s/ to the beginning of the word *top*. What word do you have now?
Phoneme substitution	The word is *hop*. Change the /h/ to /t/. What's the new word?

Source: Adapted from Armbruster, B., Lehr, F & Osborn, J. (2006). Put reading first: The research building blocks for teaching children to read. Washington, DC: National Institute for Literacy.

Figure 2.1 outlines the scope and sequence for phonemic awareness instruction beginning in pre-K and continuing through first grade (Armbruster, Lehr, & Osborn, 2006).

Phonological Awareness

Foundational Skills Standard 2   Demonstrate understanding of spoken words, syllables, and sounds (phonemes) (kindergarten).

a. Recognize and produce rhyming words.

In the Common Core Classroom
Rhyming Words: Kindergarten

The kindergartners in Ms. Cortina's class have been working on identifying pairs of rhyming words for the past several months. Students have participated in a variety of rhyming activities in their Word Work center, such as matching rhyming picture cards, using wiki sticks to highlight rhyming words in familiar nursery rhymes, and completing rhyming activities on the class iPad. Today, while the students work in a variety of centers around the classroom, Ms. Cortina decides to work with a small group of students who continue to struggle with rhyming.

> **Ms. Cortina:** I have a book here that we all know very well from story time. Can you all remember the title of this book?
>
> **All students:** *Tumble Bumble!*

Ms. Cortina: (Laughing) Wow, you all have a great memory! You're right. The title of this book is Tumble Bumble, and you might also remember that the author is Felicia Bond. Let's quickly warm up our reading muscles by taking a picture walk. While I'm showing you the pictures in this book, I want you to try to remember what the book is all about.

Ms. Cortina turns the pages in the book slowly, making sure that each student in the group can see the illustrations.

Ms. Cortina: Who can remind us what this story is all about?

Quinn: I remember! It's about a boy who goes on a walk and then . . . he meets some animals, and then . . . he goes in a house, and it's yellow, and the animals come in, too, and they all take a nap at the end.

Ms. Cortina: Smart thinking, Quinn! You remembered some important parts about this story. Today, we're going to take a closer look at this book, and we're going to try to find some of the rhyming words in this story. You might remember that I told you a great hint about rhyming words in a story . . .

Reese: They're at the end!

Ms. Cortina: Great, Reese. You're right. You can usually find rhyming words in a story at the ends of the sentences. Listen carefully as I read this page out loud.

Ms. Cortina opens the book to a page near the middle of the story and reads aloud.

Ms. Cortina: If you think you know the rhyming words on this page, whisper them out loud.

All students: (Whispering dramatically) Road, toad.

Ms. Cortina: Smart work! Let's try the next page.

Ms. Cortina turns the page and reads aloud.

All students: (Whispering) Mouse, house.

Ms. Cortina: I think you're ready to try this on your own. (While handing out materials) I'm giving each of you photocopies of the next several pages in the text, along with yellow highlighters. As I read the next few pages out loud, take your highlighters and highlight the rhyming words you see on each page.

The students work independently to highlight the rhyming words as Ms. Cortina reads aloud. After dismissing the students and sending them back to their centers, Ms. Cortina puts additional photocopies of the book with highlighters in the Word Work center so students can continue to practice this skill.

Tips for the Teacher

STANDARD 2 IDENTIFIES A WIDE RANGE of phonological awareness skills for each grade level. Teachers should recognize, however, that students are unlikely to master all of these skills after one or even several lessons. Students will need reinforcement in whole-class, small-group, and independent settings to truly internalize and meet the objectives outlined in Standard 2.

Phonics and Word Recognition

Phonics is the most widely known strategy for word study. Quite simply, *phonics* is the connection of sounds and symbols. The use of phonics requires children to learn letter sounds and combinations of letter sounds (referred to as *phonemes*) in association with their corresponding letter symbols (referred to as *graphemes*).

In the English language, there are 26 letters in the alphabet but at least 44 different sounds. This means that sound–symbol correspondence is not always consistent in English. There are many irregularities and exceptions to the rules, which are difficult for children to learn. Therefore, we must help children learn words by sight that are difficult to sound out, and we need to give them multiple strategies for figuring out unknown words.

In spite of the various difficulties with phonics, it is the major approach used to help children become independent readers. Table 2.3 highlights the standards for children's understanding of phonics and word recognition (grades K–2).

Consonants   Teaching the consonant sounds begins in preschool in a limited way. Instruction continues in kindergarten, and students have usually mastered these sounds by first grade.

TABLE 2.3 ● *Phonics and Word Recognition Standards for Grades K–2*

Kindergarten	Grade 1	Grade 2
Know and apply grade-level phonics and word analysis skills in decoding words.	Know and apply grade-level phonics and word analysis skills in decoding words.	Know and apply grade-level phonics and word analysis skills in decoding words.
a. Demonstrate basic knowledge of one-to-one letter-sound correspondences by producing the primary or many of the most frequent sounds for each consonant.	a. Know the spelling-sound correspondences for common consonant digraphs.	a. Distinguish long and short vowels when reading regularly spelled one-syllable words.
b. Associate the long and short sounds with common spellings (graphemes) for the five major vowels.	b. Decode regularly spelled one-syllable words.	b. Know spelling-sound correspondences for additional common vowel teams.
c. Read common high-frequency words by sight (e.g., *the, of, to, you, she, my, is, are, do, does*).	c. Know final -*e* and common vowel team conventions for representing long vowel sounds.	c. Decode regularly spelled two-syllable words with long vowels.
d. Distinguish between similarly spelled words by identifying the sounds of the letters that differ.	d. Use knowledge that every syllable must have a vowel sound to determine the number of syllables in a printed word.	d. Decode words with common prefixes and suffixes.
	e. Decode two-syllable words following basic patterns by breaking the words into syllables.	e. Identify words with inconsistent but common spelling-sound correspondences.
	f. Read words with inflectional endings.	f. Recognize and read grade-appropriate irregularly spelled words.
	g. Recognize and read grade-appropriate irregularly spelled words.	

Source: NGA & CCSSO (2010).

We begin teaching phonics with the most commonly used initial consonant sounds, such as *f, m, s, t,* and *h,* and then use the same sounds in ending word positions. The next set of initial and final consonant sounds usually taught is *l, d, c, n, g, w, p, r,* and *k* followed by *j, q, v;* final *x;* initial *y;* and *z.*

Most consonants are quite regular and represent a single sound. Some consonants have two sounds, such as the *g* in *go* and *girl* (often referred to as the "hard *g*"), and the *g* in *George, giraffe,* and *gentleman* (often referred to as the "soft *g*"). Other consonants with two sounds are the *c* in *cookie, cut,* and *cost* (the hard *c* sound) and the *c* in *circus, celebrate,* and *ceremony* (the soft *c* sound). The letter *x* has a "zee" sound when it appears at the beginning of a word, such as *xylophone,* but it has the "ex" sound in the word *next.* The letters *w* and *y* each have one sound at the beginning of a word and act as consonants, as in *was* and *yellow.* In the middle or at the end of a word, *w* and *y* act as vowels, as in *today* and *blow.*

Consonant blends and consonant digraphs are pairs of consonants that make new sounds. A *blend* is a cluster of two or three consonants in which the sounds of all of the consonants are heard but blended together, as in the words **blue, true, flew,** and **string.** A *consonant digraph* is composed of two consonants that when put together do not have the sound of either one but rather a new sound, such as **th** in **th**ree, *sh* in **sh**oes, **ch** in **ch**air, **ph** in **ph**otograph, and **gh** at the end of a word (e.g., *enou**gh***).

Vowels   The next phonic element we teach are the vowels. Many teachers begin teaching vowels toward the end of kindergarten and continue instruction in first grade.

The vowels are *a, e, i, o,* and *u.* We teach the short vowels first: *a* as in *cat, e* as in *bed, i* as in *hit, o* as in *hot,* and *u* as in *cut.* Next, we teach the long vowels: *a* as in *hate, e* as in *feet, i* as in *kite, o* as in *boat,* and *u* as in *cute.* Each long vowel has the sound of its letter name.

As mentioned earlier, *w* and *y* act as vowels in the middles and at the ends of words. The letter *y* has the sound of a long *e* when it comes at the end of a word, such as *baby.* The letter *y* has the sound of a long *i* when it comes at the end of a one-syllable word, such as *cry* or *try.*

In addition, vowels change sounds when they are *r* controlled. They become neither long nor short, as in *car* and *for.*

Like consonants, vowels are sometimes used in pairs. The first vowel pairs we teach are called *digraphs.* A vowel digraph includes two vowels that have a single sound, such as *ai* in *pail* and *ea* in *sea.* The next vowel pairs are called *diphthongs.* A diphthong is composed of two vowels that form a gliding sound as one vowel blends into the other, such as *oy* in *toy* and *oi* in *oil.* These vowel combinations can be difficult for students to master, as the letter sounds may change from one vowel combination to another.

At each grade level, teachers should review what has been learned and provide additional practice in medial consonants, variant consonant sounds, and blends. The phonics elements to work on after these have been mastered include some structural aspects, such as compound words, syllabication, contractions, prefixes, and suffixes. Eventually, children will learn about synonyms, antonyms, and homonyms.

Children find it easier to learn about word patterns or chunks, rather than individual sounds. Recognizing word patterns helps in decoding many different words that contain the same patterns but may have different beginning or ending sounds. Teachers should help students to learn familiar word patterns at the ends of words, which are called *rimes.* They are also referred to as *phonograms, word families,* and *chunks.* There are many common rimes, as illustrated in Figure 2.2.

FIGURE 2.2 ● Common Rimes Used in Early Literacy

ack	al	ain	ake	ale	ame	an	ank	up	ush
at	ate	aw	ay	ell	eat	est	ice	ick	ight
id	ill	in	ine	ing	ink	ip	ir	ock	oke
op	ore	or	uck	ug	ump	unk			

There are many phonics generalizations, or rules. Although many apply only to a few words, the following rules are considered to be more universal:

1. When a one-syllable word has only one vowel in the middle and it is surrounded by two consonants, the vowel is usually short. Words such as *hot, cut,* and *bet* follow this consonant-vowel-consonant (CVC) word pattern.
2. When there are two vowels in a one-syllable word and one of them is an *e* at the end, the first vowel is long and the *e* is silent. This is the consonant-vowel-consonant e (CVCe) pattern or final *e* rule. Some words that demonstrate this rule include *plate, cute,* and *bone.*
3. When a consonant is followed by a vowel, the vowel is usually long, as in *be, go,* and *because.* This is the consonant-vowel (CV) rule.
4. When two vowels appear together, the first is long and the second is silent, as in *meat, boat,* and *rain.* This is the consonant-vowel-vowel-consonant (CVVC) rule. Some people remember this rule by using the expression "When two vowels go walking, the first one does the talking."

Phonics and Word Recognition

Foundational Skills Standard 3   Know and apply grade-level phonics and word analysis skills in decoding words (first grade).

   e. Decode two-syllable words following basic patterns by breaking the words into syllables.

In the Common Core Classroom

Decoding Two-Syllable Words: First Grade

The first-graders in Ms. Williams' class have been studying short vowel sounds and consonant blends for several months, but Ms. Williams has noticed that many students are having difficulty using their phonics knowledge to accurately decode two-syllable words when reading independently. Because the majority of the class is having difficulty with this skill, she has decided to teach a whole-class lesson on this topic.

    Ms. Williams plans to teach the lesson using the text *A Mouse Told His Mother* (Roberts, 1997), which contains many two-syllable words, many of which are supported by picture clues. She gathers students in the classroom meeting area and displays a big book copy of the text in front of them. She introduces the title and author of the book, asks students to share predictions about the story, and then begins the lesson.

> **Ms. Williams:** As we read *A Mouse Told His Mother* today, you'll see that I've used sticky notes to cover the tricky words in this book. We're going to use some of our smart reading tools to figure out these words. Turn and share with your partner what reading tools you can remember. I'll listen in as you and your partner name these tools.

> *Students turn to face their partners and discuss various tools the class has been studying over the past several weeks.*

> **Ms. Williams:** I heard lots of smart ideas. You all remembered that we can use pictures as clues, look at the beginning sounds, and break longer words into smaller chunks or parts. These are some of the tools that we'll use today.

> *Ms. Williams begins to read aloud from the text, stopping at the word "pajamas," which has been covered up with a sticky note.*

> **Ms. Williams:** Readers, when I got to the tricky word, I said "blank" and then continued reading to the end of the sentence. Before I look at the letters in this word, I might able to use a picture clue to help me out. What could this word be?

> **Aneri:** *Clothes.* Because the mouse is wearing red clothes in the picture.

> **Ms. Williams:** Smart thinking! Any other ideas?

> **Rajvi:** *Pajamas.* Because right now it's bedtime, so that's probably what he's wearing.

> **Jack:** *Hat and scarf.* The mouse has those on.

> **Ms. Williams:** Let's take a look at the first part of this word. *(Removes sticky note and uncovers first syllable,* pa) Turn and whisper to your partner what you notice.

> *Students turn to one another and whisper "pa." Some say excitedly, "It's pajamas!"*

> **Ms. Williams:** So many of you are thinking the word might be *pajamas.* Let's take a look at the second part of this word. *(Removes second sticky note to show* jam)

> **Emily:** That's *jam!* Like when we learned the *am* word family.

> **Ms. Williams:** Right! *(Reveals remaining syllable)* So let's look at the last part of this word: as. So the parts we have are *pa, jam, as.* Now we need to put these parts together.

> **Students:** *Pajamas!*

> **Ms. Williams:** Let's go back and reread to check and make sure this word makes sense in the sentence. *Ms. Williams reads the line from the text aloud a second time, this time including the word "pajamas."* What do you think? Give a thumbs up if you're thinking that makes sense in the sentence and matches the picture.

Each student gives a thumbs-up to indicate that the word *pajamas* makes sense. Ms. Williams continues reading to the next sticky note and then stops so students can practice decoding another two-syllable word.

Tips for the Teacher

WHEN READING BIG BOOKS TO REINFORCE phonics instruction, using sticky notes to cover tricky words is a great way to help students practice decoding skills within the context of real reading. After students have sufficient practice decoding two-syllable words in a whole-class setting, gradually release responsibility by having them practice this skill with partners and then independently. The ultimate goal of teaching all phonics skills and strategies is for students to be able to apply what they have learned when reading independently.

Foundational Skills Standard 3   Know and apply grade-level phonics and word analysis skills in decoding words (second grade).

   b. Know spelling-sound correspondences for additional common vowel teams.

In the Common Core Classroom

Vowel Teams: Second Grade

The second-graders in Ms. Doucette's class have been studying common "vowel teams" (i.e., digraphs) for the past several weeks. During their Word Work block, they have completed word sorts and picture sorts, gone on word hunts in their independent reading books, and practiced typing word lists on the classroom computers using various fonts and colors.

Today, while students work around the classroom, engaged in self-selected Word Work activities, Ms. Doucette works with a small group of students to review several vowel teams the class has been studying. These students are able to complete word sorts and picture sorts with these vowel teams but have difficulty decoding words in context when reading independently. Ms. Doucette decides to use the book *Roller Coaster* (Frazee, 2003) with the group, because it is familiar to students and contains words with several of the vowel teams they have learned.

> ***Ms. Doucette:*** We've been working with lots of different vowel teams during Word Work. I wrote some of these vowel teams in a chart on this whiteboard, so let's quickly review the sounds.

> *As Ms. Doucette points to each vowel team (ea, ai, oa), students provide the correct sound.*

> ***Ms. Doucette:*** I have a book that we've used during our Writing Workshop. Do you all remember it? The title is *Roller Coaster*, and the author is Marla Frazee.

> ***Kylie-Ann:*** Oh, yeah! I remember it. It was about all these people going on a roller coaster and a girl going on one for the first time.

Ms. Doucette: Exactly! So today, I'm going to give you each a copy of the book, plus a whiteboard and a marker. We'll read the book quietly to ourselves, and when we find a word that has the /ea/, /oa/, or /ai/ sound, we can use what we know about these vowel teams to figure out the word. Then we'll write the word on our whiteboards under the correct heading in the chart. Take a minute to make your charts and add your headings, just like I did on my whiteboard.

The students all create charts on their whiteboards and add the vowel teams ea, ai, *and* oa *as column headings.*

Ms. Doucette: Let's take a look at the first page together. Open your books, and quietly read the first page to yourself.

The students quietly read the section of the text about people waiting in line to get on the roller coaster.

Daniella: I see one! *Waiting!* It has the *ai* vowel team.

The students write waiting *on their whiteboards under the* ai *heading.*

Ms. Doucette: Any others?

Shantae: Oh! Coaster! Like in the book title!

Ms. Doucette: Where should we add that word?

Shantae: Um, under oa. It has the long /o/ sound.

The students write coaster *on their whiteboards under the* oa *heading.*

Ms. Doucette: Great! Let's keep going. It will be your job to be word detectives as you read. If you find any words that fit our vowel teams, be sure to write them down.

Ms. Doucette monitors students as they work and encourages them to decode unfamiliar words using their knowledge of vowel teams and other letter–sound combinations. By the end of the text, the students' charts include nine words, as shown in Figure 2.3. Students who missed words are encouraged to look back in the text to locate each word and read it in the context of the sentence. Mrs. Doucette suggests that students try this activity with their independent reading books later that day.

FIGURE 2.3 ● Chart of Vowel Teams

ea	ai	oa
least	waiting	coaster
seat	train	load
releases	chain	
scream		

Plans for the Teacher

Materials Needed to Get Started

A book familiar to students, a copy for each group member, whiteboards and dry erase markers

Content of Lesson

Even though phonics lessons can occur in a whole-class or small-group setting, teachers may decide to utilize small strategy groups to reteach or review those skills that are difficult for some students. Often, students can demonstrate an understanding of phonics skills in isolation but have difficulty applying these skills to independent reading or writing.

When working with a small group on using phonics skills in context, model how to use context clues and phonics knowledge to decode unknown words. Then provide students with the opportunity to practice these skills independently.

Differentiation

When conducting a lesson with a group of students, the text you select should be at an instructional level for all group members. An independent-level text will not provide enough challenging two-syllable words for students to decode, and a text at frustration level will not provide students with enough context clues to accurately decode unfamiliar words. When working with a group of students that are having difficulty with this skill but are not at the same reading level, provide them with texts of different difficulty levels. Students do not need to use the same text to be successful with this lesson.

Assessment

Teachers should continually assess students on their mastery of phonics skills. This can be completed in a variety of ways, including independent reading and writing conferences, weekly word tests, checklists, and so on. Teachers can then utilize the data gained from these assessments to work with students independently or in small groups to reinforce those skills with which students are struggling.

Fluency

The goal of the CCSS Foundational Skills standards is to "develop proficient readers with the capacity to comprehend texts across a range of types and disciplines" (NGA & CCSSO, 2010, p. 15). To achieve this goal, children must become fluent readers.

According to the report of the National Reading Panel (2000), helping children to become fluent readers is crucial for literacy development. Prior to publication of this report, fluency was not a skill commonly emphasized in reading instruction.

TABLE 2.4 ● *Fluency Standards for Grades K–2*

Kindergarten	Grade 1	Grade 2
Read emergent-reader texts with purpose and understanding.	Read with sufficient accuracy and fluency to support comprehension. a. Read grade-level text with purpose and understanding. b. Read grade-level text orally with accuracy, appropriate rate, and expression on successive readings. c. Use context to confirm or self-correct word recognition and understanding, rereading as necessary.	Read with sufficient accuracy and fluency to support comprehension. a. Read grade-level text with purpose and understanding. b. Read grade-level text orally with accuracy, appropriate rate, and expression on successive readings. c. Use context to confirm or self-correct word recognition and understanding, rereading as necessary.

Source: NGA & CCSSO (2010).

Fluency is a combination of accuracy, automaticity, and prosody when reading. Put simply, a child who reads fluently is able to decode text automatically and accurately—without laboring over every sound. In addition, the child reads at the appropriate pace and with the appropriate expression. This aspect of language is referred to as *prosody*. Being able to read at the appropriate pace and with the appropriate expression suggests that the student comprehends the text (Kuhn & Stahl, 2003; Rasinski, Reutzel, Chard, & Linan-Thompson, 2011). The grades K–2 standards for fluency are identified in Table 2.4.

Foundational Skills Standard 4   Read with sufficient accuracy and fluency to support comprehension (first and second grades).

b. Read grade-level text orally with accuracy, appropriate rate, and expression on successive readings.

In the Common Core Classroom

Fluency: First and Second Grades

It is October, and Reading Workshop is in full swing in Ms. Kuzniacki's second-grade class. While students sit in "book nooks" around the room with their reading partners, Ms. Kuzniacki meets with students for individual conferences and a special education teacher meets with guided reading groups at a table in the back of the room. Ms. Kuzniacki has noticed several students at various reading levels struggling with reading fluently, and she plans to meet with some of them today.

Checking over her notes from previous student conferences, Ms. Kuzniacki decides to begin her conferences today by meeting with Andrew, a reader who has difficulty with decoding and, as a result, often struggles to read fluently with accuracy and expression. She selects a book for Andrew to read to work on fluency—a book that he has had read before. Andrew will be able to read the book easily and therefore focus on reading fluently.

Ms. Kuzniacki: Andrew, may I interrupt you for a few minutes? I brought over some books that I'd like to take a look at with you. Have you read either of these books before?

Andrew: Um, I read *There Is a Bird on Your Head!* and I read *Wemberly Worried*, too.

Ms. Kuzniacki: Great! I'm glad that you're familiar with these books. Today, I'd like you to pick one to read, and we're going to work on reading in a smooth voice and reading with expression.

Andrew: Um, I'll read *There Is a Bird on Your Head!*

Andrew picks up the book, opens it to the first page, and begins to read rapidly and in a monotone voice.

Ms. Kuzniacki: Andrew, may I interrupt you? This book was a great choice, because it's all about a conversation between two characters. Let's try this again, but this time, how about if I read the Elephant parts and you can be Piggie? We're also going to slow down a bit and check the punctuation for clues about how to read the sentence.

Ms. Kuzniacki begins to read with expression.

Ms. Kuzniacki: Did you notice that when I saw the exclamation point, I tried to make my voice sound excited, and when I saw the question mark, I made my voice go up at the end, like I was asking a question? These are things readers do when they read with expression. Let's try that as we continue reading.

Ms. Kuzniacki and Andrew continue to read as Elephant and Piggie, with Ms. Kuzniacki interjecting tips and encouraging remarks when Andrew reads expressively. By the end of the book, he is smiling as he reads the silly story and is reading in a smooth voice with tentative expression.

Ms. Kuzniacki: Andrew, that was great work! When you read in a smooth voice with expression, it really helps you to understand the story better. I'm going to leave both of these books with you to practice reading with expression, and you might decide to pick out some other Elephant and Piggie books from the Mo Willems bin in our library the next time you go book shopping.

As Ms. Kuzniacki leaves to meet with another student, she notices that Andrew flips back to the beginning of the book and begins to reread the book out loud. She notes in her anecdotal records to continue to work on expressive reading with Andrew by using texts on or slightly below his current reading level.

Tips for the Teacher

THE WORDING OF THE FLUENCY STANDARD reads: "Read grade-level text orally with accuracy, appropriate rate, and expression on successive readings." Many students, especially in the primary grades, are quick to announce that they are finished with a book after a first reading, rather than deciding on their own to reread the text. It is crucial that we, as teachers, model repeated readings, especially to develop expressive reading. Books with simple dialogue, such as the *Piggie and Elephant* series by Mo Willems, encourage students to develop naturally fluency as they take on the roles of the story characters.

Additional instructional techniques for fluency instruction include echo reading, choral reading, repeated reading, partner reading, Reader's Theater, and listening to stories read aloud on tape. When studying a particular theme, the teacher may decide to create a Reader's Theater piece from an informational or narrative text. Reader's Theater is a purposeful approach to fluency instruction, as students are provided with time to rehearse their parts and then read them aloud as a performance, focusing on appropriate expression and pace. Inviting students' families or members of the school community to a Reader's Theater performance will help students view reading fluency as an authentic and meaningful skill.

Foundational Skills Throughout the Day

FOUNDATIONAL SKILLS ARE TYPICALLY TAUGHT USING EXPLICIT INSTRUCTION at a particular time during the language arts block. However, teachers can embed skills teaching within reading and writing instruction when appropriate.

For example, teachers can use certain texts for syllable instruction. Prior to reading the text, the teacher should introduce the term *syllables* explicitly, and then while reading, students should practice clapping the syllables of various words or sections of the text. Certain types of stories lend themselves particularly well to this type of instruction, such as *Five Little Monkeys Sitting in a Tree* (Christelow, 1998); it has a distinct rhythm that will aid students in clapping the syllables when reading the text aloud. This activity can also be completed with simple children's songs, such as "Three Blind Mice."

When creating experience charts with young children, counting the words in a sentence helps to increase phonemic awareness. For example, *The Snowy Day* (Keats, 1962) contains many words that begin with the letter *s*. Point this out by writing all of the *s* words on a chart after reading the story.

Teachers should also look for opportunities to bring awareness to foundational skills, such as during the Morning Message or a student conversation. If a first-grade class is learning about digraphs and some come up in conversation, the teacher should take the time to point them out to students. For example, during Show and Tell, first-grader Sharon said: "Last night, it rained a lot. The showers didn't stop forever. The windows were shining from the drops of water." This would be a great time for the teacher to recognize Sharon's use of language: "Sharon just used two words that begin with *sh* digraph we are learning about. Listen and see if you hear them." Sharon raised her hand and said, "Well, there were *showers* and *shining* and there is another—my name, *Sharon*." Take every opportunity to embed or reinforce foundational skills spontaneously or purposefully into any lesson.

Summary and Conclusions

FOR MANY STUDENTS, GRADE-LEVEL EXPECTATIONS MATCH THEIR DEVELOPMENTAL level, but for many other students, the two do not align. Teachers who understand the significance of their students' level of literacy development are in a better position to teach print concepts, phonological awareness, phonics and word recognition, and fluency in a developmentally responsive way. As highlighted in the CCSS: "Good readers will need much less practice with these concepts than struggling readers will. The point is to teach students what they need to learn and not what they already know" (NGA & CCSSO, 2010, p. 15).

ACTIVITIES

1. Define the following words about foundational skills: high-frequency words, phonological awareness, phonemic awareness, diagraphs, blends, segment, prefixes, suffixes, print concepts, alphabetic principles.

2. Select three initial consonants and design a classroom experience that will teach and reinforce the sound–symbol relationship of each. Connect the letters to a thematic topic that is commonly studied in science or social studies in early childhood classrooms. Use both explicit and embedded experiences.

3. Create a lesson to teach high-frequency words using a "word wall." Include the objective, student activities, and evaluation of the lesson.

4. Identify the foundational skill that underlies each of the following activities:
   a. Make words from onsets and rimes.
   b. Sort words with similar patterns into separate categories.
   c. Create little words from a big word.

5. Use the following tools to create three phonics lessons about long vowels:
   a. an electronic whiteboard.
   b. a software program on the computer
   c. a pocket chart and word cards

6. For the most part, you will teach foundational skills systematically using explicit instruction. However, you will find situations in which skills instruction can be embedded into content areas or with children's literature. Describe three embedded situations in which you could teach foundational skills.

REFERENCES

Allington, R. L. (2009). *What really matters in fluency: Research-based practices across the curriculum.* Boston, MA: Allyn & Bacon.

Armbruster, B., Lehr, F., & Osborn, J. (2006). *Put reading first: The research building blocks for teaching children to read.* Washington, DC: National Institute for Literacy.

Bear, D. R., Invernizzi, M., Templeton, S., & Johnston, F. (2012). *Words their way: Word study for phonics, vocabulary, and spelling instruction* (5th ed.). Boston, MA: Allyn & Bacon.

Cook-Cottone, C. (2004). Constructivism in family literacy practices: Parents as mentors. *Reading Improvement, 41*(4), 208–216.

Cunningham, P. (2009). *Phonics they use* (5th ed.). Boston, MA: Pearson.

Cunningham, P. (2013). *Phonics they use: Words for reading and writing.* (6th ed.). Boston, MA: Pearson.

Kuhn, M., Schwanenflugel, P., Morris, R., Morrow, L. M., Woo, D., Meisinger, E., Sevcik, R., Bradley, B., & Stahl, S. (2006). Teaching children to become fluent and automatic readers. *Journal of Literacy Research, 38,* 357–387.

Kuhn, M. R., & Stahl, S. A. (2003). Fluency: A review of developmental and remedial strategies. *Journal of Educational Psychology, 95,* 3–21.

Levin, I., Snatil-Carmon, S., & Asif Rave, O. (2006). Learning of letter names and sounds and their contribution to word recognition. *Journal of Experimental Child Psychology, 93*(2), 139–165.

McAfee, O., & Leong, D. (1997). *Assessing and guiding young children's development and learning.* Boston, MA: Allyn & Bacon.

McCormick, C., & Mason, J. (1981). What happens to kindergarten children's knowledge about reading after summer vacation? *Reading Teacher, 35,* 164–172.

McGee, L. (2007). Language and literacy assessment in preschool. In J. Paratore & R. McCormack (eds.),*Classroom literacy assessment: Making sense of what students know and do* (pp. 65–84). New York, NY: Guilford Press.

McGee, L. M., & Morrow, L. M. (2005). *Teaching literacy in kindergarten.* New York, NY: Guilford Press.

National Governors Association Center for Best Practices & Council of Chief State School Officers (NGA & CCSSO). (2010). *Common Core State Standards.* Washington, DC: Authors. Retrieved from www.corestandards.org/assets/CCSSI_ELA%20Standards.pdf.

National Reading Panel (NRP). (2000). *Teaching children to read: Report of the subgroups.* Washington, DC: U.S. Department of Health and Human Services, National Institutes of Health.

Neuman, S., & Roskos, K. (eds.). (1998). *Children achieving: Best practices in early literacy.* Newark, DE: International Reading Association.

Rasinski, T. V., Reutzel, D. R., Chard, D., & Linan-Thompson, S. (2011). Reading fluency. In M. L. Kamil, P. D. Pearson, B. Mojc, & P. Afflerbach (eds.), *Handbook of reading research* (Vol. 4, pp. 286–319). New York, NY: Routledge.

Reutzel, D. R., & Cooter, R. B. (2009). *Teaching children to read: Putting the pieces together* (4th ed.). Upper Saddle River, NJ: Pearson/Merrill/Prentice Hall.

Snow, C. E., Burns, M. S., & Griffin, P. (1998). *Preventing reading difficulties in young children.* Washington DC: National Academy Press.

Sulzby, E. (1985). Children's emergent reading of favorite storybooks. *Reading Research Quarterly, 20,* 458–481.

Treiman, R., & Kessler, B. (2003). The role of letter names in the acquisition of literacy. In R.V. Kail (ed.), *Advances in child development and behavior* (3rd ed., pp. 105–135.) Oxford, UK: Academic Press.

Ziegler, J. C., & Goswami, U. (2005). Reading acquisition, developmental dyslexia, and skilled reading across languages: A psycholinguistic grain size theory. *Psychological Bulletin, 13*(1), 3–29.

CHILDREN'S LITERATURE CITED

Bond, F. 1996. *Tumble bumble.* New York, NY: Scholastic.

Davis, K. 1998. *Who hops?* Orlando, FL: Harcourt.

Christelow, E. (1993). *Five little monkeys sitting in a tree.* San Anselmo, CA: Sandpiper.

Cole, J. (1991). *Anna Banana 101 jump rope rhymes.* New York, NY: Scholastic.

Cole, J., & Calmenson, S. (1990). *Miss Mary Mack and other children's street rhymes.* New York, NY: Morrow Junior Books.

Cowley, J. (1999). *Mrs. Wishy-Washy.* New York, NY: Philomel Books.

Ehlert, L. (1989). *Eating the alphabet: Fruits & vegetables from A to Z.* San Diego, CA: Harcourt Brace Jovanovich.

Frazee, M. 2003. *Roller coaster.* Orlando, FL: Harcourt.

Henkes, K. (2000) Wemberly worried. New York, NY: HarperCollins.

Katz, A. (2001). *Take me out of the bathtub.* New York, NY: Scholastic.

Keats, E. J. (1963). *The snowy day.* Boston, MA: Viking Juvenile.

33tt3ption

1fff

Lobel, A. (1986). *The Arnold Lobel book of Mother Goose: A treasury of more than 300 classic nursery rhymes.* New York, NY: Random House.

Orozoco, J. (2002). *Diez deditos and other play rhymes and action songs from South America.* New York, NY: Puffin Books.

Prelutsky, J. (1986). *Read aloud rhymes for the very young.* New York, NY: Alfred Knopf.

Roberts, B. (1997). *A mouse told his mother.* New York, NY: Scholastic.

Shaw, N. E. (1986). *Sheep in a jeep.* Boston, MA: Houghton Mifflin.

Willems, M. (2007). *There is a bird on your head!* New York, NY: Scholastic.

Zelinsky, P. (1990). *The wheels on the bus.* New York, NY: Dutton Children's Books.

Reading Development: Comprehending Literature

THE ENGLISH LANGUAGE ARTS (ELA) COMMON CORE STATE Standards (NGA & CCSSO, 2010) recommend that teachers use many different types of children's literature as the main source of material for development of reading comprehension because reading quality literature provides students with opportunities to interact with texts in meaningful ways (Morrow, 2012; Morrow & Gambrell, 2011; Rosenblatt, 1978, 1994; Sipe, 2008). Students can listen to literature read aloud, read it themselves, think and talk about it, relate it to their own lives, and respond to it in any number of ways (Bryan, Tunnell, & Jacobs, 2007). All of these cognitive, social, and emotional interactions can occur within the authentic context provided by children's literature.

Monkey Business/Fotolia

In addition, reading high-quality children's literature is motivating. Reading good books makes students want to read more, and increased reading is related to overall improvement in literacy skills (Guthrie, 2011; Martinez & McGee, 2000). Reading literature helps build background knowledge, as well, which is important for all students but especially those from disadvantaged backgrounds (Moore, Alvermann, & Hinchman, 2000). Students can also develop vocabulary and comprehension skills and learn about text structures, literary genres, and author and illustrator styles from reading literature (Beck & McKeown, 2001; Gunning, 2010; Leung, 2008). Finally, making high-quality literature available in the classroom develops students' love of and appreciation for reading (Galda, 2010; Galda & Cullinan, 2003).

Reading Children's Literature in the Classroom

IN THE CLASSROOM, CHILDREN'S LITERATURE CAN BE USED successfully with a variety of instructional approaches—for instance, teacher read-alouds and independent reading—and to support theme-based instruction in the content areas. Research has proven a connection between teachers reading aloud in the classroom and students making gains in vocabulary, comprehension, background knowledge, listening, and attitudes toward reading (Baker, Chard, & Edwards, 2002; Beck & McKeown, 2001; Fisher, Flood, Lapp, & Frey, 2004; Leung, 2008; Martinez & McGee, 2000). Students' independent reading of literature is particularly effective when they are encouraged to account for what they read (Gunning, 2010). Integrating children's literature in content-based thematic instruction stimulates students' interest in concepts ranging from the weather (e.g., using *The Mitten* [Brett, 1989]) to the Civil War (e.g., using *The Red Badge of Courage* [Crane, 2005/1895]) (Fisher & Frey, 2011; Guthrie, 2011).

Research has also shown that a variety of beneficial reading outcomes result from using children's literature for guided instruction and for independent and partner reading (Edmunds & Bauserman, 2006; Neuman, 1997; Neuman & Celano, 2001; Pachtman & Wilson, 2006). Moreover, reading on a frequent basis has been associated with improvement in students' literacy skills (Guthrie, 2011; Lau, 2009).

Given the tremendous importance of infusing literature into literacy instruction, a significant portion of the CCSS is dedicated to its use. The CCSS Reading Standards focus on supporting students' ability to read and comprehend increasingly complex texts. Two standards address reading comprehension: Literature and Informational Text. In this chapter, the focus is on literature—narrative literature, in particular (e.g., folktales, fairytales, fables, picture books, and novels)—along with strategies for helping children comprehend. To accomplish this goal at the pre-K through grade 2 level, four categories of standards are provided:

1. Key Ideas and Details
2. Craft and Structure
3. Integration of Knowledge and Ideas
4. Range of Reading and Level of Text Complexity

Research Support for Reading Standards for Literature

Research has established the value of reading children's literature, including both narratives and informational texts. The standards in the first category, Key Ideas and Details, address skills such as identifying significant details in a text, retelling familiar stories, and identifying the characters, settings, and major events in a story. Among the most important strategies students should learn is how to summarize a text. Doing so involves recognizing main ideas and key details and identifying elements of story structure (e.g., character, setting, theme, major events, and resolution). Students should also be able to retell familiar stories after reading them (Almasi & Hart 2011; Gunning; 2010; Morrow, 2012). Morrow (2012) suggests that there is a significant connection between retelling and reading comprehension: "Retelling, whether it is oral or written, engages children in holistic comprehension and organization of thought" (p. 230). Students will better comprehend the central ideas of what they read if they apply the strategies mentioned earlier.

The second category, Craft and Structure, contains standards aimed at helping students to learn new words, to distinguish among different types of texts, and to learn about authors' and illustrators' styles. Knowing the meanings of words is necessary for reading comprehension. Students who lack word knowledge will have difficulty comprehending sentences, paragraphs, and full texts and will be unable to determine the meaning of what they read. Best practices for teaching word knowledge and vocabulary have been suggested by several researchers (Bear, Invernizzi, Templeton, & Johnston, 2008; Beck, McKeown, & Kucan, 2008; Blachowicz & Fisher, 2011). Knowing about different types of text structures (e.g., poetry, folktales, fables, and so on) not only improves students' comprehension, but also enhances their understanding by helping them organize information as they read and then process it. Knowing about authors' and illustrators' styles is important to students' understanding of concepts about books, as well, and deepens their appreciation for the processes that underlie reading and writing.

The standards in Integration of Knowledge and Ideas, the third category, address skills such as comparing and contrasting characters within stories and recognizing the purposes of illustrations in the stories in which they appear. Teaching kindergartners how to compare and contrast can begin with helping them understand the relationship between the illustrations and the text. Many young children pretend to read by looking at the illustrations in a book; as they develop as readers, they gradually move from the pictures to the print (Sulzby, 1985). Furthermore, as readers continue to develop, they learn that not only are pictures and print related, but also that pictures can be used to assist in word identification and comprehension (Pearson & Duke, 2002).

In the final category, Range of Reading and Level of Text Complexity, the standards focus on helping students to read and comprehend complex narrative literature at or above grade level. When teachers read aloud to the class, they should read at- or above-grade-level texts. Although students may not be able to read the same texts, they can listen to and discuss them in a critical manner. Although whole-class instruction should consist primarily of grade-level or above materials, it is crucial that children are provided with individualized, explicit instruction based on their level of achievement using instructional-level materials, which will ensure the greatest opportunity to improve their reading ability.

Several measures of text complexity should be considered. *Quantitative* text complexity is measured by these qualities:

1. the percentage of words with phonically regular relationships between letters and sounds

2. the degree of match between letter–sound relationships

3. the difficulty of the vocabulary

4. the lengths of sentences

5. the numbers of words in sentences
6. the number of different words
7. the complexity of sentence structure

The difficulty level of a text can be determined using any of several readability formulas—among them, the Fry Readability Formula (Fry, 1968) and the Dale-Chall Readability Formula (Dale & Chall, 1948). Readability software is also available, including the Lexile Framework for Reading (MetaMetrics, 2013).

An additional method of determining text complexity looks at the reader, the text, and the task. This method considers the reader's background knowledge of and inherent curiosity about the subject of the text, which can affect his or her motivation to read.

In addition, these *qualitative* features of text complexity should be addressed:

1. **Levels of meaning:** Does the text have one or several levels of meaning? A text with a single level of meaning is less challenging than one with various levels of meaning.

2. **Structure of text:** How is the text presented? In a simple text, events are usually presented in sequence, whereas in a more challenging text, events may be presented out of sequence (e.g., using flashbacks or moving into the future).

3. **Language conventions and clarity:** What is the nature of vocabulary? Simple texts use basic words and language that is concrete, straightforward, and conversational. Challenging texts use uncommon words and language that is colloquial, symbolic, and unfamiliar.

4. **Knowledge demands:** How much prior knowledge does the reader need to understand the text? Texts that require a certain level or type of prior knowledge are more challenging than texts that do not have these knowledge requirements (Malloy & Gambrell, 2013).

Each category of the CCSS Reading Standards for Literature relates to building students' comprehension of texts. These standards are designed to support students' ability to read and comprehend increasingly complex texts. As students progress through the grades, the content for each standard spirals, becoming increasingly complex and difficult and building on skills and strategies acquired in previous grades.

Putting the Reading Standards for Literature into Practice

THE SPIRALING NATURE OF THE CCSS IS UNIQUE and significant. Compared to standards of the past, some of the CCSS are less explicit and prescriptive. The CCSS are repeated across grade levels, reinforcing learning while also becoming increasingly complex. Consequently, children acquire the skills needed to read with greater depth and comprehension.

Key Ideas and Details

As noted earlier, the first category in the standards for reading literature is Key Ideas and Details (see table 3.1). For kindergarten students, Standard 1 in that category states, "With prompting and support, ask and answer questions about key details in a text." For first-graders, the skill stays the same but greater accountability is expected of students. For grade 1, the standard states, "Ask and answer questions about key details in a text"; the language about

TABLE 3.1 ● *Reading Literature Standard 1 for K–Grade 2:* **Key Ideas and Details**

Kindergarten	Grade 1	Grade 2
With prompting and support, ask and answer questions about key details in a text.	Ask and answer questions about key details in a text.	Ask and answer such questions as *who, what, where, when, why,* and *how* to demonstrate understanding of the key details in a text.

Source: NGA & CCSSO (2010).

providing "prompting and support" has been dropped. For grade 2, the standard becomes even more challenging: "Ask and answer such questions as *who, what, where, when, why*, and *how* to demonstrate understanding of the key details in the text." Across the grade levels, the activities provided to help students meet these standards will be both similar and different to reflect students' varying abilities and developing skills.

Kindergartners sometimes find it difficult to listen in whole-group settings. Because most of these children don't read yet, teachers often read aloud to them. Some first-graders will be emergent readers early in the school year, and some will read at grade level or above as the year progresses. Teachers can read books aloud to first-grade students or have them read in small groups and follow up with discussion. These approaches are also suitable for second-graders, who should be proficient in decoding and developing the skills needed for fluent, automatic, expressive reading. Teachers might read a complex book to the group and then discuss it, or students might read material of the appropriate difficulty level on their own and then discuss it with a small group of classmates.

Reading Literature Standard 1   Ask and answer such questions as *who, what, where, when, why,* and *how* to demonstrate understanding of the key details in a text (second grade).

In the Common Core Classroom
Discussing Details after a Read Aloud: Second Grade

As Ms. Tempera's second-graders hurry in from recess, they chat as they put away lunchboxes, hang up their jackets, and head over to the meeting area. Ms. Tempera is ready to greet them and share a familiar read-aloud book with the class.

Ms. Tempera: Hi, everyone. Let's get ready for our afternoon. I have a book to read to you today, and it's one we've heard before. *(Holding up a copy of* Owen*)* Today, I'm going to read this book aloud to you, and I want you to listen carefully for the key details in the story: the *who, what, where, when, why,* and *how,* just like we've been practicing. At the end of the story, I'm going to ask you to work together with your reading partners. For today, one partner will ask the questions and the other partner will answer. Let's get ready to listen carefully.

Ms. Tempera reads the story aloud and as she reads, she models asking various questions and asks students to turn and talk to discuss their answers.

Ms. Tempera: You did a great job answering some of my questions. Now it's your turn to practicing asking and answering some of your own questions.

Ms. Tempera passes out a graphic organizer to each set of designated reading partners. The graphic organizer provides a template for students to write who, what, where, when, and why questions and spaces to record partner responses. As students work around the classroom, Ms. Tempera supports various partnerships in both asking and answering questions about key details. She listens in as Austin and Ava work, leaning against the pillows on one of the classroom carpets.

Austin: Okay, I have my *who* question. Are you ready to answer it? I wrote, "Who are the main characters in this story?"

Ava: That's easy. The main characters are Owen, his mom and dad ... Oh, and also Mrs. Tweezers. Are you writing down my answer?

Austin: Yes, I've got it. Okay, here's my *what* question: "What happened at the end of this story?"

Ava: His mom fixed the problem. She cut his blanket up into little squares, so he can take them everywhere now, even to school.

Ms. Tempera: Great questions, you two. It looks like you're still working on a *when* question. Remember that a *when* question might have to do with the setting, and it also might have to do with sequence, or when events in the story took place.

Austin: Oh! Okay I have one now: "When did Owen bury his blanket in the sand?"

Ava: Um . . . that was after his parents put it in vinegar.

Austin: Yup, you're right!

Ms. Tempera notes her observations and plans to work further with the class on how to develop each type of question.

Tips for the Teacher

ALTHOUGH STUDENTS ARE REQUIRED BY STANDARD 1 to ask and answer *who, what, where, when, why,* and *how* questions, they will need a great deal of teacher modeling to have a clear understanding of how to develop and answer questions. An interactive read-aloud provides a great opportunity to model asking and answering questions about key details in a text.

Table 3.2 provides the second Key Ideas and Details standard from the CCSS for Reading Literature.

TABLE 3.2 • *Reading Literature Standard 2 for K–Grade 2:*
Key Ideas and Details

Kindergarten	Grade 1	Grade 2
With prompting and support, retell familiar stories, including key details.	Retell stories, including key details, and demonstrate understanding of their central message or lesson.	Recount stories, including fables and folktales from diverse cultures, and determine their central message, lesson, or moral.

Source: NGA & CCSSO (2010).

Retelling Stories   In Standard 2, within the category Key Ideas and Details, the teacher will help the children learn to retell stories, include key details, and demonstrate understanding of the central message or main idea (see table 3.2). To meet this standard, students must be able to demonstrate mastery with different types of children's literature, such as fables, folktales, and picture storybooks. When students retell a story—whether by speaking or writing—they are active participants in a literacy experience that supports the development of language structures, reading comprehension, and understanding of story structure (Paris & Paris, 2007).

Retelling a story immerses students in the text, fully engaging them in comprehending what they read and organizing their thoughts, and once they have some experience in retelling, they will grasp the concept of text structure. When introducing a narrative, students will be able to recount how the story begins and in what setting it takes place; then they will be able to provide details about the plot, as well as the resolution and the theme. Retelling allows students to demonstrate their understanding of story sequence, their ability to identify key details, and their ability to infer and interpret characters' speech and actions.

Many students have difficulty retelling stories, but they can learn this skill with sufficient practice and guidance. To prepare students, the teacher should tell them before they read or listen to a story that they will later retell or rewrite it (Morrow, 1996). The teacher should also model a retelling for students. The instruction the teacher provides should relate to his or her purpose for the activity. For example, if the purpose is to teach or assess students about the sequence of events in a plot, then instruction should focus on establishing the chronology. If the purpose is to teach students how to integrate details and make inferences from what is stated in the text, then instruction should guide them to think of similar things that have happened to them and to deduce aspects of the story that are not actually stated. If the purpose is to have students recall details, then instruction should teach them strategies for remembering characters, events, actions, and so on. Discussing a text before and after reading it can help develop students' retelling skills, and so can examining the illustrations in the book and using props such as feltboard characters.

To scaffold retelling for an individual student, the teacher should follow these guidelines:

1. Remind the student of a story previously read aloud. Then encourage the student to retell the story as though he or she were sharing it with a friend who has never heard it before.

2. Prompt the student's retelling as needed:
   - If the student has difficulty getting started, suggest beginning with one of these traditional openers: "Once upon a time ..." or "There once was ..."

- If the student stops before reaching the end of the story, encourage him or her to keep going. Ask general questions: "What comes next?" "Then what happened?"
- If the student stops and cannot go on even after general prompting, ask a specific question about the place in the story where he or she stopped. Try to get the student back on track.

3. If the student cannot retell a story or if he or she recounts events out sequence and leaves out key details, guide the retelling one step at a time:

- "Once upon a time …"
- "This story is about …"
- "The time of this story is …"
- "The setting [or place] of this story is …"
- "[The main character's] problem in this story is …"
- "[The main character] tries to solve the problem by … First, [he or she] … Then, [he or she] …"
- "The problem in this story gets solved …"
- "At the end of this story …" (Morrow, 1996)

The teacher can use retelling as a means of evaluating a student's comprehension of a given story and gauging his or her progress overall. During this type of evaluative retelling, the teacher's prompting should be limited to general questions (e.g., "Then what happened?" and "Can you think of anything else about the story?"). Evaluating the retelling of a narrative text will demonstrate the student's understanding of story structure. The emphasis will be on literal recall, but the student's inferential and critical-thinking abilities will be revealed, as well.

To evaluate understanding of story structure, the teacher should prepare a guide sheet that includes a four-part outline of the events of the story: setting, theme, episodes, and resolution. As the student retells the story, the teacher records the numbers of ideas and details that he or she provides for each part. The student should be given credit for all ideas and details, regardless of the order in which they are recounted; likewise, credit should be given for partial recollections (Wasik & Bond, 2001; Whitehurst & Lonigan, 2001). To evaluate the student's sequencing skills, the teacher compares the order of events from the retelling with the correct order. The student's responses will demonstrate both sequencing skills and understanding of story elements and structure. With this information, the teacher can identify where to focus instruction, and by examining a student's retellings over the school year, the teacher can evaluate his or her progress. Evaluative retellings are useful for students from kindergarten throughout the primary grades.

The following paragraph is a summary of the story *Jenny Learns a Lesson* (Fujikawa, 1980). After the summary is a retelling of the story by 5-year-old Jache, recorded verbatim. This retelling was her first retelling and was completed early in the school year.

Story Summary

A little girl named Jenny liked to play. She played with her friends Nicholas, Sam, Mei Su, and Shags, her dog. Every time Jenny played with her friends, she bossed them. Jenny decided to pretend to be a queen. She called her friends. They came to play. Jenny told them all what to do and was bossy. The friends became angry and left. Jenny decided to play dancer. She called her friends and they came to play. Jenny told them all what to do. The friends became angry and left. Jenny decided to play pirate. She called her friends and they came to play. Jenny told them all what to do. The friends became angry and left. Jenny's friends refused to play with her because she was so bossy. Jenny became lonely and apologized to them for being bossy. The friends all played together, and each person did what he wanted. They all had a wonderful day and were tired at the end of the day. (Morrow, 2014)

Jache's Retelling

Once upon a time there's a girl named Jenny and she called her friends over and they played queen and went to the palace. They had to do what she said and they didn't like it, so then they went home and said that was boring. It's not fun playing queen and doing what she says you have to. So they didn't play with her for seven days and she had an idea that she was being selfish, so she went to find her friends and said, I'm sorry I was so mean. And said, let's play pirate, and they played pirate and they went onto the ropes. Then they played that she was a fancy lady playing house. And they have tea. And they played what they wanted and they were happy. The end. (Morrow, 2014)

Jache's retelling was transcribed early in her kindergarten year. Over time and with continued practice, her retellings became more detailed and well developed. Later in the school year, Jache did a retelling of *Under the Lemon Tree* (Hurd, 1980). The next paragraph is a summary of that story, and the paragraph after that is Jache's retelling of it.

Story Summary

The story is about a donkey that lives under a lemon tree on the farm and watches out for all the other animals. A fox comes in the night to steal a chicken and duck, and the donkey hee-haws loudly to protect them. He scares the fox away but wakes the farmer and his wife, who never see the fox. This happens frequently until the farmer can no longer take the noise and moves the donkey to a tree far from the farmhouse, where he is very unhappy. The fox comes back and steals the farmer's prized red rooster. The other animals quack and cluck and wake up the farmer, who chases after the fox. When the fox passes the donkey, the donkey makes his loud noises again, frightening the fox who then drops the red rooster. The farmer realizes that the donkey has been protecting his animals and moves him back to the lemon tree, where he is happy again. (Morrow, 2014)

Jache's Retelling

Once upon a time there was a donkey, and he was in a farm. He lived under a lemon tree by the animals on the farm. He was next to the ducks, the chickens, and the roosters. It was night time. The red fox came into the farm to get something to eat. The donkey went "hee-haw, hee-haw" and the chickens went "cluck, cluck" and the ducks went "quack-quack." The farmer and his wife waked up and looked out the window and saw nothing. They didn't know what came into their farm that night. They said, "What a noisy donkey we have. When it gets dark we will bring him far away." So when it get darker they brang the donkey over to a fig tree. And he had to stay there. He couldn't sleep alone. That night the red fox came to the farm again to try and get something to eat. The ducks went "quack-quack" the turkeys went "gobble-gobble." The farmer and his wife woke up and said, "Is that noisy donkey back again?" They rushed to the window and saw the fox with their red rooster in his mouth and yelled, "Stop thief, come back." The fox passed the donkey and he shouted "hee-haw, hee-haw." The red fox heard it and dropped the rooster and ran away. The farmer and his wife said, "Aren't we lucky to have the noisiest donkey in the world?" And they picked up the rooster and put one hand around the donkey and went home and tied the donkey under the lemon tree. (Morrow, 2014)

Retellings can be used to evaluate a range of comprehension tasks. However, as stated earlier, both the directions teachers give to students before the retelling and the means of analysis should correspond with the purpose of the task. Figure 3.1 provides a guide sheet for use in evaluating an oral retelling. The teacher should check the "Yes" box for each element the student recounts in whole or in part. Each retelling should be recorded, and then recordings should be compared across time to track the student's progress.

Reading Literature Standard 2   Retell stories, including key details, and demonstrate understanding of their central message or lesson (first grade).

FIGURE 3.1 ● A Qualitative Analysis of Story Retelling

| Child's name _____ Date _____ |
| Name of story _____ |

Setting	Yes	No
a. Begins story with an introduction?	☐	☐
b. Names main character?	☐	☐
c. List other characters named here: _____		
d. Includes statement about time and place?	☐	☐

Theme

	Yes	No
a. Refers to main character's primary goal or problem to be solved.	☐	☐

Plot Episodes

	Yes	No
a. Recalls episodes.	☐	☐
b. Lists episodes recalled.	☐	☐

Resolution

	Yes	No
a. Includes solution to problem or attainment of goal.	☐	☐
b. Puts ending on story.	☐	☐

Sequence

	Yes	No
a. Tells story events in sequential order.	☐	☐

In the Common Core Classroom

Retelling Stories: First Grade

Ms. Brown has been focusing on helping her students retell familiar stories, including key details, as stated in Standard 2. Ms. Brown enjoys having her students work with storytelling materials and having them retell to identify the details in a story. She has created a literacy center in the classroom, and it is filled with puppets, props, and a feltboard with story characters. She models retelling stories using these materials, and after modeling their use, she makes them available in the center for students use at a designated time.

Once a month, with the support of parent volunteers and a classroom aide, Ms. Brown has her students video record themselves retelling a story for a specific purpose. She sets up the camera on a tripod for the students to use. The use of technology is commonplace in Ms. Brown's classroom and as a result, students are quite familiar with these tools. After recording the retellings, a child or parent volunteer takes the digital memory card from the video camera and insert it into a computer. Students view their story retellings to determine if they included all of the key details in the text. After that, they save the recordings for the teacher to watch at a later time.

During literacy center time, the children are able to use the materials Ms. Brown has provided. Anyone visiting the classroom on a given day would observe the expectations of Standard 2 being met in the following ways:

- *Alliah and Tierra are on the floor with the feltboard and characters from* Caps for Sale. *They are engaged in partner reading, taking turns reading and manipulating the figures. Aliah chants, "A peddler was trying to sell his caps" Tierra says in return, "He had red caps, blue caps, green caps and his own checked cap." As each student chants, she puts up a character on the feltboard.*

- *Anias has a big book of* The Little Red Hen *(Galdone, 2001) and gives several copies of the same story to children in the group he has gathered together. He sits in the classroom rocking chair. Role-playing the teacher, he says, "Now boys and girls, let's read the title and the name of the author together," which they do. Anias begins reading. Occasionally, he occasionally stops and asks the other children questions about the story, such as "Who is in the story?" "What does the Little Red Hen want help with?" and at the end, "Why didn't the hen give the animals any of the bread she baked?"*

- *Jack and Kevin are doing a "chalk talk" using the book* Harold's Trip to the Sky *(Johnson, 1957). Jack is telling the story, and Kevin is drawing the story. When they finish, they go back into the book to make sure they have included all of the who, what, where, when, and how details. They determine they have missed two key details, so they add the pictures that represent those parts.*

- *Another group is acting out the story* The Little Red Hen *(Galdone, 2001). They are using props from the literacy center: five stick puppets for the red hen, plus the cat, dog, pig, and goat. One student is the storyteller and uses the book to help narrate, and the others act out the events using the stick puppets.*

In all of these instances, the children are demonstrating knowledge of Standard 2 by retelling familiar stories and including key details.

Plans for the Teacher

Materials Needed to Get Started

Familiar texts, feltboards and feltboard pieces, storytelling props, puppets

Optional: video camera, tripod

Content of Lesson

Retelling stories is a skill that students will need to practice throughout the primary grades. To get started, the teacher should model retelling familiar stories, using materials such as puppets and props, and allow students the opportunity to participate in whole-class retellings. Then the teacher should provide the storytelling materials in the classroom literacy center for students' continued practice. Teachers might find it helpful for students to work with partners, especially when beginning to practice retelling stories. Eventually, teachers might encourage students to create their own storytelling props, such as feltboard pieces and puppets, to retell stories independently.

Differentiation

Some students will grasp the elements of story retelling quickly, while others will struggle with this skill. Teachers can support students who are having difficulty by prompting them to scaffold their development. Additionally, teachers should provide students with books that follow a predictable structure, such as *Brown Bear, Brown Bear, What Do You See?* (Martin, 1983). These kinds of books will be easier for students who are just beginning to retell stories.

Assessment

Retellings can be assessed using the Qualitative Analysis of Story Retelling, as discussed earlier in this chapter (see Figure 3.1).

Table 3.3 provides the third Key Ideas and Details standard for CCSS Reading Literature.

TABLE 3.3 ● *Reading Literature Standard 3 for K–Grade 2: Key Ideas and Details*

Kindergarten	Grade 1	Grade 2
With prompts and support, identify settings, characters, and major events in a story.	Describe characters, settings, and major events in a story, using key details.	Describe how characters in a story respond to major events and challenges.

Source: NGA & CCSSO (2010).

Reading Literature Standard 3   Describe how characters in a story respond to major events and challenges.

In the Common Core Classroom
Describing the Characters in the Story: Second Grade

Standard 3 states that students should be able to describe how characters respond to the major events and challenges in a story. This is a skill Ms. Anderson has been practicing with her second-graders. She has decided to model this skill by thinking aloud for her students and showing them how she notices characters' responses while she reads.

> **Ms. Anderson:** Today, I'm going to read aloud a book that you all know very well. *(She holds up* Lilly's Purple Plastic Purse *(Henkes, 2006) and sees that many students signal excitedly to show they are familiar with it.)* As I read, I want you to listen in as I do some thinking about how Lilly responds to the events and problems she has in the story. Then I'm going to ask you to do some thinking about this.

Ms. Anderson begins to read aloud. She pauses at the point when Lilly, the main character, writes a mean note about her teacher, Mr. Slinger, after he confiscates her purse because she plays with it in class.

> **Ms. Anderson:** *(Thinking aloud)* Hmm, I'm going to stop here, because this seems like a big event or problem. We know how much Lilly loves her teacher, Mr. Slinger, but here she is, writing a mean note about him. I'm thinking that Lilly doesn't really mean what she's writing. She's writing this note because she's really angry with Mr. Slinger now, but later, she might decide that this isn't the best way to solve her problem. Readers, did you notice how I stopped after a big event or problem and noticed how the character responded? Then I tried to think of whether how the character responded fits with what I know about her. Let's keep reading.

Ms. Anderson reads on until the point when Lilly finds a nice note from Mr. Slinger in her purse after he returns it to her.

> **Ms. Anderson:** I'm stopping because this seems like another big event in the story. Let's pay attention to how Lilly responds.

Ms. Anderson continues reading until the point when Lilly returns home and writes a new note about Mr. Slinger.

> **Ms. Anderson:** Turn and talk to your partner. Think about everything you know about Lilly. How she does respond to Mr. Slinger's nice note? Why do you think she responds this way?

Tips for the Teacher

TO HELP STUDENTS MEET THE GOALS of Standard 3, teachers have many instructional options. They might have students use a graphic organizer to record details about characters and how they respond to the major events of the story. They might also hold interviews in which one student acts as a favorite character and answers questions posed by a student "reporter."

Ms. Anderson moves around the room and listens in as students engage in discussions with their preassigned partners.

Cyrus: She makes a nice note, like as a way to apologize to Mr. Slinger. She probably feels really bad now, and she really likes Mr. Slinger, so she doesn't want him to be mad.

Brooke: Maybe she feels bad, too, that she didn't listen to him when he asked her not to play with her purse. That's probably why she made the new note—like to say she's sorry for not listening.

Ms. Anderson jots down the names of several students with whom she plans to practice this skill in a small group. Then she wraps up the lesson.

Ms. Anderson: Smart thinking, everyone. This is a good strategy for you to use as readers. When there's a big event or problem in a story, stop to notice how the characters respond. Think about all you know about each character and why he or she might have responded this way.

Craft and Structure

The standards in this category address children learning about genres of children's literature and how they differ from each other (see table 3.4). The standard deals with vocabulary in the books and differences in types of books and their structures, such as books with rhymes or repeated phrases and books that explore characters' feelings.

The CCSS suggest that in the course of the school year, children should become familiar with a variety of literary genres. Teachers should consider the following narrative genres:

- **Picture storybooks:** In these books, the text and illustrations are so closely linked that both are necessary to tell the complete story. Quality picture storybooks follow the traditional story structure and have a setting, a well-defined theme, episodes tied to the theme, and a resolution. Books in this genre are available on many topics.

- **Traditional literature:** This genre includes familiar stories (e.g., nursery rhymes, fables, folktales, fairytales) that originated in the oral tradition of storytelling and are part of our heritage. Teachers sometimes assume that students know stories such as "Goldilocks and the Three Bears," but in fact, many students are not familiar with them.

TABLE 3.4 • *Reading Literature Standard 4 for Grades K–2: Craft and Structure*

Kindergarten	Grade 1	Grade 2
Ask and answer questions about unknown words in a text.	Identify words and phrases in stories or poems that suggest feelings or appeal to the senses.	Describe how words and phrases (e.g., regular beats, alliteration, rhymes, repeated lines) supply rhythm and meaning in a story, poem, or song.

Source: NGA & CCSSO (2010).

- **Realistic literature:** The stories in this genre are about real-life problems. A good example is the *Arthur series of* books by Marc Brown; they address issues experienced by young children—for instance, wearing glasses and losing a tooth. Additional topics might include bedtime fears and the difficulties of having a new baby in the family. Some works of realistic fiction explore sensitive personal issues—for instance, divorce and death. Teachers can read books in this genre to the entire class if they address common or shared issues, but discretion is advised in choosing topics and titles. Teachers might recommend specific titles to the parents of children that are facing private issues.

- **Poetry:** Collections of children's literature often leave out poetry, but many theme-based children's poetry anthologies have been compiled. A good example is *Fathers, Mothers, Sisters, Brothers: A Collection of Family Poems* (Hoberman, 1991). Teachers should make sure that poetry books are available to students in the classroom literacy center.

- **Novels:** These longer works of fiction are usually organized into chapters. Young students are interested in these so-called chapter books, because they associate the books with older readers. Most young students will not be able to read a novel on their own, but they will understand a book that is read aloud to them. Reading a novel aloud to kindergartners is a good way to introduce them to the genre.

- **Digital texts:** This genre includes texts that are read on a computer or a device such as a cell phone, Kindle, or iPad—for instance, digital stories, emails, web pages, and computer games. Because students read digital texts in addition to print-and-paper-based books, these texts should be available in the early childhood classroom.

Young children enjoy other kinds of texts, as well: joke and riddle books, graphic novels and comic books, craft books and cookbooks, participation books (which involve touching, smelling, manipulating), books related to television programs and pop culture (which are age appropriate), and series books about individual characters. These kinds of texts should be available in the library corner or literacy center. In addition, magazines and newspapers should be available for students to read. Not only do these types of texts provide a friendly format and address a range of topics, but they are written for readers of all ability levels. Print materials such as menus, directions, and maps can also be made available as texts.

Young children enjoy predictable forms of literature, which incorporate rhymes, repeated words and responses, clever phrases, and conversations. Predictable texts often feature well-known sequences (e.g., letters of the alphabet, days of the week, counting numbers) and cumulative patterns, in which events are added or repeated as the story develops. Predictable books tend to be well structured and feature simple, basic illustrations with the text. Their clear structure helps students to understand the text. Students also learn about patterns from these books, which make them easy to comprehend. Students might use these books as models for their own writing.

Directed Listening/Thinking Activity or Directed Reading/Thinking Activity for Narrative and Expository Texts   The standards in the category Craft and Structure focus on developing skills for learning new words and for using characters' voices and expressions to understand their points of view. These skills and many others can be taught using the directed listening/thinking activity (DLTA) or directed listening/reading activity (DRTA). In a DLTA or DRTA, a purpose for reading or listening is set at the start of the activity and followed throughout it.

In the DLTA or DRTA format, the listener or reader is also provided with a strategy for getting information from the text and then organizing it. When students use the strategy on a regular basis (and it is reinforced by the teacher), they will internalize it and be able to apply it when they read or listen to a text on their own (Morrow, Gambrell, & Freitag, 2009; Roskos, Tabor, & Lenhart, 2009). The framework of a DLTA or DRTA includes these three elements:

1. Prepare for reading or listening by reviewing prereading questions and setting a purpose for reading.
2. Read or listen to the story with no or few interruptions.
3. After reading, discuss the story.

A DLTA or DRTA can be conducted to achieve a variety of objectives; in any case, the after-reading discussion should focus on those objectives (Baumann, 1992; Pearson, Roehler, Dole, & Duffy, 1992). In the following DRTA/DLTA for the picturebook *When Sophie Gets Angry-Really Really Angry* (Bang, 1999), students will read to achieve these two objectives:

1. Develop vocabulary.
2. Recognize reasons the author may have selected to use these words in the text.

After students have practiced and internalized the DLTA/DRTA format, they can set their own purposes for reading. Eventually, they will also be able to determine which strategies to use to retrieve and organize information when reading or listening.

Reading Literature Standard 4   Identify words and phrases in stories or poems that suggest feelings or appeal to the senses (first grade).

In the Common Core Classroom

Words and Phrases That Suggest Feelings: First Grade

For first grade, Standard 4 states that students should be able to identify words and phrases in literature that suggest feelings. Mr. Mertz has selected the book *When Sophie Gets Angry—Really, Really, Angry . . .* (Bang, 1999) to work on this skill with his first-graders. The students have gathered on the carpet and are holding their reading notebooks on their laps. Mr. Mertz holds up a copy of the book and introduces it to the class. Then he introduces today's activity.

> *Mr. Mertz:* Readers, as I read today, I want you to listen for words and phrases that give you clues about how Sophie is feeling. Jot down these words and phrases in your notebook so we can talk about them and why the author might have decided to use them in the book.

Mr. Mertz begins to read the book aloud. As he reads, he pauses to give students the chance to record words and phrases in their notebooks. After he has finished reading the book, he asks several students to share what they have written. He records these words and phrases on a sheet of chart paper mounted on an easel at the front of the room.

> **Mr. Mertz:** Readers, before I started reading, I asked you to listen for words and phrases that give us clues about how Sophie is feeling throughout the book. Let's take a look at our list. I see the words *scream* and *smash* and *roar*. Why do you think the author, Molly Bang, decided to use these words when she wrote about Sophie's fight with her sister? Turn and discuss with your partners.

Mr. Mertz listens in as students discuss the author's word choices with their partners.

> **Claire:** I think it's because Sophie felt angry, and those are angry words. Like if I was angry, I might want to scream and smash things.
>
> **Rohan:** Yeah, and think about the words she used at the end of the book.
>
> **Claire:** *(looking up at the list on the easel)* Yeah, like *comforts.* That's a word from the end of the story, when she calmed down. I think maybe the author wanted to show us that Sophie was calmer now and not angry anymore.

As students' discussions wind down, Mr. Mertz brings the whole class together again.

> **Mr. Mertz:** It seems like many of you noticed that the author used angry words, like *explodes,* when Sophie was angry, and calmer words, like *comforts,* when Sophie calmed down. This is something that writers do. They pick words and phrases that give us clues about how characters are feeling. When you're reading on your own, give this a try: Try to pick out words that give you clues about how a character is feeling. You might notice that the author chooses different words to show how a character's feelings change in the story.

The students return to their desks and take out their independent reading books. They also take out some sticky notes and open their reading notebooks to record the words and phrases about feelings they find in their own books.

Tips for the Teacher

STANDARD 4 FOCUSES ON LANGUAGE AND word choice within texts. A read-aloud, like the one conducted in the vignette, is one instructional strategy teachers can use to point out words and phrases in stories that suggest feelings or appeal to the senses. Teachers might also have students keep vocabulary notebooks or post a list titled "Juicy Words" in the classroom for students' reference. When teachers model how they notice words and phrases in stories or poems that suggest feelings or appeal to the senses, students will be more likely to identify these kinds of words while they read independently.

Table 3.5 provides the fifth Craft and Structure standard from the CCSS for Reading Literature.

TABLE 3.5 ● *Reading Literature Standard 5 for K–Grade 2: Craft and Structure*

Kindergarten	First Grade	Second Grade
Recognize common types of texts (e.g., storybooks, poems, fables, folktales).	Explain major differences between books that tell stories and books that give information, drawing on a wide reading of a range of text types.	Describe the overall structure of a story, including describing how the beginning introduces the story and the ending concludes the action.

Source: NGA & CCSSO (2010).

Reading Literature Standard 5   Recognize common types of texts like storybooks, poems, fables, folktales for kindergarten.

In the Common Core Classroom

Types of Texts: Kindergarten

Ms. Dench has labeled the books in her classroom library with colored stickers to represent the various genres to which they belong. Every time new books are purchased, the class helps label them before they are added to the classroom library. Using this system helps students become familiar with the different types of text, the goal of Reading Literature Standard 5.

This month, the kindergartners are learning about insects, and several new books related to this theme have just arrived. Ms. Dench has gathered the class on the carpet in the library center and pulls the first book out of the box to show the children.

Ms. Dench: This book is called *Why Mosquitoes Buzz in People's Ears,* and is written by Verna Aardema. Oh my! The title of this book really gives away what kind of book it is, doesn't it? This book is going to explain why mosquitos buzz in people's ears. That's something that happens in real life, but it doesn't seem like this picture book is going to give us facts about mosquitos. What kind of book is it if it tries to explain something that happens in real life by using a made-up story instead of true facts?

Joey: A folktale.

Ms. Dench: That's right, Joey. Come, put the sticker on the book for *folktale.* Here is the next book, *The Caterpillar and the Polliwog,* by Jack Kent. Look at the picture on the front cover. I see a clue that will help me decide if this this book is going to tell a made-up story or teach us about these animals. Do you see it, too?

Taylee: That bug's got a scarf on her head!

Ms. Dench: Yes, Taylee, that's the clue I see, too! What kind of book do you predict this is going to be?

Taylee: A storybook, 'cause bugs don't wear scarves.

Ms. Dench: Good point. Listen as I read this page to see if Taylee's prediction is correct.

Ms. Dench opens up to a preselected page and reads aloud. The class confirms that *The Caterpillar and the Polliwog* is a storybook. Ms. Dench also tells students that this book hides some true facts in the story and shares an excerpt to demonstrate this feature. Students decide together that it best fits in the *storybook* category.

The class continues this process with the other new books, with Ms. Dench prompting and scaffolding when needed. At the end of this experience, the new books are displayed in a row on a low shelf in the classroom library.

Plans for the Teacher

Materials Needed to Get Started

Stickers, books to add to the classroom library

Content of Lesson

Prior to this activity, the teacher should have several books already labeled with stickers that represent the genres of the books. To build students' background knowledge about genres of books, the teacher should devote a significant amount of time to showing examples of different types of books. The teacher should model the process of determining a book's genre until students have built enough background knowledge to join in.

Differentiation

Additional practice, whether in small groups or one on one, should be offered to students still developing this skill.

Assessment

The teacher can use a checklist to organize data about each student's ability to identify the targeted genres.

Table 3.6 provides the sixth Craft and Structure standard from the CCSS for Reading Literature.

TABLE 3.6 ● *Reading Literature Standard 6 for K–Grade 2: Craft and Structure*

Kindergarten	First Grade	Second Grade
With prompting and support, name the author and illustrator of a story and define the role of each in telling a story.	Identify who is telling the story at various points in a text.	Acknowledge differences in the points of view of characters, including by speaking in a different voice for each character when reading dialogue aloud.

Source: NGA & CCSSO (2010).

Reading Literature Standard 6   Identify who is telling the story at various points in a text for first grade.

In the Common Core Classroom

Story Narration: First Grade

Ms. Fidura sits with a small group of students at the kidney-shaped table in her classroom, planning to work with them to identify who is telling the story at various points in a text. She holds up a copy of *The Pain and the Great One,* by Judy Blume.

Ms. Fidura: I have a new book to share with you today. The title is *The Pain and the Great One,* and the author is Judy Blume. Let's look at the picture on the cover and take a picture walk. Does anyone have any predictions for what this book might be about?

Joey: I think there is a brother and a sister and maybe they don't like to play together.

Nicholas: I think the brother and sister fight all the time and get in trouble.

Ms. Fidura: Good predictions. Let's read to find out. While I read aloud, I want you to pay attention to who is telling the story in the first part of the book and who is telling the story in the second part of the book.

Ms. Fidura begins to read the text aloud. After the first few pages, she stops reading.

Ms. Fidura: Who do you think is telling the story at this part in the book?

Samay: I think it's the sister.

Ms. Fidura: How do you know?

Samay: Because she's telling all about how her brother always bothers her and is a pain.

Ms. Fidura: What else?

Joey: And it says "I." It doesn't say "she." So it's her talking.

Ms. Fidura: Right! So right now we're hearing the story from her point of view.

Ms. Fidura continues reading until she comes to the second part of the story.

Ms. Fidura: Who do you predict is telling the next part of this story?

Nicholas: The brother. Now it's his turn to tell all about the sister.

Ms. Fidura: Good prediction. Let's read to find out. *(Reads a few pages and pauses)* Were we correct?

Nicholas: Yes! It says "I" again, but this time the brother is telling all about how his sister gets to do everything and he doesn't.

Ms. Fidura continues reading to the end of the book.

Ms. Fidura: Why do you think it's important to know who is telling the story in each part?

Samay: If we didn't know, we might get confused. We might not know who is talking, so we wouldn't understand the story.

Ms. Fidura: Smart thinking. In this story, it's important to know which character is telling the story, and this is something we can practice when I read stories to you or when you read stories by yourself. Good work.

Tips for the Teacher

BOOKS WRITTEN IN THE FIRST PERSON, such as *The Pain and the Great One*, lend themselves particularly well to meeting this standard. Other books that primary teachers might find helpful include the following:

Alexander and the Terrible, Horrible, No-Good, Very Bad Day, by Judith Viorst

The Polar Express, by Chris Van Allsburg

My Great-Aunt Arizona, by Gloria Houston

The True Story of the Three Little Pigs, by Jon Scieszka

Integration of Knowledge and Ideas

Standards 7, 8, and 9 pertain to the Integration of Knowledge and Ideas. These standards involve students in discussing the text and illustrations and comparing how they support each other (see table 3.7 for the first standards table in this group). In addition, these standards have students compare and contrast different texts and illustrations by different authors. (Note that Standard 8 is not applicable to literature and is therefore not included in the following section.)

TABLE 3.7 ● *Reading Literature Standard 7 for K–Grade 2:* **Integration of Knowledge and Ideas**

Kindergarten	Grade 1	Grade 2
With prompting and support, describe the relationship between illustrations and the story in which they appear (e.g., what moment in a story an illustration depicts).	Use illustrations and details in a story to describe its characters, setting, or events.	Use information gained from the illustrations and words in a print or digital text to demonstrate understanding of its characters, setting, or plot.

Source: NGA & CCSSO (2010).

Reading Literature Standard 7   With prompting and support, describe the relationship between illustrations and the story in which they appear (e.g., what moment in a story an illustration depicts) (kindergarten).

In the Common Core Classroom

Using Illustrations: Kindergarten

Ms. Farley is sitting with a group of four kindergartners at a table in the back of her classroom. She has decided to work on the goals of Standard 7, which states that students should, with prompting and support, be able to describe the relationship between illustrations and the story in which they appear. In today's activity, she will use the book *Owen's Marshmallow Chick* (Henkes, 2002). She has made photocopies of the illustrations in the book and distributed a set to each student.

> **Ms. Farley:** Kindergartners, today we are going to talk about the illustrations in a story. Remember, *illustrations* is another word for *pictures*. I'm going to read aloud the book *Owen's Marshmallow Chick*. As I read, I want you to listen carefully to the words and hold up the picture that matches the words in each part of the story.

Ms. Farley introduces the book to students and helps them spread out their copies of the illustrations so they can see them clearly. When everyone is ready, she begins reading. She reads aloud the part of the book in which Owen sees his Easter basket but does not show students the illustration of this scene. She pauses as students look through their photocopies to find the illustration that matches this part of the story. One by one, students hold up their copies.

> **Ms. Farley:** Great job, kindergartners! Turn and tell the person next to you why you picked that illustration.

Two students exchange these ideas about the illustration they both have selected.

> **Ryan:** I see a basket in the picture, like in the words.
> **Robert:** It has an Easter basket. There was candy in the basket.

Ms. Farley shares Robert's ideas with the rest of the class.

> **Ms. Farley:** Robert remembers a detail from the words. He remembers that the book told us that Owen's basket was filled with candy—just like the picture you all picked. The picture matches the words. Any time you are reading a book, remember that the words and the pictures have to match. You can use details from the words and the pictures to make sure they match.

Ms. Farley continues this strategy while she reads the rest of the book, reminding students of how they can use the strategy when they read.

Tips for the Teacher

BEGINNING IN KINDERGARTEN, STUDENTS SHOULD RECOGNIZE that both the illustrations and the words provide information about a story. Standard 7 asks kindergartners to describe the relationship between the illustrations and the story in which they appear—noting that they may need prompting and support to do so. Older students will be expected to analyze photos and drawings more closely, so that by grade 5, students will be able to analyze how visual and multimedia elements contribute to the meaning, tone, or beauty of a text.

Table 3.8 provides the ninth Integration of Knowledge and Ideas standard from the CCSS Reading Literature.

TABLE 3.8 • *Reading Literature Standard 9 for K–Grade 2:* Integration of Knowledge and Ideas

Kindergarten	Grade 1	Grade 2
With prompting and support, compare and contrast the adventures and experiences of characters in familiar stories.	Compare and contrast the adventures and experiences of characters in stories.	Compare and contrast two or more versions of the same story (e.g., Cinderella stories) by different authors or from different cultures.

Source: NGA & CCSSO (2010).

Reading Literature Standard 9   With prompting and support, compare and contrast the adventures and experiences of characters in familiar stories for kindergarten.

In the Common Core Classroom

Comparing and Contrasting Characters: Kindergarten

Ms. Bonanne is sitting in her rocking chair at the front of the meeting area and looking at her kindergarten class sitting in rows on the carpet. On the classroom easel, a Venn diagram is displayed and the character names "Biscuit" and "Clifford" are written at the tops of the two sides.

Ms. Bonanne: Boys and girls, we have read many *Biscuit and Clifford* books over the past few weeks, and I know these are two characters that you know well. Today, I want to show you something new. On the easel, you can see two large circles that are overlapping in the middle. This is called a *Venn diagram.* Today, we will use this Venn diagram to compare two characters we know well: Biscuit and Clifford.

Ms. Bonanne explains to the class that they will write down one character's characteristics on each side of the Venn diagram and that shared characteristics will go in the overlapping area of the two circles.

Ms. Bonanne: Let's look at the "Biscuit" side first. Think about what we know about Biscuit that is NOT true about Clifford. Turn and talk to share your ideas.

Ms. Bonanne listens in as the kindergartners turn to share ideas with their partners. After a minute, she stops them.

Ms. Bonanne: Boys and girls, turn and look back up here. I heard great ideas. Let's add them to our Venn diagram.

Ms. Bonanne records two ideas: Biscuit is small *and* Biscuit is yellow. *The class repeats this process to discuss the character traits of Clifford. Ms. Bonanne records these two ideas:* Clifford is really big. *and* Clifford is red.

Ms. Bonanne: Great work! We've contrasted these characters by telling what's different about them. Now let's compare them by telling what's the same or mostly the same. We'll write those facts in the middle of the two circles. Turn and talk to share your ideas.

Ms. Bonanne moves around from partnership to partnership to scaffold students' conversations and listen to their ideas. After a minute or two, she stops the class again.

Ms. Bonanne: Boys and girls, you did some very smart thinking work. Let's record your ideas to compare these two characters.

In the overlapping section of the Venn diagram, Ms. Bonanne records these ideas:

They are both dogs.
They both have girl owners.
They are both silly puppies.
They both sometimes get into trouble.
They both like to play.

Ms. Bonanne: Kindergartners, we can compare any two characters in our stories using Venn diagrams. We will practice this skill again all together, and then I will ask you to try this with your reading partner using two characters that you both know well.

Ms. Bonanne knows that several partnerships will have difficulty comparing and contrasting characters on their own, so she plans to provide additional support and guidance to these pairs to ensure success for all students.

Plans for the Teacher

Materials Needed to Get Started

Book characters with similarities and differences that are familiar to students, Venn diagrams

Content of the Lesson

Kindergartners will need a great deal of support and guidance to compare and contrast the adventures and experiences of characters in familiar stories. Given this, teachers should begin addressing this standard in a whole-class setting, introducing the concept of a Venn diagram and recognizing character similarities and differences. Teachers should also ensure students' familiarity with characters by reading and rereading stories before expecting students to be able to compare and contrast characters' traits.

Differentiation

As the complexity of the text increases, the complexity of the characters typically increases, as well. As students read more difficult texts, they will need further instruction on identifying and comparing character traits, as well as additional text support.

Assessment

Teachers can assess students' completed Venn diagrams to observe progress toward this standard. Teachers can also choose to confer with individual students to determine their mastery of this standard.

Range of Reading and Level of Text Complexity

For grades K–2, the final category of standards encourage wide and varied reading—both in large groups, when students listen to complex texts being read, and when they read on their own (see table 3.9 for the first standards table in this group). When reading complex texts with large or small groups, teachers should provide frequent opportunities for scaffolding.

TABLE 3.9 • *Reading Literature Standard 10 for K–Grade 2:* *Integration of Knowledge and Ideas*

Kindergarten	Grade 1	Grade 2
Actively engage in group reading activities with purpose and understanding.	With prompting and support, read prose and poetry of appropriate complexity for grade 1.	By the end of the year, read and comprehend literature, including stories and poetry, in the grades 2–3 text complexity band proficiently, with scaffolding as needed at the high end of the range.

Source: NGA & CCSSO (2010).

Before reading the book, the teacher should discuss with students what it's about. To do so, the teacher should review all of the book's features—the subheadings, illustrations, captions, and so on—and then discuss them with students. The teacher should also review complex words and phrases that students will need to understand to comprehend the text.

After reading the full book, the teacher and students should have a detailed discussion of the features identified earlier. In reading the book a second time, the teacher should conduct an *echo reading*. In this format, the teacher reads a portion of the book and then the students repeat it, following along in their own copies of the text or looking at an enlarged version. A third reading should be a *choral reading,* in which the teacher and students read together. Approaching a complex text this way (along with repeated readings) will give students the support they need.

Standard 10 also recommends integrating complex texts into the content areas. Students should be able to read and comprehend a variety of challenging texts. To achieve this goal, classrooms should be filled with literary texts from across all of the genres, and the complexity of the texts should increase throughout the year.

Reading Literature Standard 10   By the end of the year, read and comprehend literature, including stories and poetry, in the grades 2–3 text complexity band proficiently, with scaffolding as needed at the high end of the range (second grade).

In the Common Core Classroom

Complex Texts: Second Grade

Ms. Judy has selected the novel *The Classroom at the End of the Hall,* by Douglas Evans, to read aloud to the class. This text lies within the grades 2–3 text complexity band and will be a challenging book for many of her students. Ms. Judy scaffolds her students' experience with this book to develop their comprehension in meeting Reading Literature Standard 10.

Today, Ms. Judy introduces the novel to the students and reads aloud the title chapter: "The Classroom at the End of the Hall." In her introduction, Ms. Judy purposefully uses vocabulary words from the text as a way to prepare students for the language that appears in the story.

Ms. Judy: Gather around, youngsters, and listen to this peculiar story of the extraordinary events that happen in the classroom at the end of the hall in W. T. Melon Elementary School. As you listen, I want you to make predictions about what is going on in this school. Write your predictions down on your sticky notes as they pop into your head.

Ms. Judy begins to read and mimics the actions of the janitor as he addresses the students in the opening scene. At the end of the first page, she pauses to allow her students to write down their predictions. She continues to read and pauses again when the janitor asks the children in the story to guess the identity of a mysterious character. Ms. Judy finishes reading the chapter aloud and asks the students to write down their final predictions. When they are done writing, Ms. Judy initiates a discussion.

Ms. Judy: In the first part of the chapter, Mr. Leeks, the janitor, is talking to the third-graders on the first day of school. He is telling them that he hears sounds coming from the classroom at the end of the hallway when there is no one there. Turn and tell your partner what you wrote on your first sticky note.

Students turn and discuss their predictions with their partners.

Ms. Judy: Can someone share what their partner said?

Alexi: Lucy said she thinks there is a ghost in the room, and it's going to spook the kids all year.

Ms. Judy: Lucy, what makes you think it's a ghost?

Lucy: Well, Mr. Leeks said the parents think the room is haunted, and then there's all that noise.

Ms. Judy: Good point. In the next part, Mr. Leeks tells what happened last night. He saw a man sitting at the teacher's desk, pointing. Please turn to your partner and share your second prediction.

The students again turn and talk with their partners.

Ms. Judy: Who can tell us what his or her partner said?

George: Trip said he thought it was the teacher, and he was kinda right, too, because it was W. T. Melon. Except that W. T. Melon is not alive, so it has to be a ghost.

Ms. Judy: Interesting idea! In the final part of the chapter, we do find out that it was Walter T. Melon, like George said, and that he has been dead for 20 years. Mr. Leeks leaves the kids by telling them to have a good school year. Tell your partner your final prediction. You can add to it if you need to.

The students share their ideas with their partners.

Ms. Judy: What did your partners say?

Olive: Eva thinks that something bad is going to happen and the kids are going to disappear one by one.

Ms. Judy: Eva, what clues gave you that idea?

Eva: Well, it's like how he said to have a good school year. I think that it's going to be the opposite, with the ghost and stuff. I think it's a hint that they're not going to have a good school year.

Tips for the Teacher

MANY OF THE EXPERIENCES STUDENTS HAVE with complex texts in the primary grades involve read-aloud procedures. However, if an activity is going to help students develop their comprehension, then the read-aloud must involve much more than the teacher reading a piece of literature out loud. Ms. Judy incorporates strategy instruction in her lesson that pushes her students to actively think about the text as they listen. Using the comprehension strategies you have modeled for your students will help them deepen not only their comprehension of the selection being read aloud but also their understanding of what it means to be a competent reader.

Throughout the month, Ms. Judy continues to read the story aloud with the class, one chapter at a time. For each chapter, she previews the vocabulary, sets a purpose for the activity, uses comprehension strategies with sticky notes, acts out portions of the story, summarizes, and holds discussions. Providing this level of scaffolding makes the text accessible to all students.

Using Narrative Literature Throughout the Day

LITERACY INSTRUCTION MUST HAPPEN ALL DAY LONG IF children are to become fluent readers by the end of third grade. If students are not reading on grade level by the end of third grade, only 10% of those who are below level will ever reach grade-level expectancies. Moreover, students who do not achieve grade-level expectancies for reading are more likely to drop out of school. Therefore, nothing is more important in the primary grades than to teach children to read.

During the time specified for explicit reading instruction—including decoding, comprehension, writing, speaking, listening, and language development—teachers will use the CCSS to plan and carry out instruction. Additionally, teachers can use these standards during music, art, math, science, social studies, and physical education.

Teachers must purposely place the CCSS skills into their lessons in the content areas. For example, in a social studies unit on helping others and what it means to be a good citizen, students can focus on the details in a story such as *The Lion and the Rat* (Wildsmith, 1995). In a science unit about winter, children's learning of scientific facts can be supported with stories about the winter and snow, such as *The Mitten* (Brett, 1989). After reading the story to the children, the teacher can ask them to recall and list the animals that went into the mitten to get warm. During art, as motivation to making winter collages, the teacher can read *The Snowy Day* (Keats, 1962). In all of his books, Keats uses watercolors and collage materials. Children can look through this book to find the collage materials to generate ideas for their own snow collages.

Activities like these will engage children in practicing skills that will help them with their comprehension of narrative text and enhance their knowledge about the themes they are studying. Using reading skills in the context of a theme puts them to use for a purpose and makes them both relevant and motivating.

Summary and Conclusions

THIS CHAPTER HAS REVIEWED THE CSSS READING STANDARDS for Literature for grades K–2, along with research that supports the standards. In addition, this chapter has proposed using schema theory to frame the standards and suggested how teachers can apply the CCSS as they work with students in their classrooms. Applying the standards will help teachers support students' development of literacy.

The role of children's literature in effective literacy instruction has become increasingly important and visible. Given the prevalent use of literature in teaching the language arts, the CCSS emphasize the reading of literary texts. Students should develop the skills needed to read a large variety and quantity of literature, and they should discuss literature by analyzing and synthesizing what they have read.

ACTIVITIES

1. Create a series of workshops for parents and teachers about the CCSS. Include the standards' purposes, characteristics, and applications. For this chapter, use the Reading Standards for Literature section of the CCSS.

2. Go through your classroom library to determine how many books and what types of narrative literature (e.g., fables, folktales, picture storybooks, etc.) you currently have. If you are missing any of the genres, develop a plan to get them for your classroom library.

3. Select a literary theme, such as authors of picture storybooks. Select three or four well-known authors and compare and contrast their styles of writing and illustration. Then select one author and work together with students to write a story using his or her writing and illustration style.

4. Create a theme for an early childhood class. Using the CCSS Reading Standards for Literature as a guide, create activities for the theme that include art, music, physical education, science, social studies, and, of course, the language arts. Include in your theme abundant opportunities for reading narrative literature.

5. Review your language arts block to determine if you are addressing all of the CCSS included in the Reading Standards Literature. Be sure that all of the categories within this standard are explicitly addressed when teaching language arts.

REFERENCES

Almasi, J. F., & Hart, S. J. (2011). Best practices in comprehension instruction. In L. L. Morrow & L. B. Gambrell (eds.), *Best practices in literacy instruction* (pp. 250–275). New York, NY: Guilford Press.

Baker, S., Chard, D. J., & Edwards, L. (2002). *The Story Read-Aloud Project: The development of an innovative instructional approach to promote comprehension and vocabulary in first grade classrooms* (CFDA 84.305G). Washington, DC: U.S. Department of Education, Institute of Education Sciences.

Baumann, J. F. (1992). Effect of think aloud instruction on elementary students' comprehension monitoring abilities. *Journal of Reading Behavior, 24*(2), 143–172.

Bear, D. R., Invernizzi, M., Templeton, S., & Johnston, F. (2008). *Words their way: Word study for phonics, vocabulary, and spelling instruction* (4th ed.). Upper Saddle River, NJ: Prentice-Hall.

Beck, I. L., & McKeown, M. G. (2001). Text talk: Capturing the benefits of read-aloud experiences for young children. *The Reading Teacher, 55*(1), 10–20.

Beck, I. L., McKeown, M. G., & Kucan, L. (2008). *Creating robust vocabulary: Frequently asked questions and extended examples*. New York, NY: Guilford Press.

Blachowicz, C. L., & Fisher, P. J. (2011). Best practices in vocabulary instruction revisited. In L. L. Morrow & L. B. Gambrell (eds.), *Best practices in literacy instruction* (pp. 224–249). New York, NY: Guilford Press.

Bryan, G., Tunnell, M., & Jacobs, J. (2007). A most valuable player: The place of books in teaching children to read. *Canadian Children, 32*(2), 25–33.

Dale, E., & Chall, S. (1948). A formula for predicting readability. *Education Research Bulletin, 27*, 11–20, 37–54.

Edmunds, K. M., & Bauserman, K. L. (2006). What teachers can learn about reading motivation through conversations with children. *The Reading Teacher, 59*, 414–424.

Fisher, D., Flood, J., Lapp, D., & Frey, N. (2004). Interactive read-alouds: Is there a common set of implementation practices? *The Reading Teacher, 58*, 8–17.

Fisher, D., & Frey, N. (2011). Best practices in content-area literacy. In L. L. Morrow & L. B. Gambrell (eds.), *Best practices in literacy instruction* (pp. 343–360). New York, NY: Guilford Press.

Fry, E. (1968). A readability formula that saves time. *Journal of Reading, 11*(7), 513–526, 575–578.

Galda, L. (2010). First things first: Why good books and time to respond to them matter. *New England Reading Association Journal, 46*(1), 1–7.

Galda, L., & Cullinan, B. E. (2003). Literature for literacy: What research says about the benefits of using trade books in the classroom. In J. Flood, D. Lapp, J. R. Squire, & J. M. Jensen (eds.), *Handbook of research on teaching the English language arts* (2nd ed., pp 640–648). Mahwah, NJ: Lawrence Erlbaum Associates.

Gunning, T. G. (2010). *Creating literacy instruction for all children* (7th ed.). Boston, MA: Allyn & Bacon.

Guthrie, J. T. (2011). Best practices in motivating students to read. In L. L. Morrow & L. B. Gambrell (eds.), *Best practices in literacy instruction* (pp. 177–198). New York, NY: Guilford Press.

Lau, K. (2009). Reading motivation, perceptions of reading instruction and reading amount: A comparison of junior and secondary students in Hong Kong. *Journal of Research in Reading, 32,* 366–382.

Leung, C. B. (2008). Preschoolers' acquisition of scientific vocabulary through repeated read-aloud events, retellings, and hands-on scientific activities. *Reading Psychology, 29,* 165–193.

Malloy, J., & Gambrell, L. (2013). Reading literature: The common core state standards. In L. M. Morrow, T. Shanahan, & K. K. Wixson (eds.), *Teaching with the common core standards for English language arts: What educators need to know (Book 1: Grades PreK–2)*. New York, NY: Guilford Press.

Martinez, M., & McGee, L. (2000). Children's literature and reading instruction: Past, present, and future. *Reading Research Quarterly, 35*(1), 154–169.

MetaMetrics. (2013). The Lexile framework for reading. *Lexile.com.* Retrieved from http://www.lexile.com.

Moore, D. W., Alvermann, D. E., & Hinchman, K. A. (eds.). (2000). *Struggling adolescent readers: A collection of teaching strategies.* Newark, DE: International Reading Association.

Morrow, L. M. (1996). Story retelling: A discussion strategy to develop and assess comprehension. In L. B. Gambrell & J. F. Almasi (eds.), *Lively discussions: Fostering engaged reading* (pp. 265–285). Newark, DE: International Reading Association.

Morrow, L. M. (2014). *Literacy development in the early years* (8th ed.). Boston, MA: Pearson.

Morrow, L. M., & Gambrell, L. B. (2011). *Best practices in literacy instruction* (4th ed.). New York, NY: Guilford Press.

Morrow, L. M., Gambrell, L. B., & Freitag, E. (2009). *Using children's literature in preschool to develop comprehension: Understanding and enjoying books.* Newark, DE: International Reading Association.

National Governors Association Center for Best Practices & Council of Chief State School Officers (NGA & CCSSO). (2010). *Common Core State Standards.* Washington, DC: Authors. Retrieved from www .corestandards.org/assets/CCSSI_ELA%20Standards.pdf.

Neuman, S. B. (1997). *Getting books in children's hands: The book flood of '96. Final report to the William Penn Foundation.* Philadelphia, PA: Temple University.

Neuman, S. B., & Celano, D. (2001). Books aloud: A campaign to "put books in children's hands." *The Reading Teacher, 54,* 550–557.

Pachtman, A. B., & Wilson, K. A. (2006). What do the kids think? *The Reading Teacher, 59,* 680–684.

Paris, A. H., & Paris, S. G. (2007). Teaching narrative comprehension strategies to first graders. *Cognition and Instruction, 25*(1), 1–44.

Pearson, P. D., & Duke, N. K. (2002). Comprehension instruction in the primary grades. In C. C. Block & M. Pressley (eds.), *Comprehension instruction* (pp. 247–258). New York, NY: Guilford Press.

Pearson, O. D., Roehler, L. R., Dole, J. A., & Duffy, G. G. (1992). Developing expertise in reading comprehension. In S. J. Samuels & A. E. Farsturp (eds.), *What research has to say about reading instruction* (2nd ed., pp. 145–199). Newark, DE: International Reading Association.

Rosenblatt, L. M. (1978). *The reader, the text, the poem: The transactional theory of literacy work.* Carbondale, IL: Southern Illinois University Press.

Rosenblatt, L. M. (1994). The transactional theory of reading and writing. In R. B. Ruddell, M. R. Ruddell, & H. Singer (eds.), *Theoretical models and processes of reading* (4th ed., pp. 1057–1092). Newark, DE: International Reading Association.

Roskos, K. A., Tabor, P., & Lenhart, L. (2009). *Oral language and early literacy in preschool: Talking, reading and writing.* Newark, DE: International Reading Association.

Sipe, L. R. (2008). *Storytime! Young children's literary understanding in the classroom.* New York, NY: Teachers College Press.

Sulzby, E. (1985). Children's emergent reading of favorite storybooks. *Reading Research Quarterly, 20,* 458–481.

Wasik, B. A., & Bond, M. A. (2001). Beyond the pages of a book: Interactive book reading and language development in preschool classrooms. *Journal of Educational Psychology, 93*(2), 243–250.

Whitehurst, G. J. & Lonigan, C. J. (2001). Emergent literacy: Development from prereaders to readers. In S. B. Neuman & D. K. Dickinson (eds.), *Handbook of early literacy research* (pp. 11–29). New York, NY: Guilford Press.

CHILDREN'S LITERATURE CITED

Aardema, V. (1992). *Why mosquitoes buzz in people's ears: A West African tale.* New York, NY: Dial.

Bang, M. (1999). *When Sophie Gets Angry—Really, Really Angry . . .* New York, NY: Blue Sky Press.

Baum, L. F. (1982). *The Wizard of Oz* (M. Hague, Illus.). New York, NY: Holt, Rinehart & Winston. (Original work published 1900)

Bemelmans, L. (1998). *Madeline.* New York, NY: Puffin Books.

Blume, J. (2002). *The pain and the great one.* (I. Trivis, Illus.). New York, NY: Atheneum.

Brett, J. (1989). *The mitten.* New York, NY: Putnam.

Bridwell, N. (2010). *Clifford the big red dog.* New York, NY: Scholastic.

Brown, M. T. (1979). *Arthur's eyes.* Boston, MA: Little, Brown.

Capucilli, A. S. (1999). *Biscuit* (P. Schories, Illus.). New York, NY: HarperCollins.

Crane, S. (2005). *The red badge of courage.* New York, NY: Simon & Schuster. (Original work published 1895)

Daley, A. (1999). *Goldilocks and the three bears* (C. Russell, Illus.). London, UK: Ladybird Books.

Evans, D. (1996). *The classroom at the end of the hall.* New York, NY: Scholastic.

Fujikawa, A. (1980). *Jenny learns a lesson.* New York, NY: Harcourt.

Galdone, P. (2001). *The little red hen.* New York, NY: Clarion Books.

Henkes, K. (2006). *Lilly's Purple Plastic Purse.* New York, NY: Greenwillow Books.

Henkes, K. (1993). *Owen.* New York, NY: Greenwillow Books.

Henkes, K. (2002). *Owen's Marshmallow Chick.* New York, NY: Greenwillow Books.

Hoberman, M. A. (1991) *Fathers, mothers, sisters, brothers: A collection of family poems.* New York, NY: Little, Brown.

Houston, G. (1992). *My great-aunt Arizona* (S. C. Lamb, Illus.). New York, NY: HarperCollins.

Hurd, E. (1980). *Under the lemon tree.* Boston, MA: Little Brown.

Johnson, C. (1998). *Harold and the purple crayon.* New York, NY: HarperCollins.

Johnson, C. (1957). *Harold's trip to the sky.* New York, NY: HarperCollins.

Kann, V., & Kann, E. (2006). *Pinkalicious.* New York, NY: HarperCollins.

Keats, E. J. (1962). *The snowy day.* New York, NY: Viking Press.

Kent, J. (1985). *The caterpillar and the polliwog.* New York, NY: Aladdin.

Lionni, L. (1963). *Swimmy.* New York, NY: Knopf/Dragonfly Books.

Lobel, A. (1970). *Frog and Toad are friends.* New York, NY: Harper & Row.

Martin, B. (1983). *Brown bear, Brown bear, what do you see?* (E. Carle, Illus.). New York, NY: Henry Holt.

O'Connor, J. (2006). *Fancy Nancy* (R. Preiss Glasser, Illus.). New York, NY: HarperCollins.

Scieszka, J. (1996). *The true story of the 3 little pigs* (L. Smith, Illus.). New York, NY: Puffin Books.

Slobodkina, E. (1947) Caps for sale. Reading, MA: Addison-Wesley.

Van Allsburg, C. (1985). *The Polar Express.* Boston, MA: Houghton Mifflin.

Viorst, J., & Cruz, R. (1972). *Alexander and the terrible, horrible, no good, very bad day.* New York, NY: Atheneum.

Wildsmith, B. (1963). *The lion and the rat: A fable.* New York, NY: F. Watts.

Zemach, M. (1991). *The three little pigs.* New York, NY: Tandem Library.

Reading Development: Comprehending Informational Text

THE ENGLISH LANGUAGE ARTS (ELA) COMMON CORE STATE Standards (CCSS) emphasize the use of informational literature at all grade levels. A primary reason for this emphasis is that in adult life, we read this type of text more than we read narrative literature. Another purpose for this new emphasis on informational text is to prepare students for college and careers.

Erin Kramer

This addition of informational text is a significant change, particularly in early childhood education, where narrative stories have traditionally been the major source of text for reading and listening. According to the CCSS (NGA & CCSSO, 2010), texts presented during instruction in the primary grades should be 50% narrative and 50% informational.

It used to be said that in the primary grades, children learn to read, and after that, they read to learn (Chall, 1983). It has been questioned whether kindergarten-aged children are capable of learning from informational text, but research strongly suggests that they are (Duke, Bennett-Armistead, & Roberts, 2003). For example, kindergarten children can comprehend and learn the language and structure of an informational text if it is read aloud to them (Pappas, 1993).

Reading Informational Texts in the Classroom

THE BENEFITS OF READING INFORMATIONAL TEXTS ARE NUMEROUS and varied. For some students, informational texts provide an alternate avenue into literacy. These students prefer to read informational text rather than narrative text. The photographs featured in many expository texts are quite attractive to these students, as is the concrete, factual nature of these texts. Informational texts are quite meaningful, exposing children to things they know about in the real world and motivating them to want to learn more. Informational texts often attract students' attention to topics that are completely new and engaging.

In the classroom, many of the benefits of using narrative texts are the same as for using informational texts. For example, informational texts cause children to think about the content, talk about it, and relate it to their own lives (Bryan, Tunnell, & Jacobs, 2007). High-quality informational books are motivating; they encourage children to want to read more, which is associated with overall gains in literacy achievement (Guthrie, 2011).

Other benefits of reading informational texts are unique to this genre. Reading nonfiction builds background knowledge about people, places, and events, which is useful for all students but especially students from disadvantaged backgrounds (Moore, Alvermann, & Hinchman, 2000). Informational books also expose children to new vocabulary, new ways to comprehend, new text structures and genres, and new author and illustrator styles (Gunning, 2010; Leung, 2008). It enhances vocabulary, content knowledge, and fluency (Fingeret, 2008; Hiebert, 2008). Finally, children who read more than one type of text have higher reading achievement.

The entire set of CCSS standards are not called the *CCSS for English Language Arts and Literacy;* rather, they are called the *CCSS for English Language Arts and Literacy in History, Social Studies, Science, and Technical Subjects.* This designation makes a statement about the importance of integrating multiple texts and topics in literacy instruction. Namely, the teaching of literacy skills must be imbedded in the content areas so children can read about and understand them.

Why Use Informational Texts with Young Children?

Equal amounts of nonfiction and fiction texts should be used in all classrooms. Both the initial analysis of the reading needs for college and career and the response from college faculty underscore the importance of informational reading.

The National Assessment of Educational Progress (NAEP) has incorporated assessment of informational text in its fourth-grade assessments. At the fourth-grade level, the NAEP assessment includes an equal number of literary and informational passages, and by the tenth grade, 70% of the passages are informational and 30% are literary (NAGB, 2012). Waiting until the third grade to introduce children to informational text is not prudent when children's ability to read and understand this text type is evaluated before fourth grade, in some cases.

The more attention that early childhood teachers give to developing students' familiarity with informational texts, the more likely students will be able to read them critically and be successful in using more complex literature—a primary goal of the CCSS.

Criteria for Selecting Quality Informational Texts

Knowing the criteria for selecting informational texts is important. According to Sudol and King (1996), *accuracy* of content is a key criterion for selection; therefore, it is necessary for teachers to read nonfiction thoroughly before using it. Information changes and increases with time. In particular, the content should be checked in hybrid informational books, in which the author is presenting a story as well as information.

Informational texts must be also *accessible* for reading and listening. Teachers should consider whether a text will be understood by the readers for which it is intended. Although teachers hope that they can help children navigate complex texts, they must be careful not to overwhelm children with books that have complex sentence structure and related concepts and vocabulary.

Teachers should also make sure that a text is *appropriate* for the children who are going to read or listen to it and appropriate for the skills being taught. Informational texts are often selected around a theme being studied, such as learning about animals, or for a holiday or special event. You may find a book about the ocean, but does it address the information you want your children to learn? Always check to see whether an informational text has the features of books students should learn to use, such as a table of contents, glossary, and index.

Finally, does the book have *appeal*? We use informational texts to motivate children. Several characteristics make an informational book more appealing, including its size and whether the colors and illustrations are attractive and of high quality. Many informational books are illustrated with photographs, which are exceptionally engaging. Most of all, the topic must be appropriate and of interest for those students who will be reading or listening to it.

Informational Texts for the Classroom Library

Classrooms must be rich with children's literature. We must be sure that our classroom libraries have the same amounts of narrative and informational texts. The following types of books should be included in a classroom library and added if they are not already present:

- **Books about social studies, science, and the arts** are called *informational books.* There are two different types: (1) *informational texts,* which provide us with knowledge about our natural or social world, and (2) *procedural books,* which provide us with directions or procedures.

- **Biographies and autobiographies** fit into the nonfiction category. Teachers can read biographies and autobiographies to kindergartners to expose them to the genre, and although these students often cannot read these books, they can listen to and comprehend them. Young readers are attracted to these texts, because they provide information on pop-culture icons, famous people, and historical figures of interest.

- **Digital texts** include any texts that students read on the computer, a cell phone, Kindle, iPad, or other device. These might include digital books, e-mails, web pages, and computer games. Because digital texts are being used today as well as printed texts, they should be introduced and incorporated in the early childhood classroom.

In addition to the categories of books mentioned, young children enjoy other kinds of nonfiction texts, such as joke and riddle books, craft books, cookbooks, and participation books (which involve them in touching, smelling, and manipulating). Magazines, newspapers, menus, directions, and maps should also be part of the informational collection. These types of texts provide nonthreatening formats and topics for students with diverse interests and ability levels. Reading them requires different skills, however, which the teacher must model for children.

Knowing the structure of a book helps readers to comprehend the text, since they are familiar with the pattern and organization of the writing. Several structures are characteristic of informational books:

- **Description:** The author identifies the characteristics of the topic.
- **Sequence:** The author discusses items in order, usually chronologically or numerically.
- **Compare and contrast:** The author focuses on two or more elements, identifying their similarities and differences.
- **Cause and effect:** The author states an action and then shows the effect it has.
- **Problem/solution:** The author states a problem and one or more solutions

As noted earlier, a hybrid book presents information in the context of a narrative story, although presenting information is its main purpose. Some people refer to this type of book as a *mixed text, blended book,* or *fraction. The Magic School Bus* series (Cole) is well known for being a hybrid book. In each of these books, a school bus takes the children and teacher on a fictional field trip, such as inside the human body or to the moon, and the facts about the topic are correct. Hybrid books can present problems, however, since some have not been well researched and their information is incorrect. Also, children may get caught up more in the story than the facts (Kletzien & Dreher, 2004).

Reading Informational Texts Aloud

We take it for granted that teachers know how to read aloud to children. Teachers may know how to read aloud narrative texts, but they may be less proficient in reading informational or expository texts aloud to children.

An informational text should be read with appropriate expression, just like a narrative text. In fact, the teacher needs to be particularly dramatic when reading aloud an informational text. Children will learn the language and concepts, but to do this, they need to hear the text more than once. The teacher should use different techniques for sharing informational books, such as echo reading, partner reading, reading the book alone, and retelling the content.

More discussion occurs when an expository text is used, because children encounter content they want clarified. Teachers should ask simple, literal questions about the book and address more difficult, reflective issues. Teachers should have the children think about the text and how it relates to their lives. Children should also consider similarities between different texts on the same topic. After reading aloud an informational book to children, have them summarize the content. A strategy that improves comprehension with nonfiction is to help students identify the structure of the text, such as description, sequence, compare and contrast, cause and effect, and problem/solution.

Putting the Reading Standards into Practice

THE CCSS READING STANDARDS FOR INFORMATIONAL TEXTS ARE organized into four categories:

1. Key Ideas and Details
2. Craft and Structure
3. Integration of Knowledge and Ideas
4. Range of Reading and Level of Text Complexity

Key Ideas and Details

The CCSS are very text based, which means readers should focus on developing a deep understanding of the text they read. In the first category, Key Ideas and Details, children must be able to use specific examples when explaining what a text means. Third-graders are expected to be able to explain sequences of events, procedures, and concepts, and fifth-graders should be able to explain "relationships or interactions" between people or events, ideas or concepts. For students to do these things, discussion of informational texts must begin in the primary grades.

In the Key Ideas and Details standards for early childhood, children must learn to ask and answer literal questions, such as *who, what, where, when, why,* and *how*. They must be able to identify the main idea in a paragraph or several paragraphs. Finally, they must be able to identify and explain connections between ideas or concepts and sequence events in both social studies and science.

Table 4.1 outlines the CCSS in this area. Following the table is a In the Common Core Classroom feature that illustrates key ideas and details.

TABLE 4.1 ● *Reading Informational Text Standard 1 for K–Grade 2:* **Key Ideas and Details**

Kindergarten	Grade 1	Grade 2
With prompting and support, ask and answer questions about key details in a text.	Ask and answer questions about key details in a text.	Ask and answer such questions as *who, what, where, when, why,* and *how* to demonstrate understanding of key details in a text.

Source: NGA & CCSSO (2010).

Reading Informational Text Standard 1   Ask and answer questions about key details in a text (first grade).

In the Common Core Classroom

Ask and Answer Questions: First Grade

It is October 1, and the first-graders are preparing their classroom for a new theme. This month, the topic of bats will peak students' interest and provide excitement as their work leads up to a culminating activity: a bat-themed Halloween party.

Whenever the theme changes, the first-graders help redesign the classroom drama center. This month, students are going to become cave explorers. To help them plan the new drama center, their teacher, Mr. Vinski, is reading the book *Inside a Cave,* by Gracie Moss as told to Carolyn Duckworth (Moss, 1997). During this reading, Mr. Vinski will ask questions about key details in the text to work on Standard 1 for Reading Informational Text.

The first-graders in Mr. Vinski's class come to the carpeted area with clipboards and pencils for notetaking. As they listen, they draw or write about things they would like to include in the center.

Mr. Vinski: When I came upon this book, I said, "Ah ha! That's it!" because I knew that I had found the perfect book to help us design our new drama center for our bats theme. Take a look at the front cover. The title is *Inside a Cave.* How could a book called *Inside a Cave* help us with our drama center? What do you think it has to do with bats?

Keagan: A cave is for bats! It's their home.

Mr. Vinski: That is a great idea. Does anyone want to add to that?

Janica: Maybe the bats sleep there?

Tate: We're going to turn our classroom into a cave and pretend to be bats.

Mr. Vinski: We are going to make our drama center into a cave. We'll be cave explorers that look for bats. As I read this story, let's make notes about what a cave explorer might need and how we can make and decorate a pretend cave.

Mr. Vinski reads the beginning of the text and pauses to ask questions and write a list of items students need for their drama center. The book begins with a photograph of Gracie Moss in all of her gear. She mentions that her gear keeps her safe and warm.

Mr. Vinski: Check the picture. What is Gracie wearing or carrying that might keep her safe? What will keep her warm? What did you hear about the helmet light?

The children use the pictures and words to help them answer Mr. Vinski's questions. So far, their list of needed items contains the following: helmet, headlamp, flashlight, elbow and knee pads, backpack, hip pack, and sweatshirt. Mr. Vinski continues to read to students about stalactites and stalagmites; other rocks with fancy shapes; and blind, colorless cave creatures, including a salamander, crayfish, and pill bug. Again, Mr. Vinski pauses to ask questions.

Mr. Vinski: What did Gracie find inside the cave? What was special about the rocks? What animals were there? What was special about the animals?

Students add items to their list that will help them design their cave. Then Mr. Vinski continues reading the book. He finally comes to the part about bats. The text says that bats sleep upside down in the cave during the day and come out for bugs at night.

Mr. Vinski: If we're going to have bats in our cave, where should we put them?

Keagan: Hang them from the ceiling by their feet! They'll be sleeping during the day!

When Mr. Vinski finishes reading *Inside a Cave,* the students have compiled a great list of items to help them transform their drama center into a cave and they have developed a solid understanding of the key details in the text. The following week, they hold a ribbon-cutting ceremony. They have created signs to hang around the classroom that advertise the event and provide details about their cave.

Parents have volunteered time and supplies such as cardboard boxes to help create a cave. They have also sent in elbow and knee pads, flashlights, old sweatshirts, and plastic insects, which have been spray painted white to look like the ones in the book. Mr. Vinski brought in the headlamps he uses when camping with his family, which he has attached to the construction worker helmets in the classroom. The paper bats that students made hang upside down in the cave.

Next to the cave, the class decides to include an office for the cave explorers, where they will record their discoveries. Blank paper is available for students to draw and label bat pictures, and small notebooks are used as journals to write about their experience. An old issue of *Scholastic News* hangs on the wall, and it has a diagram of a bat with labeled body parts. Several nonfiction books about bats are placed in the office for students to read.

Tips for the Teacher

MR. VINSKI GAVE HIS STUDENTS PRACTICE answering questions about key details from an informational text by reading aloud an engaging text for an authentic purpose: to find information that will help the class redecorate its dramatic play area. Clearly, asking and answering questions about key details in a text is widely applicable in many other situations, as well.

When selecting questions for practice with this standard, be sure to craft them carefully so students are explicitly drawing on information from the text. Avoid questions that students can answer using their own background knowledge (e.g., "Have you ever seen a bat?"), which do not help students develop proficiency with this standard. If you want students to ask the questions, model the process for them and prompt them to share what they wonder about from the text (e.g., "I wonder why she needs a helmet?").

Table 4.2 provides Reading Informational Text Standard 2 from the CCSS, which focuses on retelling the main ideas and details.

TABLE 4.2 ● *Reading Informational Text Standard 2 for K–Grade 2: Key Ideas and Details*

Kindergarten	Grade 1	Grade 2
With prompting and support, identify the main topic and retell key details of a text.	Identify the main topic and retell key details of a text.	Identify the main topic of a multiparagraph text as well as the focus of specific paragraphs within the text.

Source: NGA & CCSSO (2010).

Reading Informational Text Standard 2   Identify the main topic of a multiparagraph text as well as the focus of specific paragraphs within the text (second grade).

In the Common Core Classroom

Identifying Main Topics: Second Grade

Ms. Kramer's second-grade class has been learning about common features in informational texts. They have spent a considerable amount of time identifying and using headings, subheadings, bold print, captions, and labels. In a lesson last week, they used headings and subheadings to set purposes for reading and make predictions. They discussed how headings help "get their brains ready" for what they are about to read. Many students shared how reading the headings helped them understand the text better.

This week, the class will focus on Standard 2 for Reading Informational Text during whole-group and small-group lessons. This standard states that second-graders should be able to "identify the main topic of a multiparagraph text as well as the focus of specific paragraphs within the text" (NGA & CCSSO, 2010, p. 13).

Yesterday, Ms. Kramer introduced students to the text *Super Storms,* by Seymour Simon (2002). The class read along with her and paused to create a Popplet graphic organizer on their iPads to map the main idea and details in a web. Today, they will build on yesterday's lesson, as well as their previous lessons on text features.

Each student has a copy of the text. Ms. Kramer puts up the main idea and details graphic organizer on the interactive whiteboard, and she refers to it as she reminds the students about yesterday's lesson.

Ms. Kramer: Yesterday, we read *Super Storms,* by Seymour Simon. I used the title to decide that the main idea of this text was going to be "Some storms are super storms." We wondered what a *super storm* was but figured it out as we read. After reading, Gianna suggested that we add more to the main idea so now it says, "Some storms are super storms, which can be dangerous and destructive." We also paused to write down the four examples of super storms in the rectangles surrounding the main idea: *thunderstorms, hail, tornadoes,* and *hurricanes.* Don't you think these examples of super storms would make great headings? If Seymour Simon ever made a new edition of this book and decided to include headings to help his readers get their brains ready, where do you think he'd put them? Let's look through the book to find the best places for these four headings. Raise your hand when you think you've found the right spots.

The students identify the appropriate places for the four headings and add them in their texts with sticky notes.

Ms. Kramer: Now that we have added headings, we have divided the story into sections, kind of like chapters. Each of these sections is going to have its own main idea and details.

With a series of taps and swipes on the iPad, Ms. Kramer attaches popple rectangles to the four details.

Ms. Kramer: Now, I want us to finish our graphic organizer. I think it would be better to turn the words *thunderstorms, hail, tornadoes,* and *hurricanes* into main idea statements before we find the details. Help me do that for *thunderstorms*. If the main idea for the whole text is "Some storms are super storms, which can be dangerous and destructive," what should be the main idea of the Thunderstorms section?

Anika: "Thunderstorms are super storms."

Ms. Kramer: Good. Let me type that in. Now when I reread, I'm going to look for details in the Thunderstorms section that tell me more about how thunderstorms are dangerous and destructive. Remember that's important, because that's how we defined *super storms*. I can't just write any random fact. Let's all reread silently and look for facts that tell us more about thunderstorms being dangerous and destructive. Raise your hand when you think you've found something to write down as a detail.

Tyrone: In a thunderstorm millions of gallons of water drop each minute.

Jamie: I got the next one: Trees and houses can be destroyed.

Ms. Kramer: Here's one I remember: Lightning can start fires. Who can find one more?

Jose: I think I have one, but it's about hail. Does that count?

Ms. Kramer: Yes, remember that we learned that hail happens during some thunderstorms. Let's hear it!

Jose: Okay: Hail damages crops, buildings, and cars.

After having this scaffolded discussion, the students break into three small groups and focus on one of the remaining sections. Group members work together as they reread and identify the details in their assigned sections. Groups then report their information to the whole class, who analyze it and add it to the Popplet.

Ms. Kramer reinforces these skills throughout the week. Students are asked to select informational texts for independent reading this week and to record information about the main idea and details of these texts in their reading journals. Students may choose to organize the information into a web, like they did for the whole-group lesson. During guided reading, each group has at least one lesson on identifying the main idea and details of an informational text.

Plans for the Teacher

Materials for Getting Started

An informational text with multiple paragraphs (preferably, a copy for each child), sticky notes, main idea/details graphic organizer, such as Popplet (technology optional).

Content of Lesson

Before conducting this lesson, the teacher will need to provide other lessons that develop students' understanding that *headings* serve as titles for the sections in an informational text and often suggest the main ideas of those sections. During the initial reading of the text, the whole class should fill out the graphic organizer together, identifying the main idea and details. In a separate lesson, add headings to the text using the details identified earlier (or review the headings of the various sections if the text you selected already has this text feature). Model adding to the main idea/details graphic organizer by selecting one section and explaining your thinking aloud. Then divide the children into groups to complete the remaining sections by identifying the main idea and key details for each one. Finish the lesson by having the groups share and provide rationales for their thinking.

Differentiation

Pair a less-able reader with a partner who is more proficient.

Assessment

Listen to students as they report their thinking, and check their graphic organizers to ensure the main idea and details match the section they reviewed.

Table 4.3 provides the Reading Informational Text standard from the CCSS, which focuses on understanding connections within informational texts.

TABLE 4.3 ● *Reading Informational Text Standard 3 for K–Grade 2: Key Ideas and Details*

Kindergarten	Grade 1	Grade 2
With prompting and support, describe the connection between two individuals, events, ideas, or pieces of information in a text.	Describe the connection between two individuals, events, ideas, or pieces of information in a text.	Describe the connection between a series of historical events, scientific ideas or concepts, or steps in technical procedures in a text.

Source: NGA & CCSSO (2010).

Reading Informational Text Standard 3   With prompting and support, describe the connection between two individuals, events, ideas, or pieces of information in a text (kindergarten).

In the Common Core Classroom

Describing Connections: Kindergarten

The children in Ms. Meek's kindergarten class gather on the carpet for a choral reading activity during the whole-group portion of their reading block. Ms. Meek is using a document camera to project the book *What Is a Food Chain?* by Heather Nicole (2006), onto the whiteboard. Projecting the book allows all of the students to see the text, which is especially important if they are to read along with the teacher.

Ms. Meek's class has read this book twice before, making this a repeated reading. Repeated and choral reading procedures provide scaffolding for reading this complex text.

The children are developing an understanding of interdependence in nature as a part of their science unit on habitats. During the initial reading, the class enjoyed the way this text builds using the natural sequence of a food chain. For the second reading, the class used the cloze procedure to fill in the covered words by checking the pictures (e.g., "The _____ eats the insect."). In today's lesson, they will focus on Standard 3 for Reading Informational Text by describing the connections among the animals, the foods they eat, and the animals that eat them.

Ms. Meek starts off the lesson by reintroducing the story. Throughout the lesson, she refers to the appropriate pages and points to the pictures whenever they discuss parts of the food chain.

Ms. Meek: Today, we are going to reread the book *What Is a Food Chain?* Who remembers some of the important parts of the food chain this book teaches you about?

Eva: The bug.

Ms. Meek: That's right, Eva. There was a bug. The book used another word for *bug*. It's a two-clap word. Does anyone remember the word that means "bug" and has two claps?

Canyon: *Insect.*

Ms. Meek: Good. What other parts of the food chain do you remember?

Dylan: Us, us! We are the top. Nothing eats us!

Ryan: There was fish.

Ms. Meek: Great memory. This book talked about children and fish as a part of the food chain. There are two more parts of the food chain we didn't say yet. Let's look at the pictures.

Jessica: The plants and the bird.

Ms. Meek: Wonderful! Now let's say them all in order as I flip through the pages.

Everyone: Plants, insect, fish, bird, children.

Ms. Meek: Wow! I think you are ready to read this book along with me. As we read, pay attention to the parts of the food chain that are connected.

Everyone reads the text together aloud, following the teacher's pace and imitating her uses of expression.

Ms. Meek: Thank you for trying so hard. That book is really fun to read. I have some questions for you about the parts of the food chain that are connected. I'm going to ask you questions, and you can answer by holding up the picture that matches my question.

Ms. Meek distributes a set of pictures on craft sticks to each child. The students indicate their answers by holding up the appropriate picture. Ms. Meek carefully observes students' responses to assess the progress being made in the lesson.

Ms. Meek: *(Pausing slightly between questions)* What two things is the insect connected to? What does the insect eat? What eats the insect? What are the children connected to? What do the children eat? What eats the children? What three things is the fish connected to? What does the fish eat? What eats the fish? What are the plants connected to? What eats the plants? What is the bird connected to? What does the bird eat?

The students do a phenomenal job of making connections between important parts of this informational text, and all of them are involved during the lesson. Ms. Meek notes that two students answered several of the questions incorrectly, and she will work with them later during small-group instruction. To wrap up the lesson, helpers collect the pictures. The pictures will be used in a future retelling lesson and then placed in the classroom library to be used during centers the following week.

Plans for the Teacher

Materials for Getting Started

An informational text for emergent readers with strong connections between ideas, reproduced pictures from the text attached to craft sticks

Content of Lesson

Prior to this lesson, read the text together with the children multiple times so they are familiar with the content. To begin, review the parts of the text that depict the ideas about which students will later describe the connections. If you use *What Is a Food Chain?* as Ms. Meek did, you should first review the different plants and animals presented in the text. Next, reread the story with the purpose of focusing on the connections between the ideas. Finally, ask students guided questions that prompt them to identify the connections as they hold up the pictures of items that are connected.

Differentiation

Alter the level of text and/or provide additional lessons in small groups or with individuals.

Assessment

Watch students as they hold up the pictures to answer the questions.

Craft and Structure

The second category of standards, Craft and Structure, is different for informational texts than for narrative texts. In narrative texts, stories follow one general structure and have a setting, theme, plot episodes, and a resolution. In contrast, informational texts are structured in many ways, including description, sequence, compare and contrast, cause and effect, and problem/solution. A single informational text can contain more than one of these structures. There are text features to learn about, as well, such as the table of contents, glossary, captions, and index.

Increasing vocabulary is another important goal of the Craft and Structure standards in the primary grades. Children should learn new vocabulary and phrases from different types of informational texts in the different content areas. Learning vocabulary improves children's ability to comprehend what they read (Manzo, 2000).

Table 4.4 presents CCSS Standard 4 for Craft and Structure. The following In the Common Core Classroom feature shows a classroom engaged in activities for meeting that standard.

TABLE 4.4 ● *Reading Informational Text Standard 4 for K–Grade 2: Craft and Structure*

Kindergarten	Grade 1	Grade 2
With prompting and support, ask and answer questions about unknown words in a text.	Ask and answer questions to help determine or clarify the meaning of words and phrases in a text.	Determine the meaning of words and phrases in a text relevant to a grade 2 topic or subject area.

Source: NGA & CCSSO (2010).

Reading Informational Text Standard 4 Ask and answer questions to help determine or clarify the meaning of words and phrases in a text (first grade).

In the Common Core Classroom
Word Meaning: First Grade

It is an early spring day, with the wind whipping across the schoolyard, and the first-graders in Ms. O'Cleary's class are restless. She recognizes a teachable moment and spontaneously picks up the book *Wind,* by Susan Canizares and Betsey Chessen (1998), which, thankfully, will get the students moving around. As she reads the book aloud to the children, Ms. O'Cleary naturally models the asking of questions to determine the meanings of words in this simple text, helping her students develop the skills identified in Reading Standard 4 for Informational Text.

> **Ms. O'Cleary:** Here's a great book for today. It's called *Wind* and was written by two authors, Susan Canizares and Betsey Chessen. It tells what can happen when the wind blows. What do you think might happen to some of the things outside when the wind blows?
>
> **Trina:** *(Waving)* The leaves wave.
>
> **Paulie:** *(Bowing)* The grass bows, like in that poem we read.

Ms. O'Cleary: That's right, Paulie. You're remembering "Afternoon on a Hill" by Edna St. Vincent Millay.

Ms. O'Cleary: This book will give us more great action words, like *wave* and *bow*. I want to pick people who are sitting criss-cross with their hands in their laps and their eyes on me to show us the right movements.

After the students scramble to sit in perfect form, Ms. O'Cleary begins to read. She pauses to model asking questions to clarify the meanings of some of the action words. She stops on the action words to allow students to demonstrate the appropriate movements.

Ms. O'Cleary: This says *scatter*, and I'm thinking in my head that I'm not sure what that means. I asked myself, "What does *scatter* mean?" Let's check the picture. I know it's something a seed does when the wind blows. I bet seeds go all over the place! Now I've figured out that *scatter* means "to go all over." Can I have five student volunteers who are sitting correctly, looking and listening, to come up front in a group and then show us what *scatter* means?

A group of students perform the action for the class and then return to their spots as Ms. O'Cleary reminds the class how they should sit if they want a turn. Turning to another page of the book, she again demonstrates how to ask questions to clarify the meaning of a word by doing a think-aloud.

Ms. O'Cleary: Hmm, *ripples*. I'm thinking in my head, "What does *ripple* mean?" Lift one finger if you're also thinking that. Good. Let's look at the picture. I know it must be something the sand does when the wind blows, and I see lines dug into the sand making high piles and low lines—going up and down, up and down. Aha! I've just figured out that *ripples* must mean "going up and down, up and down." Who has on a big T-shirt and can come up front to make ripples with the bottom of his or her shirt?

Ms. O'Cleary asks other volunteers to show and use words to describe the meanings of the other action words in the book. After the class has read the book through one time, they stand up, spread out around the room, and act out the entire book together, doing the motions for each page as Ms. O'Cleary reads it a second time. The students fall gracefully like leaves, scatter like seeds, roll like waves, and bend like palm trees. The class has so much fun with this book that Ms. O'Cleary decides to put it in a center, to be reread and acted out again.

Tips for the Teacher

STANDARD 4 FOR READING INFORMATIONAL TEXTS is taking a strategic approach in determining the meanings of unknown words in an informational text. In the primary grades, we ask students questions and demonstrate how to use context clues, prior knowledge, related words, and grade-appropriate reference tools. In second grade, students should independently determine the meanings of words found in grade-level texts, according to the CCSS. Much of the work needed to meet this standard can take place in small-group instruction, such as guided reading.

Table 4.5 lists Reading Informational Text Standard 5, which focuses on using parts of an informational book. After kindergarten this includes text features.

TABLE 4.5 ● *Reading Informational Text Standard 5 for K–Grade 2: Craft and Structure*

Kindergarten	Grade 1	Grade 2
Identify the front cover, back cover, and title page of a book.	Know and use various text features (e.g., headings, tables of contents, glossaries, electronic menus, icons) to locate key facts or information in a text.	Know and use various text features (e.g., captions, bold print, subheadings, glossaries, indexes, electronic menus, icons) to locate key facts or information in text efficiently.

Source: NGA & CCSSO (2010).

Reading Informational Text Standard 5   Identify the front cover, back cover, and title page of a book (kindergarten).

In the Common Core Classroom

Text Features: Kindergarten

Ms. Healey sits down with a guided reading group of four kindergartners who are reading at a midkindergarten level. Her students are studying animals in science, and she has found the perfect book for this group: *Animal Coats,* by Jo Windsor (1999). This book features beautiful close-up photographs of different animal coats, and the text is written in simple four-word sentences. The first part of this lesson focuses on identifying the book's front cover, back cover, and title page, all addressed in Standard 5 of Reading Informational Text.

> **Ms. Healey:** Today, we're going to read a book called *Animal Coats.* It was written by Jo Windsor. Just like the title says, this book will show us photographs of different animal coats. I know that a *coat* is something that I put on to keep warm when it's cold out. Surely, they don't mean that the animals are wearing coats in this real-life, nonfiction book. What do you think they're talking about when they use the words *animal coats*?

> **Nerie:** My dog has a fur coat.

> **Juan:** It's like their skin or hair or fur.

> **Ms. Healey:** That's right. *Animal coats* is talking about the animal's body covering— whatever the animal has that covers its body. We've already thought of three different animal coats. Nerie's dog is covered in fur. Juan also said that skin and hair are animal coats. That's what our bodies are covered in.

> *Ms. Healey hands out the books upside down, aiming the top corner at each child.*

Ms. Healey: Let's look at the cover. *(Pausing and noting that all students flip the book over and turn it so it is facing upright)* What kind of animal is on the cover?

Trudy: A bird.

Ms. Healey: What kind of animal coat does the bird have?

Juan: It's got feathers.

Ms. Healey: That's right! A bird has feathers. Now let's open the cover and look at the next page.

Ms. Healey: *(Reading) Animal Coats,* written by Jo Windsor. This page tells us the title and author again. What do we call this page?

Victor: The *title* page!

Ms. Healey: And what animal coat do we see on the title page?

Trudy: A snake.

Ms. Healey: It could be a snake. What does a snake have covering its body?

Juan: I know it's got scales, because I go to *Scales and Snakes* after school.

Ms. Healey: Oh, that's why you know so much about animal coats! That's right, Juan. A snake has scales, and this is a picture of scales, so it could be a snake. Let's flip through the rest of the pages to see what animals there are and what animal coats they have. Maybe we'll find this same picture of scales in the book and find out what animal it belongs to.

The group does a book walk, flipping through the text and discussing the pictures without reading. They identify the animals in the pictures, along with their body coverings. Ms. Healey makes sure students use the language from the text and even pauses to have them "frame" some of the words with their fingers. Using this strategy helps her emerging readers with word identification. When students get to the picture that matches the title page, they find out that the scales actually belong to a fish. On the last page, Ms. Healey briefly reviews the index to expose her students to this text feature, which they will need to be able to use in future grades.

Ms. Healey: I wonder if the back cover has a picture on it, too. *(Pausing and noting that every student closes the book and looks at the appropriate cover)* Nope, no picture here. I think we're ready to read. Let's go back to the front cover and touch the title with our fingers. *(Noting that students can easily identify the front cover)*

Ms. Healey's class choral reads the text together, touching each word as it is pronounced. Then the students read the book a second time independently as Ms. Healey listens in. She notices that two students say "chicken" instead of "hen." After reading, the class does a brief lesson on the *-en* word family and then rereads that page together.

As Ms. Healey begins to meet with her next guided reading group, Nerie, Juan, Victor, and Trudy work together to sort a set of animal pictures on the feltboard by their coverings. When they are finished, they will take a digital photograph to record their work, which Ms. Healey will check and print for them after she finishes with her new group.

Tips for the Teacher

HIGH-QUALITY INFORMATIONAL TEXTS FOR YOUNG READERS come onto the market continually and are available for use during content area instruction and small-group reading lessons. As a response to the widespread adoption of the CCSS, even books for emergent readers are beginning to include the text features identified in the standards.

The provisions of Standard 5 for Reading Informational Text begin in kindergarten by requiring students to identify basic parts of books (i.e., front cover, back cover, and title page) and quickly move to include features specific to expository texts (i.e., headings, captions, labels, and bold print). Young students will need multiple experiences with these text features before incorporating them into their schemata for expository texts.

Fill your classroom library with the very best informational texts on the market. Newbridge, National Geographic, and Peoples Education are three publishers that offer high-quality texts for young readers. Also keep old issues of magazines in the classroom library, such as *Scholastic News* and *TIME for Kids,* because they will expose your students to the text features that the standards require them to know and use.

Table 4.6 provides Reading Informational Text Standard 6.

TABLE 4.6 ● *Reading Informational Text Standard 6 for K–Grade 2: Craft and Structure*

Kindergarten	Grade 1	Grade 2
Name the author and illustrator of a text and define the role of each in presenting the ideas or information in text.	Distinguish between information provided by pictures or other illustrations and information provided by the words in a text.	Identify the main purpose of a text, including what the author wants to answer, explain, or describe.

Source: NGA & CCSSO (2010).

Reading Informational Text Standard 6   Identify the main purpose of a text, including what the author wants to answer, explain, or describe (second grade).

In the Common Core Classroom

Author's Purpose: Second Grade

For the past month, Mr. Haria's second-grade has been working on a famous Americans theme that incorporates both language arts and social studies. In language arts, students have been learning about biographies and had many opportunities to interact with this type of informational text. In social studies, students have worked with partners to research the life of one famous American and create a poster to teach their classmates about him or her. Partners have just finished presenting their posters to their peers, and now, they are preparing for the second-grade play, in which they will present their famous Americans to their parents.

> **Mr. Haria:** We will be writing our own lines for our famous Americans play. When we write the script, we need to make sure we put in three things about each person: the reason the person is famous and two interesting facts about the person's life. In order to determine the reason the person is famous, you need to reread the biography you used to make your poster.
>
> To give you an example, I am going to read aloud the biography of Johnny Appleseed, the famous American I want to dress up as. By now, everyone remembers that the purpose of a biography is to tell about a person's life. If I think about what the author wanted to tell us about Johnny Appleseed's life as I read, then I can figure out what the author's purpose was for writing this biography. If I know the author's purpose, I can easily determine why Johnny Appleseed is famous.

To help his students meet Standard 6 for Reading Informational Texts, Mr. Haria uses think-aloud procedures to demonstrate the kinds of thoughts a competent reader has when determining the author's purpose. When Mr. Haria reads about Johnny's childhood, he makes a comment to reveal his thinking.

> **Mr. Haria:** I see that the author makes a point of telling us that Johnny used to walk in the forest and check out the plants and animals. I think the point is that Johnny was always interested in nature.

A few pages later, the biography tells that Johnny planted apple trees along the Ohio River Valley.

> **Mr. Haria:** That seems important, but I'm not sure that planting apple trees would be enough to make a person as famous as Johnny Appleseed became. I wonder why planting trees made Johnny famous. Maybe if I find that out, I'll be able to figure out the author's purpose for writing this biography.

Mr. Haria goes on to read about the settlers that moved into the valley and how Johnny taught them how to plant apple trees, which provided them food for the entire year.

> **Mr. Haria:** I remember when we learned about colonial life in November that it was really hard for many reasons. One of the reasons was because there wasn't much food. Having apple trees must have made a big difference for these settlers. I think I know the author's purpose now, but let's keep reading to see if we find out more.

Three pages later, Mr. Haria reads that Johnny Appleseed could make medicine from the plants.

> **Mr. Haria:** Now that's important, too. Another reason colonial life was so hard was because people got sick and didn't have medicine. Many people died from things we can easily cure today. Johnny Appleseed helped these settlers a lot!

After finishing the book, Mr. Haria articulates the author's purpose and identifies the reason Johnny Appleseed is famous.

Mr. Haria: The author wanted to teach us that Johnny Appleseed's life was dedicated to helping others. He planted apple trees that fed many settlers and made medicine to help the sick. That is why he is so famous. When I write my lines, I want to make it sound like I'm Johnny Appleseed. I'll probably start by introducing myself: "Hi, I'm John Chapman, but you might know me as Johnny Appleseed." Then I'll tell why I'm famous: "There are a lot of new settlers in these parts that don't know much about the land. So I teach them, and together we plant apple trees to feed their families. The apples and the medicine I make from plants help them stay alive."

Mr. Haria flips through the book one more time to pick out his two favorite facts about Johnny Appleseed's life and finishes composing his lines. Then the children work with their partner to reread the biographies they have chosen. On a graphic organizer, each pair writes down the author's purpose in the top box, draws the face of their famous American in the oval, writes the reason that person is famous in the speech bubble, and then fills in two interesting facts on the remaining lines. Mr. Haria checks over the graphic organizers as his students complete them and allows those who finish early to start writing their lines.

Plans for the Teacher

Materials for Getting Started

Biographies written for young students, such as *Rookie Biographies,* published by Scholastic; graphic organizer

Content of Lesson

Prior to this lesson, students need to have read the biographies they selected at least once, so that they already have begun to build background knowledge of the people they are researching. To begin the lesson, model the process of thinking about the author's purpose and the main idea of the text, as Mr. Haria did while reading a biography aloud to his class. Demonstrate how to complete the graphic organizer using the information you shared during the think-aloud portion. Finally, allow students to work independently or in pairs, or guide them individually as they reread their texts to determine the author's purpose. If you want students to use the graphic organizer as a tool for writing the lines for their play, complete the lesson by modeling the writing process.

Differentiation

Provide texts for struggling readers that are written on their level, or support their reading with an audiorecording. Go to the website Bookflix.com (www.bookflix.com), which is a subscription site that makes a handful biographies available that will read the text aloud. Guide those students who need help with this standard by listening to them think aloud as they read and adding your own thoughts when necessary.

Assessment

Check students' graphic organizers to see how well they identified the author's purpose and other details.

Integration of Knowledge and Ideas

The third category of standards is Integration of Knowledge and Ideas. The standards in this category relate to children understanding the information within a single text and across two texts. These standards ask us to help children learn to integrate the use of various forms of information in a text to enhance comprehension, such as illustrations and diagrams, a glossary, an index, and digital information. Students will be asked to compare and contrast key ideas in two texts on the same topic. They will also begin to suggest reasons for what the author has written. The integration of knowledge in the CCSS emphasizes teaching literacy skills concurrently, so that reading, writing, listening, and speaking are not viewed as separate. Rather, all areas of literacy support each other.

Integrating literacy skills into the content areas also allows children to continue to practice literacy strategies. Thematic instruction is suggested as a way to integrate literacy skills into content area teaching, having children read, write, listen, and speak about science, social studies, math, art, and music. Doing so provides the opportunity for making literacy a means by which students gather information. Thematic instruction is also motivating and engaging. Teachers plan interesting experiments and give children choices about what they will read and write. Children pose questions about what they want to learn, and they prepare food, go on field trips, and explore and experiment with electricity, magnets, and other topics of interest. Studying themes of interest to children, such as insects and weather, makes school relevant to them. They become motivated to read and write, because they are interested in learning more about the theme and completing a project in which they are engaged.

Table 4.7 provides Standard 7 in the category Integration of Knowledge and Ideas. The table is followed by a classroom vignette on integrating literacy and language arts across the curriculum.

TABLE 4.7 ● *Reading Informational Text Standard 7 for K–Grade 2: Integration of Knowledge and Ideas*

Kindergarten	Grade 1	Grade 2
With prompting and support, describe the relationship between illustrations and the text in which they appear (e.g., what person, place, thing, or idea in the text an illustration depicts).	Use the illustrations and details in a text to describe its key ideas.	Explain how specific images (e.g., diagram showing how a machine works) contribute to and clarify a text.

Source: NGA & CCSSO (2010).

Reading Informational Text Standard 7   With prompting and support, describe the relationship between illustrations and the text in which they appear (e.g., what person, place, thing, or idea in the text an illustration depicts) (kindergarten).

In the Common Core Classroom
Integrate and Evaluate Images: Kindergarten

The kindergartners are having morning play time and enjoying the transportation-themed additions to their classroom. Several students sit around a town created from blocks, zooming new toy cars and trucks down the streets. Others are in the dramatic play area, sitting in rows of chairs and pretending they are passengers on an airplane. Two children are counting the blocks on a transportation graph that students update daily to show how they got to school.

A parent volunteer sits in the library corner with two lucky students who are excited to be the Snuggle Readers of the day. Their teacher, Ms. Torino, started the Snuggle Reader program to get parents involved and give her students the opportunity to get a little extra attention. For this program, parents and school workers (i.e., the principal, secretary, physical education teacher) sign up to come in during morning play time to read to two students. The program is called Snuggle Readers because the two students get to sit right next to the volunteer as he or she reads. Today's volunteer, Ms. Ionny, is a regular volunteer who comes in once a week. She is excellent with the children and works with all of them throughout the year.

Today, Ms. Ionny reads the book *Fast Food,* by Saxton Freymann (2006). The illustrations in this creative book are photographs of food sculptures that have been made into different vehicles, and the text is written in verse. Since the purpose of this text is to teach children about different modes of transportation, it is considered informational–poetic (Duke, 2000).

Ms. Torino has asked Ms. Ionny to pose questions to the students about the illustrations to practice Standard 7 for Reading Informational Text. Ms. Ionny begins to read and pauses to let the students take turns pointing to and talking about the text.

Ms. Ionny: Which one has the skates on? *(Student points)* Which vehicle has something to hold on to? *(Student points)* What did the book say that kind of vehicle is called?

Vidal: A scooter. I got a scooter!

Ms. Ionny reads a couple more pages and pauses again.

Ms. Ionny: Who is riding the bike? Who is riding the trike?

Tanji: The mushroom guy has a trike. He's the little brother. See this guy here. He's big. He's got a bike made of oranges! *(Laughs)*

With the next page flip, Vidal points and shouts out excitedly before Ms. Ionny even asks her question.

Vidal: That's SANTA! He's in his sleigh. Sleighs go across snow, and Santa lives in the North Pole where it's snow everywhere! He also flies all around the world when he delivers presents.

Ms. Ionny: That's right. Let's hear what the book says.

When Ms. Ionny and the students get to the pages about boats, there are lot of questions to ask.

Ms. Ionny: Which boat probably has a motor? *(Student points)* Where is the submarine? *(Student points)* Which boat moves when the wind blows? *(Student points)* What is that called?

Tanji: A sailboat. I love these little mushroom guys just sailing along!

Vidal and Tanji loved the book so much they decide to act like the pictures. Tanji says that he is a "mushroom guy" and sails around for the rest of playtime, looking into the air and exclaiming, "A little help here!" Vidal flies around in his imaginary banana airplane and decides to join the children in the dramatic play area as their pilot.

In addition to being excited participants, Vidal and Tanji are also good at determining the relationship between the illustrations and the text. When asked short, prompting questions, they can easily match the pictures to the ideas they represent. Ms. Ionny shares this information with Ms. Torino as she gathers her things and says goodbye.

Tips for the Teacher

IN THE ELEMENTARY GRADES, STANDARD 7 for Reading Informational Text focuses on using the illustrations to enhance understanding of the topic presented in an informational text. At the kindergarten level, students should be able to point out who or what idea from the text a picture represents. As we go up the grade levels, students are expected to make use of these visuals independently to develop their understanding of the key idea of the text. Students as young as second grade are expected to be able to explain what the image adds that the text alone lacks. To accomplish this goal, a lot of work needs to be done early on with informational texts. Early childhood and elementary teachers need to use images in big books or projected versions of informational text with their students. Explicit instruction involving modeling and think-alouds becomes more and more necessary as the complexity of the text increases and students get older.

Table 4.8. provides Reading Informational Text Standard 8, which focuses on the author's reasoning provided in the text.

**TABLE 4.8 ● *Reading Informational Text Standard 8 for K–Grade 2:*
Integration of Knowledge and Ideas**

Kindergarten	Grade 1	Grade 2
With prompting and support, identify the reasons an author gives to support points in a text.	Identify the reasons an author gives to support points in a text.	Describe how reasons support specific points the author makes in a text.

Source: NGA & CCSSO (2010).

Reading Informational Text Standard 8   Identify the reasons an author gives to support points in a text (first grade).

In the Common Core Classroom

Identify Reasons: First Grade

Ms. Shannon is sitting down with a small group of first-grade students that read on level for the end of the year. She introduces three books in what is called a "booktalk," and the group selects *On the Ranch,* by Ellen Catala (2004), to read together. Today, the group will focus on Standard 8 for Reading Informational Text. As the children read, Ms. Shannon listens in and asks guiding questions.

Ms. Shannon: *(Speaking to Brian)* You just read about the special clothing that cowboys used in the past. The author explains the reason that their boots had heels. Can you tell me the reason the author gave? Why did their boots have heels?

Brian: It's so their feet didn't slip out of the stirrups.

Ms. Shannon: Oh, that's a good reason. And why did they wear hats?

Brian: Because it was sunny. I wear a hat for baseball so I don't have to scrunch up my eyes.

Next, Ms. Shannon listens to Elizabeth. She stops Elizabeth at the part where the author draws comparisons between cowboys of the past and today.

Ms. Shannon: *(Speaking to Elizabeth)* What reasons does the author give that tell us how cowboys today are like the cowboys in the past?

Elizabeth: They both wear the same things. They camp and work hard.

Ms. Shannon: Tell me more. What do they wear that's the same?

Elizabeth: *(Looking at the book)* Hats, boots, and chaps.

Ms. Shannon: Why do they work hard?

Elizabeth: There's a lot to do. It says they don't walk so far, though.

Ms. Shannon moves on to Jeremy. He is a couple of pages ahead of Elizabeth.

Ms. Shannon: *(Speaking to Jeremy)* What reason does the author give to explain why ranchers should be good at riding?

Jeremy: They ride horses to round up the cattle. You see the rope there? That's a lasso. I don't know how they swing it around in a circle. I tried and it's hard.

The students have finished their initial reading. Ms. Shannon was able to listen in and interact with three students. She wrote down notes about their reading and how well they were able to identify the specific reasons the author gave to support key points in the text. Now, the group fills out a graphic organizer together to record the most important points and the reasons the author gives to support those points.

Ms. Shannon: Who remembers one important detail about ranchers and cowboys from this book?

Scott: Cowboys wear special clothes.

Ms. Shannon: Okay, let's write that in the first box. In the box next to it, we need to write down some reasons the author gave to tell us why cowboys wear special clothes.

Jeremy: They need them for their job.

Ms. Shannon: Right, but let's get a little more than that. Why do they need them for their job? Let's look back at that page.

Elizabeth: The heels kept their feet in the stirrups and the hats gave their faces shade.

Ms. Shannon: Good, Elizabeth. Let's write that down. *(Modeling writing)* Heels keep feet in stirrups. Hats give shade.

The group continues to fill out the graphic organizer together. Then, the students do a second reading of the text alone, and Ms. Shannon listens to the remaining two students read. She notes that they are developing their ability to identify reasons given by the author but that they will need more time with this skill.

Plans for the Teacher

Materials for Getting Started

Informational text at students' instructional reading level, graphic organizer

Content of Lesson

Listen to students as they read independently. Have them pause to explain the reason the author gives about a specific point that you have questioned them about. Refer to the text and illustrations together to guide this activity. When most of the students have finished reading, distribute the graphic organizer. Guide students to record the reasons the author gives to explain specific points in the text. Allow students to look back at the text when necessary.

Differentiation

Vary the level of support offered to students as needed.

Assessment

Take notes on each student's ability to identify reasons. Refer back to these notes during future lessons.

Table 4.9 provides Reading Informational Text Standard 9 in the category Integration of Knowledge and Ideas. This standard focuses on comparing and contracting texts.

TABLE 4.9 ● *Reading Informational Text Standard 9 for K–Grade 2:* **Integration of Knowledge and Ideas**

Kindergarten	Grade 1	Grade 2
With prompting and support, identify basic similarities and differences between two texts on the same topic (e.g., in illustrations, descriptions, or procedures).	Identify basic similarities in and differences between two texts on the same topic (e.g., in illustrations, descriptions, or procedures).	Compare and contrast the most important points presented by two texts on the same topic.

Source: NGA & CCSSO (2010).

Reading Informational Text Standard 9   Compare and contrast the most important points presented by two texts on the same topic (second grade).

In the Common Core Classroom
Compare and Contrast Texts: Second Grade

The second-graders in Ms. Kyle's class have been comparing and contrasting all year long. They have used characters within the same story (i.e., Henry and Mudge), characters from similar stories (i.e., Clifford and Mudge), and different versions of folktales. They know all about Venn diagrams and can easily draw the two overlapping circles when asked to compare and contrast. Students have done well in developing these skills, and so it is no surprise when many of them choose to compare and contrast two informational texts on the same topic for their reading journal activity.

During whole-group instruction, Ms. Kyle reads aloud *Penguin Chick,* by Betty Tatham (2001). The lesson that accompanies this reading focuses on drawing conclusions, and the students use details from the story to decide that the life of an emperor penguin is hard. In the classroom literacy center, Ms. Kyle has set up a browsing box of penguin books. *Penguins Through the Year,* by Robin Bernard (1995), is one of the most popular selections because of its many similarities to *Penguin Chick.* Justin and Eric decide to work together to compare and contrast these two books and create Venn diagrams in their reading journals.

> *Justin:* Let's put *PTY* above the left circle for *Penguins Through the Year* and *PC* above the right circle for *Penguin Chick.*
>
> *Eric:* Okay, but make your circles closer together. We're going to need a lot of room in the middle where they overlap, because there are a lot of similarities.
>
> *Justin:* I have the first one: "Baby penguins are born in a rookery." It goes in the middle.
>
> *Eric:* The emperor penguins don't have a nest. The egg sits on the father's feet. The penguins in *Penguins Through the Year* make a nest of pebbles. Oh, and the emperor penguins only have one egg and these have two! Those are two differences. They go inside the circles in the part where they're not overlapping.
>
> *Justin:* (*Speaking as he writes*) PTY: Nest of pebbles. PC: No nest. PTY: Two eggs. PC: One egg.
>
> *Justin:* In *Penguins Throughout the Year,* they say the egg is laid in spring, but in *Penguin Chick,* they say it's winter. That is another difference.
>
> *Eric:* When I read *Penguins Throughout the Year* the first time, I didn't notice that there were so many differences! Maybe there's not as much to write in the middle as I thought! See, here it says both parents take care of the egg. But the emperor penguin father takes care of the egg the whole time. Wait, look at this little speech bubble! We need to move "No nest" into the middle. This cartoon penguin talks about how some penguins carry the egg on their feet. That's a similarity!
>
> *Justin:* I have one for the middle, too. Both parents take care of the chick. Oh, and the chick has fluffy, gray, down feathers.
>
> *Eric:* In *Penguins Throughout the Year,* the speech bubble says the group of chicks is called a *kindergarten,* but in *Penguin Chick,* they call it a *crèche,* a nursery.

Justin: In the middle, we should put "Lose baby feathers." I think they can swim once they've lost their down.

Eric: They both end by talking about having more eggs and making new families.

The boys complete their Venn diagrams and return their reading journals to the appropriate spots. They both have demonstrated mastery of Standard 9 for Reading Informational Text, as they were able to compare and contrast the main details from two informational texts on the same topic.

Tips for the Teacher

THE STUDENTS IN THE PREVIOUS VIGNETTE are already independently meeting Standard 9 for Reading Informational Texts. Their teacher has spent a lot of time on comparing and contrasting in general and on building knowledge of informational texts. To get students to be able to compare and contrast key ideas from two informational texts on the same topic, this background work must be done. In kindergarten, the teacher might begin by informally noting when two texts are on the same topic. Then, the teacher might involve students in comparing and contrasting the illustrations from two different texts. For texts that are very familiar to students, descriptions and procedures can be compared with support from the teacher. In first grade, the teacher can work with young readers in small groups to guide this process. Providing graphic organizers with premade T-charts and Venn diagrams would be an effective way to approach this standard with first-grade students.

Range of Reading and Level of Text Complexity   The final category in Reading Information Text is Range of Reading and Level of Text Complexity. The CCSS offer a three-part framework for determining text complexity:

1. qualitative evaluation of the text
2. quantitative evaluation of the text
3. matching the reader to the text and task

Qualitative evaluation focuses on text characteristics, including level of meaning, support of graphic elements, and print format. *Quantitative* evaluation, which is also referred to as *readability,* is typically calculated with formulas such as the Lexile Framework for Reading (MetaMetrics, 2013), the Coh-Metrix (which measures text cohesion by accounting for additional text- and sentence-level variables) (Graesser, McNamara, & Kulikowich, 2011), the Fry Readability Formula (Fry, 1968), and the Dale-Chall Readability Formula (Dale & Chall, 1948). Matching the reader to the text must also consider characteristics such as the reader's motivation and purpose for reading a book. The many variables just discussed help to determine the complexity of a text. The teacher must think about all of these characteristics that can affect how well a reader can comprehend a particular text.

Text complexity is not as big an issue in kindergarten and first grade as it is in higher grades. Since young children are often not conventional readers, they are working mostly on learning how to read. Therefore, during explicit instruction of reading, we cannot use a complex text; rather, we must use a text at the students' instructional level. However, we can expose students to a complex text when reading aloud to them. Although the vocabulary may be new, students will remember unusual words and things out of the ordinary. For instance, 4-year-olds will remember the names and characteristics of a hippopotamus or brontosaurus when introduced to them. Teachers can support the reading of a more complex text by explaining difficult vocabulary and performing repeated readings of difficult material. Providing this type of exposure motivates children to want to hear more complex texts.

Students should also be exposed to a variety of informational texts on the same topic, just as they are exposed to a range of types of fiction. Having multiple experiences with informational texts enables students to develop a schema for understanding what the author has presented to the reader. When exposed to complex texts and many types of informational texts and levels of complexity, children will have models to connect to their writing. In addition, children will likely be more willing to explore other informational texts. Teachers need to help students build on what they know, challenge their ideas, and expand their knowledge and understanding.

Table 4.10 provides the CCSS for the category Range of Reading and Level of Text Complexity. A vignette follows about working on this standard in the classroom.

TABLE 4.10 ● *Reading Informational Text Standard 10 for K–Grade 2: Range of Reading and Level of Text Complexity*

Kindergarten	Grade 1	Grade 2
Actively engage in group reading activities with purpose and understanding.	With prompting and support, read informational texts appropriately complex for grade 1.	By the end of year, read and comprehend informational texts, including history/social studies, science, and technical texts, in the grades 2–3 text complexity band proficiently, with scaffolding as needed at the high end of the range.

Source: NGA & CCSSO (2010).

Reading Informational Text Standard 10   By the end of the year, read and comprehend informational texts, including history/social studies, science, and technical texts, in the grades 2–3 text complexity band proficiently, with scaffolding as needed at the high end of the range (second grade).

In the Common Core Classroom

Supporting Comprehension for Complex Texts: Second Grade

Ms. Kelly's class is engaged in an online wiki project with a class on the other side of the country. They are collecting and sharing weather data for the month of February. For this project, the children use real weather tools (i.e., thermometers, barometers, and hygrometers) to gather their data, record it in a chart on their class's wiki page, and use the data to predict tomorrow's weather.

Ms. Kelly puts up an article on the interactive whiteboard titled "Understanding Barometer Readings," by Isaiah David, which is from the *eHow* website. This is a complex text for second-graders but will teach them how to use a barometer to predict tomorrow's weather. Ms. Kelly provides support for this text by reading it aloud to the students and then discussing and clarifying the procedures it describes.

Ms. Kelly: I was doing a search on Google to see if I could find a webpage that could explain how to predict the weather, and I came across this *eHow* article. It is exactly the kind of information I was looking for. It's not really written for second-graders, but it's not too hard to understand. Let's read it carefully together and see if we can figure out how to predict the weather using a barometer.

Ms. Kelly reads the opening paragraph and makes several comments.

Ms. Kelly: Our barometer is marked with numbers, just like the one in the picture. Instead of the words *stormy, rain, change, fair,* and *very dry,* our barometer has pictures of a sun, a sun covered by a cloud, and a rain cloud. This article says that I need to know two things to predict the weather: (1) I need to know the current air pressure, which is what I will find on my barometer, and (2) I need to know the change in air pressure. To get that information, I compare yesterday's measurement to today's measurement.

Ms. Kelly reads the first, second, and third items in the Instructions section. She reviews what air pressure is and how changes in air pressure happen by referring to pictures in the book What Will the Weather Be? *by Lynda DeWitt (1991), which the class read together a few days ago.*

Ms. Kelly: *(Showing pages 22 and 23)* Air pressure is the weight of the air that pushes on the Earth and your body. Remember the picture of the basketball that has no air inside? If there's no force inside the ball to balance out the force from the air pressure, the ball gets crushed. *(Showing page 25)* When the air pressure is high, the air is falling toward the earth. The weather is usually dry and sunny. *(Showing pages 12 and 13 and then page 24)* When cold air blows into the area forming a cold front, the warm air is pushed up—it rises—creating a drop in the air pressure. Of course if there's a good amount of water vapor in the air, the clouds will fill up and it will rain.

Ms. Kelly reads item 4 in the Instructions and explains what it means.

Ms. Kelly: When the author says "rising pressure," he means that today's pressure was higher than yesterday's. So if yesterday we read that the air pressure was 995 hPa, is 1,000 hPa higher?

Tyler: Yes! 1,000 is higher than 995.

Ms. Kelly: Right. So if it was 995 hPa yesterday and 1,000 hPa today, we might predict that tomorrow, it will not be raining. Maybe it will be partly cloudy.

Ms. Kelly reads item 5 in the Instructions and sums up the article.

Ms. Kelly: If the pressure is high, the air is falling to the earth and the sky is clear. If the pressure is low, the air is rising, and so is the water vapor, so the weather may be rainy. If yesterday's air pressure was lower than today's, we might predict that the weather is going to clear up. If yesterday's air pressure was higher than today's, we might predict that a cold front is coming and the clouds are filling up.

Ms. Kelly checks her students' understanding by pulling up an image of a barometer on the interactive whiteboard. She draws a blue arrow to represent yesterday's barometer reading and a red arrow to show today's barometer reading. The class uses this hypothetical information to forecast the weather and review the information in the article. Finally, each student gets a printed copy of the online article to reread. Another copy is added to the Resources page of their wiki, in case they need to access it one more time when they are collecting data and forming their predictions.

Tips for the Teacher

FINDING TEXT WITH THE RIGHT LEVEL of complexity for your students may be difficult at first. We used to think about text in the frustrational range as something that was better to leave out. Now, we think that these texts may be beneficial after all. The key to making a complex text useful to young students is providing the right amount of support during students' initial experience with the text. Make sure you activate students' prior knowledge and review challenging vocabulary words before reading the text. During reading, pause to rephrase complex concepts and use visuals if necessary. After reading, summarize the text with the whole class and then have students work with partners for a second reading.

Foster Children's Motivation

Research has identified many teacher practices that are associated with higher levels of student motivation (from Brophy, 1987):

- Induce curiosity and suspense.
- Make abstract materials more concrete and understandable.
- Provide informative feedback.
- Adapt academic tasks to student interests.
- Provide novel content as much as possible.
- Provide unusual ways to learn content with hands-on activities.
- Give students choices between alternative tasks.
- Allow students some autonomy in doing tasks.
- Provide tasks with an appropriate level of challenge/difficulty.

Selecting informational texts about interesting topics is very important (Guthrie, McRae, & Klauda, 2007; Jiménez & Duke, 2011). As early as preschool, children have developed topics of interest to them, so grouping children for reading instruction by common interests is sometimes advised (Guthrie & McCann, 1996).

We also recommend keeping individual children's interests in mind when identifying books and other texts that they can choose from for independent or home reading. Having a choice fosters motivation. So, rather than approach a reading group with "The book we are going to read today is...," consider offering two or three titles from which the children can choose.

Using Informational Texts Throughout the Day

THE CCSS WERE CREATED TO COORDINATE THE EDUCATION of the children across the United States. Families move often, which makes it critical to provide some continuity in the teaching of reading throughout the country.

The CCSS Reading Standards recommend that teachers expose children to equal amounts of informational text and narrative literature. In line with the CCSS, children should read magazines, poetry, novels, newspapers, and new literacy media. In addition, children should be exposed to information to increase vocabulary.

When we integrate literacy strategies into content areas such as social studies and science, we can accomplish the goals discussed in this chapter. The CCSS can easily be integrated into small-group, differentiated, explicit literacy instruction, as well as whole-class and individual instruction. Teachers have used themes in the past but not necessarily with the intention of teaching and reinforcing literacy skills. The CCSS recommends that literacy be taught intentionally within the content areas.

See Chapter 6 for a discussion of integrating language arts/literacy into the content areas and a thematic science unit that uses both informational text and narrative literature.

Summary and Conclusions

THE CCSS EMPHASIS ON USING INFORMATIONAL TEXT IS a very positive shift in literacy instruction, since as adults, we spend most of our time engaged in reading expository material. Motivation is an important element in creating engaged readers. Informational texts provide students with materials that meet their interests, present authentic purposes for reading, and allow for choice. Children are most likely to be motivated when they have opportunities for choice, challenge, collaboration, and success.

Activities should allow students some responsibility in forming and completing tasks. Instruction in reading comprehension must be carefully designed, drawing attention to the craft and structure of text and engaging children in discussion. Teachers should incorporate a range of texts within the classroom environment and throughout the school day. The CCSS advocate the teaching of literacy all day, not just in the language arts period. The English language arts should also be incorporated as a major part of content area instruction. Doing so is required for our children to become fluent readers.

ACTIVITIES

1. In your series of CCSS workshops for parents and teachers, include a workshop on informational texts. Have books to share, point out the features in these texts, and compare and contrast these texts with narrative literature. Have a discussion about the values of sharing informational text with children.

2. Count the numbers and types of informational books in your classroom library. Organize these books so they are accessible to children. Add informational books that are missing from your collection.

3. Select a science or social studies theme to study that is appropriate for your class. Collect as many theme-related informational texts as possible, including not only books but also magazines, newspapers, brochures, maps, posters, charts, digital media, picture books, cookbooks, and pamphlets with directions.

4. Read an informational text that is slightly above grade level for your children. Begin by talking about the vocabulary students will encounter, and put the words on the board with pictures accompanying them if possible. Do a book walk and have students look at the pictures and discuss what they might learn in the book. Ask the students to pose questions about what they want to learn. Read the book aloud to the children, and have them follow along in their own copies. After the first reading, discuss the vocabulary, as well as what students learned from the book and whether they learned what they wanted to learn. In the second reading, have the children echo read the book with you. On another day, have them read the story with partners.

5. Arrange for the author of an informational text to visit your classroom. Make sure the children have read some of his or her work in advance of the visit. Also have questions prepared that include (a) how or why the author decided to write informational text instead of narrative literature, (b) how he or she decides what topics to write about, and (c) how children can write their own informational texts.

REFERENCES

Brophy, J. (1987). *On motivating students*. East Lansing, MI: Institute for Research on Teaching, Michigan State University.

Bryan, G., Tunnell, M. O., & Jacobs, J. S. (2007). A most valuable player: The place of books in teaching children to read. *Canadian Children, 32*(2), 25–33.

Chall, J. S. (1983). *Stages of reading development*. New York: McGraw-Hill.

Dale, E., & Chall, S. (1948). A formula for predicting readability. *Education Research Bulletin, 27,* 11–20, 37–54.

Duke, N. K. (2000). 3.6 minutes per day: The scarcity of informational texts in first grade. *Reading Research Quarterly, 35*(2), 202–224.

Duke, N. K., Bennett-Armistead, V. S., & Roberts, E. M. (2003). Filling the great void: Why we should bring nonfiction into the early-grade classroom. *American Educator, 27*(1), 30–35.

Fingeret, L. (2008). "March of the Penguins": Building knowledge in a kindergarten classroom. *The Reading Teacher, 62,* 96–103.

Fry, E. (1968) A readability formula that saves time. *Journal of Reading, 11*(7), 513–516 and 575–578.

Graesser, A. C., McNamara, D. S., & Kulikowich, J. M. (2011). Coh-Metrix: Providing multilevel analyses of text characteristics. *Educational Researcher, 40,* 223–234.

Gunning, T. G. (2010). *Creating literacy instruction for all children* (7th ed.) Boston, MA: Allyn & Bacon.

Guthrie, J. T. (2011). Best practice for motivating students to read. In L. M. Morrow & L. B. Gambrell (eds.). *Best practices in literacy instruction* (4th ed.). New York, NY: Guilford Press.

Guthrie, J. T., & McCann, A. D. (1996). Idea circles: Peer collaborations for conceptual learning. In L. Gambrell & J. Almasi (Eds.), *Lively discussions!* (pp. 87–105). Newark, DE: International Reading Association.

Guthrie, J. T., McRae, A., & Klauda, S. L. (2007). Contributions of concept-oriented reading instruction to knowledge about interventions for motivations in reading. *Educational Psychologist, 42,* 237–250.

Hiebert, E. H. (2008). The word zone fluency curriculum: An alternative approach. In M. R. Kuhn and P. J. Schwanenflugel (eds.), *Fluency in the classroom* (pp. 154–170). New York, NY: Guilford Press.

Jiménez, L. M., & Duke, N. K. (2013). *The effect of high and low interest on multiple text reading comprehension in elementary-age readers.* Unpublished manuscript.

Kletzien, S. B., & Dreher, M. J. (2004). *Informational text in K–3 classrooms: Helping children read and write.* Newark, DE: International Reading Association:

Leung, C. B. (2008). Preschoolers' acquisition of scientific vocabulary through repeated read-aloud events, retellings, and hands-on science activities. *Reading Psychology: An International Quarterly, 29,* 165–193.

Manzo, K. K. (2000). Schools begin to infuse media literacy into the three R's. *Education Week, 20*(14), 6–8.

MetaMetrics. (2013). The Lexile framework for reading. *Lexile.com.* Retrieved from http://www.lexile.com.

Moore, D. W., Alvermann, D. E., & Hinchman, K. A. (2000). *Struggling adolescent readers: A collection of teaching strategies.* Newark, DE: International Reading Association.

National Assessment Governing Board (NAGB). (2012). Reading framework for the 2009 National Assessment of Educational Progress. Washington, DC: U.S. Government Printing Office.

National Governors Association Center for Best Practices & Council of Chief State School Officers (NGA & CCSSO). (2010). *Common Core State Standards.* Washington, DC: Authors. Retrieved from www.corestandards.org/assets/CCSSI_ELA%20Standards.pdf

Pappas, C. (1993). Is narrative "primary"? Some insights from kindergarteners' pretend readings of stories and information books. *Journal of Reading Behavior, 25,* 97–129.

Sudol, P., & King, C. M. (1996). A checklist for choosing nonfiction trade books. *The Reading Teacher, 49,* 422–424.

CHILDREN'S LITERATURE CITED

Bernard, R. (1995). *Penguins through the year.* New York, NY: Scholastic.

Canizares, S., & Chessen, B. (1998). *Wind.* New York, NY: Scholastic.

Catala, E. (2004). *On the ranch.* Austin, TX: Steck-Vaughn.

David, I. (n.d.). Understanding barometer readings. *eHow.* Retrieved from http://www.ehow.com/how_4532234_understanding-barometer-readings.html.

DeWitt, L. (1991). *What will the weather be?* New York, NY: HarperCollins.

Ditchfield, C. (2003). *Johnny Appleseed.* New York, NY: Children's Press.

Freymann, S. (2006). *Fast food.* New York, NY: Arthur A. Levine.

Moss, G. (1997). *Inside a cave.* New York, NY: Scholastic.

Nicole, H. (2006). *What is a food chain?* Orlando, FL: Harcourt.

Simon, S. (2002). *Super storms.* San Fransisco, CA: Chronicle.

Tatham, B. (2001). *Penguin chick.* New York, NY: HarperCollins.

Windsor, J. (1999). *Animal coats.* Orlando, FL: Harcourt.

Writing Development

ACCORDING TO DONALD GRAVES (1983), CHILDREN WANT TO write. They want to write as soon as they can hold a pencil or marker in their hands. They want to write prior to starting school and will commonly mark up walls and newspapers with crayons, chalk, pens or pencils, or anything that makes a mark. This chapter discusses how teachers can channel students' early motivation to write, fostering the skills and strategies necessary to mastering the skills outlined in the Common Core State Standards (CCSS).

Petro Feketa/Fotolia

Early Writing Acquisition

CHILDREN'S EARLY LITERACY EXPERIENCES ARE EMBEDDED IN THE familiar situations and real-life experiences of the family and community (Ritchie, James-Szanton, & Howes, 2003). In fact, because these literacy events are so natural, many parents do not realize how these experiences serve to enhance their children's writing and reading until it is pointed out to them (Schickedanz & Casbergue, 2004; Soderman & Farrell, 2008). Many of the things family members do on a regular basis involve writing; for instance, they leave each other notes, make to-do lists, send greeting cards, write directions, and draw pictures.

Early writing development is characterized by children's moving from playfully making marks on paper, to communicating messages on paper, and finally to creating texts. Children are initially unconcerned about the products of their "writing," and they lose interest in these products almost immediately. However, once children begin to understand that the marks they make can be meaningful and fun to produce, they are determined to learn how to write (Tompkins, 2003).

Children learn the uses of written language before they learn the forms (Bromley, 2007; Gundlach, McLane, Scott, & McNamee, 1985). In observing children scribbling and inventing "texts," researchers have noted that they seem to know what writing is well before they are able to form letters correctly in their writing. The letters to friends and relatives, greeting cards, and signs that children produce are not typically conventional forms of writing. Yet children seem to have an understanding of the functions of written texts from an early age.

Drawing should play an integral role in early childhood literacy practices because it affords the child a voice, creativity, and the ability to interact with both the real and the imaginary. Most children naturally enjoy the act of drawing, yet in today's early childhood classrooms, it is becoming less and less prioritized. Affording early childhood students ample time for the creative act of drawing provides a stepping stone to future literacy practices and supports students in their visual literacy development. Early childhood teachers should pay close attention not only to what children draw but also their metacognition, as demonstrated by their thinking aloud while drawing.

Children's writing develops through constant invention and reinvention of the forms of written language (Calkins, 1994; Dyson, 1986; Graves, 1994; Spandel, 2008). Children invent ways of making letters, words, and texts, moving from primitive forms to closer approximations of conventional forms (Hansen, 1987; Jalongo, 2007). Parents and teachers of preschool children need to show an interest in their youngsters' early writing and accept and support these early approximations. Children invent forms of writing based on their observations of environmental print and through observing, modeling, and interacting with the more literate individuals who write in their presence.

Children learn about writing through receiving explicit instruction from teachers and by observing more skilled writers. Children need to be guided and taught about writing by supportive adults, and they need to observe adults participating in authentic writing activities. These adults, who serve as examples of proficient writers, play an important modeling role in children's writing development (Jalongo, 2007; Temple, Nathan, Burris & Temple 1988; Tompkns, 2003).

Children want to write about real experiences that are relevant and meaningful to their lives. To provide authentic writing instruction, teachers need to spend time with their young writers, engaging them in conversations about their work. In doing so, teachers should attend to students' intended meaning, though their writing is unlikely to contain conventional spelling. Children must know that others are interested in what they are trying to express through their writing. Teachers should confer with young writers about the decisions they make as they figure out what to write down (Calkins, Hartman, & White, 2005).

An authentic writing unit of study could include the study of different formats of children's literature. With this objective in mind, children might learn about authors' and illustrators' styles, and teachers might select mentor texts as examples of different models of writing and illustration. For example, Dr. Seuss and Eric Carle are both authors and illustrators who possess distinct writing and illustration styles and can provide young writers with authentic models for their own writing and illustrating. Primary-grade teachers might also decide to share books that include opinions or explanations, which serve as models for children's writing for these genres.

It is imperative that children write independently on a daily basis. When they write by themselves, they are involved in practicing aspects of writing: letter formation and differentiation, similarities and differences between drawing and writing, and conventions such as spelling and punctuation. When children engage in independent writing, they provide teachers with concrete evidence of what they know. However, children also need to write in social settings. When children write with each other, with a teacher, or with a more literate peer or adult, they have the opportunity to share their writing and engage in discussions by asking questions and suggesting revisions.

Writing development is part of a child's journey to literacy development. Literacy learning starts with drawing and proceeds to writing and reading (Vygotsky, 1978). Children's main resource for literacy learning is their knowledge of ways to symbolize experiences and to communicate through those symbols. This theoretical framework can be summarized as follows:

1. Literacy development encompasses the development of reading, writing, listening, speaking, and viewing.

2. Literacy development involves learning to use the symbols involved in reading, writing, listening, speaking, and viewing.

3. The symbols in literacy development also include the development of social and cultural meanings (Hansen, 2012).

For most children, writing development occurs as a series of events that progress along a continuum. Under normal circumstances, children's early literacy development begins with learning to communicate—first nonverbally, next by talking, then with symbolic play, and finally by drawing. Each new phase is rooted in earlier phases and forms a network of communication skills.

Literacy learning originates in the interactions of family and community life. Through these interactions, children move from playing with written language to using it to communicate. They invent and reinvent forms. When children first begin making marks on paper, most do so with no knowledge of the alphabetic nature of the system of symbols that comprise written language. Soon, however, children view letters as referring to actual people and things. And quite a bit later, children realize that writing represents language (Spandel, 2001).

Relationships Between Reading and Writing

CHILDREN LEARN ABOUT READING AND WRITING IN SIMILAR ways; they are reciprocal skills. Children experiment and pretend play at reading and writing and engage in trial and error as they practice the literacy skills they are learning. Children are inventive when learning to write. They decorate letters, symbols, and words; they mix drawing and writing; and they invent messages in various forms and shapes. Similarly, when children read, they invent what they think the text says by reading the pictures, provide voices for the characters in the books, and predict outcomes in stories and create their own endings, as well. When children are learning to read, we teach them phonics skills so they can decode text independently. Similarly, when children are beginning to write, they need to use the same phonics skills to create written pieces.

It is important for teachers to realize how similar reading and writing are and to engage children in both daily. When children read, they strengthen writing skills, and when children write, they strengthen reading skills. We have always known that we must allow time to teach reading, but often in the past, we have not given the same amount of time to writing instruction. This disparity is further widened by the fact that many students take longer to develop writing skills than reading skills.

Teaching the mechanics of writing involves a different focus of instruction compared to writing to express ideas. Given this, the CCSS have provided separate Language standards to address mechanics. In this standard, the conventions of standard English are emphasized when children write and speak. This standard also calls for being able to write the letters of the alphabet, punctuate sentences properly, and spell correctly. In the past, instruction paired the mechanics of writing and spelling with generating ideas for writing content, but today, the generation of ideas is the most important component of writing. While mechanics are needed, they are not crucial to the development of ideas and content. When mechanics are separated from the writing task, children are free to learn to express ideas in writing and, at a later stage in developing writing skills, to focus on editing the mechanics so they match the expectations of standard English.

The CCSS and Writing

THE CCSS AFFORD WRITING A MUCH MORE PROMINENT place in literacy development than it has been given in the past. The report of the National Reading Panel (2000) did not study or mention writing. In the CCSS, the concept of integrating the language arts means that reading, writing, listening, speaking, and language are afforded equal emphasis. This is an important point, as these skills are interrelated; the development of one serves to improve the others.

Children's writing allows us to observe the foundational skills they have acquired, as we note how they spell words and punctuate sentences. Writing also helps us to gain knowledge of a child's vocabulary and how it is developing and expanding. In addition, writing allows us to observe how well children understand what they have read or what has been read to them.

The purposes for reading and writing are similar, as well: Both processes serve to construct meaning. Readers create meaning by responding to what they have read, while writers create meaning by constructing text (Bromley, 2011). When reading and writing, children engage in the following similar activities: generating ideas, organizing ideas, monitoring thoughts, and revising their understanding as they work through a text.

The CCSS expect children to generate ideas, write in different genres, think critically, and write informational, narrative and opinion texts. Prior to the CCSS, little emphasis had been placed on young children writing informational or opinion text.

The following sections provide tables that identify the CCSS for writers in kindergarten through grade 2. Overall, there are three categories of Writing standards for grades K–2, resulting in a total of seven standards.

The first category, Text Types and Purposes, presents three standards that match three types of written pieces: opinion, informative/explanatory, and narrative. Within each category, there is a progression of skills from kindergarten through grade 2. The expectations become increasingly complex as students progress through each grade level.

The second category of Writing standards is Production and Distribution of Writing, and it contains two standards for grades K–2. One standard focuses on the addition of details and encourages children to develop, by grade 2, the ability to strengthen writing via revision and editing. The second standard requires the use of digital tools to produce and publish writing.

The third category, Research to Build and Present Knowledge, also includes two standards for grades K–2. The first standard requires that children participate in shared research and writing projects, and the second standard addresses the recall of information gained from experiences or the gathering of information to answer a question. Over the course of grades K–2, children develop the skills that allow them to move from away from relying on guidance and support and toward engaging independently in research-related tasks.

Putting the Writing Standards into Practice

THIS SECTION, WHICH IS ORGANIZED STANDARD BY STANDARD, identifies all seven standards and includes classroom vignettes that provide a snapshot of Common Core-aligned activities taking place in primary grade classrooms. Some of the vignettes also include examples of student writing within the specified genre. As we move through the standards, you will notice that each vignette aligns with a specific grade-level standard, but because the standards follow a horizontal progression, activities can be adapted for students in the grade level below or above the one described in the vignette.

Text Types and Purposes

Table 5.1 introduces the standards under the category of Text Types and Purposes for grades K–2 and includes the first standard in this category.

TABLE 5.1 ● *Writing Standard 1 for K–Grade 2:*
Text Types and Purposes

Kindergarten	Grade 1	Grade 2
Use a combination of drawing, dictating, and writing to compose opinion pieces in which they tell a reader the topic or the name of the book they are writing about and state an opinion or preference about the topic or book (e.g., *My favorite book is...*).	Write opinion pieces in which they introduce the topic or name the book they are writing about, state an opinion, supply a reason for the opinion, and provide some sense of closure.	Write opinion pieces in which they introduce the topic or book they are writing about, state an opinion, supply reasons that support the opinion, use linking words (e.g., *because, and, also*) to connect opinion and reasons, and provide a concluding statement or section.

Source: NGA & CCSSO (2010).

Writing Standard 1   Write opinion pieces in which they introduce the topic or name the book they are writing about, state an opinion, supply a reason for the opinion, and provide some sense of closure (first grade).

In the Common Core Classroom

Opinion Pieces: First Grade

The students in Ms. Monaco's first-grade class are gathered on the carpet in their classroom. Ms. Monaco has just read aloud the text *Click, Clack, Moo: Cows That Type* (Cronin, 2000), and students are engaged in a whole-class discussion of how Duck has used opinion and persuasive letters to acquire electric blankets and a diving board from Farmer Brown.

With prompting, the students quickly realize that, like Duck, they can use persuasive letter writing to solve problems. They make a plan to tour their school the following day to hunt for problems they might help solve through their writing. The next day, while touring the school, a student approaches Ms. Midura, the school librarian.

Danielle: *(Walking excitedly up to Ms. Midura, clipboard and pencil in hand)* Are there any problems at our school that we can help you with?

Ms. Midura: Hmm, good question. Well, I do need more shelves in the library to store new books.

The first-graders quickly jot down this idea on their clipboards and continue their tour, recording many authentic ideas to use in the persuasive letters they will write. Back in the classroom, students share their ideas while Ms. Monaco records them on a chart posted on the easel. The chart has two columns: "Problems to Fix" and "Who Can Help Solve Them."

Ms. Monaco: Writing persuasive letters is a great way to solve problems. We found lots of interesting problems while we were on our school tour. Now we need to figure out the person we can write to so that we can help solve these problems. What was one problem that you wrote down?

Isabella: Ms. Midura needs more shelves in the library.

Ms. Monaco: Right! That was a good one. *(Records suggestion in "Problems to Fix" column)* Now, let's think of someone we can write to so that we might be able to help Ms. Midura solve this problem?

Christina: What about the principal? She can order more shelves.

Ms. Monaco: That's a great idea! *(Records suggestion in "Who Can Help Solve Them" column)* Any other thoughts?

Justin: Um, maybe the custodian? He might have some extra ones the library can use.

Ms. Monaco adds Justin's idea to the chart, as well, and the class continues to discuss problems and solutions in a similar manner.

Over the next few weeks, students come together daily in whole-class mini-lessons that focus on the format and content of their letters—specifically, stating an opinion clearly, supplying factual reasons for the opinion, and providing some sense of closure. Additionally, students work on brainstorming letter-writing ideas. Ms. Monaco provides time each day for students to write

● independently or with a partner while she meets with individuals or groups of students. Over the course of the persuasive letter-writing unit, the following persuasive writing activities occur in this first grade classroom:

Dylan and Noah ask for the names of the mayors of two shore towns. They want the mayors to add more fishing spots so they can catch more fish over the summer. They are coordinating their letters so that neither of them forgets any important reasons.

Alexis is writing to the state governor, asking him to enforce smoking laws more strictly. It bothers her when her grandfather smokes, and she wants to make sure he won't be able to smoke in public places. She also hopes that the governor's help will ensure that kids won't start smoking.

Several students are composing a letter to the school custodian. On their tour of the school, they noticed several cracks in the floors and walls and are concerned that students might trip. They have come up with several reasons to support their opinion, including that the cracks are unattractive, might make kids fall, and could leak water if it's raining.

Grace is writing to Timmy to let him know that it bothers her that he is leaving her out of the Cookie Club, and she is writing to persuade him to include her. She makes sure to let him know that he hurt her feelings and that it is not very nice to have a club that only includes some students.

Each of these examples portrays an authentic, meaningful, and collaborative way in which students are able to meet Standard 1.

At the close of the unit, each student selects two letters to revise, edit, and publish. Ms. Monaco gives students envelopes and stamps, which were provided by parents in response to a letter sent home that asked for contributions. Students record addresses on their envelopes, as they chat excitedly about their letters going in the "real mail." Here are two of the students' published letters, ready for the mail:

Amy Monaco

Dear Mayor Pucci,

Hello. I am a 1st grader who goes fishing at Thompson Park. I only catch sunfish. Can you put bass and catfish and crappies in the pond? That's all. Good-bye, Mayor Pucci.

Love, Noah

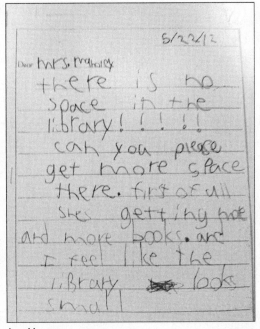

Amy Monaco

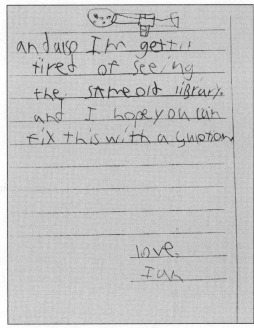

Amy Monaco

Dear Mrs. Mahoney,

There is no space in the library! Can you please get more space there? First of all, she's getting more and more books. And I feel like the library looks small. And also I'm getting tired of seeing the same old library. And I hope you can fix this with a solution.

Love, Ian

Plans for the Teacher

Materials Needed to Get Started

Letter-writing paper, envelopes, stamps, the book *Click Clack Moo: Cows That Type*, chart paper
(As noted in the vignette, the teacher might decide to ask parents to donate stamps and envelopes)

Content of Lesson

To begin this unit, teachers may choose to have students tour the school to search for problems they might help solve. Doing so helps students to become interested immediately and to view letter writing as an authentic and meaningful activity. The teacher should confer with individual students regularly throughout the letter-writing process, as both content and writing conventions are critical to this unit. (The recipients of the letters must be able to decipher their mail!) The teacher should encourage students to write letters about topics that are personally meaningful and continue to meet in a whole-class setting if students have difficulty in generating topics.

Differentiation

Teachers can form strategy groups to meet the needs of struggling writers. Having individual writing conferences allows teachers to differentiate instruction to meet the needs of all learners.

Assessment

Develop a rubric to assess final writing pieces. Teacher observation and anecdotal records may be used throughout the unit to plan for future teaching points.

Table 5.2 lists writing standard 2 for Text Types and Purposes for grades K-2.

TABLE 5.2 ● *Writing Standard 2 for K–Grade 2: Text Types and Purposes*

Kindergarten	Grade 1	Grade 2
Use a combination of drawing, dictating, and writing to compose informative/explanatory texts in which they name what they are writing about and supply some information about the topic.	Write informative/explanatory texts in which they name a topic, supply some facts about the topic, and provide some sense of closure.	Write informative/explanatory texts in which they introduce a topic, use facts and definitions to develop points, and provide a concluding statement or section.

Writing Standard 2   Write informative/explanatory texts in which they introduce a topic, use facts and definitions to develop points, and provide a concluding statement or section (second grade).

In the Common Core Classroom

Informative/Explanatory Texts: Second Grade

The students in Ms. Tucker's second-grade class are sitting in a circle in the classroom meeting spot, and a sea of expository texts are scattered in the center of the circle. The class has been studying conventions of nonfiction texts and is planning to use what they have learned to create their own informational texts.

Mia: *(Reaching for the book* Flowers*)* Look! It's a diagram, like we learned about! *(Points to diagram of flower, which has parts labeled, such as petals, pistil, stamens)*

Jordan: *(Picking up* From Seed to Plant*)* Mia, look! There's a diagram in this one, too! It has the same parts and some other information under each label.

Angelina: I found the table of contents in *Baby Dolphin's Tale*! And all of the headings match the names in the table of contents!

Ms. Tucker: Angelina, can you hold that up to share with everyone?

Angelina holds up the book and turns it to the left and then to the right to show her classmates.

Ryan: *(Grabbing* Rescue Dogs*)* Are these captions? *(Points to the words under photos)*

Another student confirms that the words are captions, and Ms. Tucker nods in agreement.

The second-graders are exploring these texts with the intention of writing their own informative texts, in which they will introduce a topic, use facts and definitions to develop points, and provide a concluding statement or section. Students are permitted to self-select topics of interest, and their subjects range from dogs to flowers to football.

After students select their topics, Ms. Tucker collects related books from the classroom and checks out books from the school library. Using these books, students research their topics carefully to be sure to include a variety of information in their own informative texts. Ms. Tucker also provides students with various writing templates, which helps them to include several nonfiction conventions in their texts, such as a table of contents, how-to writing, Fun Facts, a diagram, a glossary, and so on.

As students work, Ms. Tucker meets with a small group of students who need assistance with adding Fun Facts pages to their books.

Ms. Tucker: Brianna, you're writing about horses. Let's think of some Fun Facts that you can add about your topic.

Brianna: Um, I know that a baby horse has a special name, but I can't think of it.

Nadia: Brianna, I know. It's called a *foal*.

Ms. Tucker: That sounds like an interesting fact to use. Here's a copy of the book *Horse Life Cycle* from our "True Animal Books" bin. Look through it and see if it helps you to find any interesting facts. Nadia, I see you have an interesting fact written about a tennis racket. What else are you planning to add?

Nadia: My mom told me that Venus Williams is a great tennis player. I want to add that, but what else can I say about her?

Ms. Tucker: Let's see if we can find some information online, and I'll print it out for you.

When students have finished writing their informational texts, they use the classroom laptops to design and print book covers. Each cover includes a title, a graphic to represent the topic, and, of course, the student's name as the author. Ms. Tucker laminates the cover of the each student's book and binds together the cover and the pages. At the class's writing celebration, family members are invited to share in reading the completed informational texts. Later, students add their books to the classroom library for classmates to read during independent reading time.

Here are examples of chapters in the students' informational texts:

Words to Know

- *Whiskers*: The little lines coming out from the fur
- *Fences*: A fence is like a gate. It could be made out of wood.
- *Pet*: An animal you keep.
- *Claw*: A claw is sharp. Some pets have claws.
- *Cage*: A pet cage is used for taking a pet out to the vet.
- *Love*: Love is something you like and love is needed to take care of a pet.

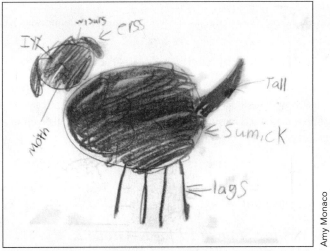

Eyes, Whiskers, Ears, Mouth, Tail, Stomach, Legs

Amy Monaco

Plans for the Teacher

Materials Needed to Get Started

Nonfiction mentor texts, writing templates (table of contents, how-to writing, Fun Facts, diagram, glossary, and so on)

Content of Lesson

To set the stage for this writing unit, begin by seating students in a circle on the carpet or meeting area and allowing them to explore informational texts, with a focus on nonfiction conventions. Students should be able to point out the types of chapters they can include in their own informational texts. Create an anchor chart by having students list and briefly describe each convention. Supply students with a writing template for each format, so they can successfully insert information on their individual topics according to the formats of conventional nonfiction texts.

Differentiation

Students will be at varying levels of proficiency in terms of both writing content and conventions. When observing student writing, prioritize your teaching points based on the skills critical to success in this unit and by taking into consideration the current abilities of each writer. You may also choose to modify the writing templates you provided based on the writers in your class.

Assessment

You may choose to rely on anecdotal notes as a means on assessing students in this unit. If you choose to assess students' final pieces of writing utilizing a rubric, be sure to recognize that students' finished products may not be indicative of their unassisted writing ability.

Below is the final Writing standard in the category Text Types and Purposes, table 5.3, which addresses narrative writing.

TABLE 5.3 • *Writing Standard 3 for K–Grade 2: Text Types and Purposes*

Kindergarten	Grade 1	Grade 2
Use a combination of drawing, dictating, and writing to narrate a single event or several loosely linked events, tell about the events in the order in which they occurred, and provide a reaction to what happened.	Write narratives in which they recount two or more appropriately sequenced events, include some details regarding what happened, use temporal words to signal event order, and provide some sense of closure.	Write narratives in which they recount a well-elaborated event or short sequence of events, include details to describe actions, thoughts, and feelings, use temporal words to signal event order, and provide a sense of closure.

Source: NGA & CCSSO (2010).

Writing Standard 3   Use a combination of drawing, dictating, and writing to narrate a single event or several loosely linked events, tell about the events in the order in which they occurred, and provide a reaction to what happened (kindergarten).

In the Common Core Classroom

Narratives: Kindergarten

This vignette describes a kindergarten class in which the majority of children are not yet writing but can participate in emergent writing with some dictation, drawing, and letter strings or simply scribble writing. The purpose of the lesson is to encourage students to see themselves as purposeful writers and to help them to see ways in which writing is relevant and meaningful to their lives.

The kindergarten students in Ms. Rosso's class sit on the classroom carpet with whiteboards and markers on their laps. Ms. Rosso reaches into a jar containing wooden craft sticks, one with each student's name, and the students watch eagerly to find out which student they will write about in this session of interactive writing. When Ms. Rosso reads aloud the name "Nikolas," the kindergartners all turn to Nikolas and smile.

Ms. Rosso: So, Nikolas, what would you like us to write about today?

Nikolas: Um, my brother and I played soccer outside yesterday.

Ms. Rosso: Okay, everyone. Let's get ready to clap the words.

Students: *(Clapping as they say each word in the sentence out loud)* Nikolas and his brother played soccer outside yesterday.

As students clap to count each word, Ms. Rosso draws a line on the chart paper for each word in the sentence and asks, "So how many words will we write today?" The students respond that the sentence is eight words long. One student is called up to make a quick sketch of Nikolas and his brother outside with a soccer ball. Students are then instructed to pick up their markers and get ready to write.

The class goes through each word in the sentence, writing on their whiteboards while Ms. Rosso records the sentence on chartpaper. Ms. Rosso supports students as they write.

Ms. Rosso: Nikolas's name is on our word wall. We can find it on the word wall to spell it! Turn and look under "N" on the word wall to find *Nikolas.* Don't forget to begin this word with a capital letter!

Mary-Lou: I found it!

Ms. Rosso hands Mary-Lou the marker and has her come up to the whiteboard.

Ms. Rosso: *And* is a word we know! We have had this word as a sight word! Who would like to come up and write the word *and*?

Ms. Rosso selects a student to come up to record the word on the chartpaper.

Ms. Rosso: *Soccer* is a tricky word. *Soccer* begins with the /s/ sound. Let's all make that sound. Can someone come up to write the first letter in the word *soccer*?

Ryan: *Soccer* begins with *s.* *(Walks up to write on the whiteboard)*

Ms. Rosso: *Yesterday* is a word we can stretch out. Help me to stretch out the word *yesterday.*

Students use their hands to demonstrate stretching out the word while saying each syllable slowly: "yes-ter-day."

Ms. Rosso: I'll write the first parts of this word. Who would like to help us with the ending? *Day* is spelled the same way as in *Monday.* Take a peek at our class calendar to help you.

Ms. Rosso continues to support students in this way until they complete the sentence. She is also sure to watch students as they write on their individual whiteboards, correcting them quietly if she notices errors, as this is a time for students to practice conventional spelling. When the sentence has been completed, the class reads it aloud together in a choral reading. Ms. Rosso ceremoniously tears off the page of the chart paper pad and presents it to Nikolas, who smiles proudly. She encourages him to practice reading the sentence aloud to his family later that night.

Tips for the Teacher

ALTHOUGH THIS LESSON DESCRIBES AN INTERACTIVE writing lesson, Standard 3 should also be addressed though independent writing, in which students use a combination of drawing and writing to "narrate a single event or several loosely linked events" in chronological order. Although it is critical that students write independently every day—ideally, about self-selected topics—interactive writing can provide a strong model of how to generate story ideas, stretch out words to spell phonetically, and refer to a word wall to spell conventionally. Students should engage in both independent and interactive writing every day in the kindergarten classroom.

Production and Distribution of Writing

Table 5.4 lists standard 5 for Writing, the first standard under the category Production and Distribution of Writing.

TABLE 5.4 ● *Writing Standard 5 for K–Grade 2:* Production and Distribution of Writing

Kindergarten	Grade 1	Grade 2
With guidance and support from adults, respond to questions and suggestions from peers and add details to strengthen writing as needed.	With guidance and support from adults, focus on a topic, respond to questions and suggestions from peers, and add details to strengthen writing as needed.	With guidance and support from adults and peers, focus on a topic and strengthen writing as needed by revising and editing.

Source: NGA & CCSSO (2010).

Writing Standard 5   With guidance and support from adults and peers, focus on a topic and strengthen writing as needed by revising and editing (second grade).

In the Common Core Classroom

Peer Revision: Second Grade

One of the most important stages of the writing process approach is *revising*. Teachers must help students to view revision as a positive stage of the writing process, rather than simply the correcting of mistakes. Revision serves to improve writing, as the first draft is seldom exactly right. In the vignette that follows, after students quickly draft their informational pieces, they meet with each other and the teacher to discuss what changes will enrich their writing.

A study of the butterfly life cycle is in full swing in Ms. Leston's second-grade class. Near the back of the classroom, several students crowd around the butterfly house, in which caterpillars wrapped in their chrysalises hang, waiting to emerge as monarch butterflies. The second-grade scientists stand holding their clipboards and butterfly observation notebooks, recording their observations and chatting about whether there will be butterflies by spring break. Near the classroom library, another group sits in a small circle, reading *Butterfly Life Cycle* (Bauer, 2007) and poring over pictures of various types of butterflies, drawing and labeling their favorites. The remaining students meet in partnerships throughout the classroom, as Ms. Leston circulates among the pairs.

Over the past several days, students have been working on writing and illustrating their own books on the butterfly life cycle, and they are now ready for the revision stage of the writing process. Ms. Leston walks up to Leena and Rose, who sit on a small rug, each leaning against a pillow. Rose's book is positioned between them, and they are engaged in conversation.

Leena: Rose, don't forget. When the butterfly comes out of the chrysalis, its wings are damp and it has to dry them.

Rose: Oh, yeah. Then it flaps its wings and they get dry. But where can I write that?

Leena: Maybe here? After the part about the butterfly coming out? You can add it right underneath.

Rose rereads the page out loud, carefully considering if the page Leena suggests is the right spot to add the new sentence.

Rose: Alright. That's a good spot. Did you bring your revision pen? I want to write it in red so I can remember that I added it in. I want to show Ms. Leston.

Rose writes carefully at the bottom of her page and turns to Ms. Leston, who smiles.

Ms. Leston: Nice suggestion, Leena. I think that is a great spot to add that detail. What will the two of you work on next?

Rose: We're going to read Leena's book. We want to see if anything's missing.

Rose picks up the book From Caterpillar to Butterfly *(Heiligman, 1996), which the girls will use to check life cycle facts.*

Ms. Leston: That sounds like a great plan.

Ms. Leston stands up and walks over to another pair of students.

Tips for the Teacher

ALTHOUGH THIS LESSON DESCRIBES AN ACTIVITY in which students revise their written texts on the butterfly life cycle, Standard 5 can be addressed using virtually any written piece to take students through the writing process. In looking at the horizontal progression of Standard 5 across the grade levels, it is clear that the CCSS expect students to take increasing responsibility for revising and editing, working with classmates to "strengthen writing as needed."

Table 5.5 lists Writing Standard 6 under the category Production and Distribution of Writing for grades K-2.

TABLE 5.5 ● *Writing Standard 6 for K–Grade 2:* Production and Distribution of Writing

Kindergarten	Grade 1	Grade 2
With guidance and support from adults, explore a variety of digital tools to produce and publish writing, including in collaboration with peers.	With guidance and support from adults, use a variety of digital tools to produce and publish writing, including in collaboration with peers.	With guidance and support from adults, use a variety of digital tools to produce and publish writing, including in collaboration with peers.

Source: NGA & CCSSO (2010).

Writing Standard 6   With guidance and support from adults, use a variety of digital tools to produce and publish writing, including in collaboration with peers (kindergarten–grade 2).

In the Common Core Classroom

Publishing: Kindergarten–Grade 2

The CCSS strongly recommend that children learn twenty-first century technology skills and new literacies (NGA & CCSSO, 2010). Of course, both include the use of digital tools. In the following vignette, Ms. Sano's class is engaged in an activity to develop familiarity with digital tools.

The students in Ms. Sano's first-grade class sit in a row of chairs at the front of the room, looking out at an audience of family members. The first-graders have participated in many writing celebrations over the course of the school year, but today is the culmination of how far they have come as writers since September. They are publishing their final pieces of writing for the year.

The class has worked for several weeks on a study of weather and the seasons in science. To complete the unit, each student has developed a final piece of writing that provides information about his or her favorite season, activities that take place during that time of year, and facts about the weather in that season. The students have worked with Ms. Sano to revise, edit, and type their informational pieces on the classroom computers. After each student completed this process, Ms. Sano transferred his or her typed work to the website StoryJumper (www.storyjumper.com). Also, using funds from a grant, Ms. Sano has purchased enough hardcover copies of the class book, titled *Wild About Weather,* for all of the students to take home. Students have practiced reading their sections aloud fluently and are ready to share their sections with their families today.

During the writing celebration, Ms. Sano uses the StoryJumper website to display the class book of weather information. As she clicks to each first-grade author's portion of the book, the student stands up, walks over to a microphone set up at the front of the room, and reads his or her writing aloud to a smiling audience.

Leah: My favorite season is winter. In winter, you can go sledding, drink hot chocolate, and have a snowball fight. In winter, there is a lot of snow, and snowflakes are made of ice crystals.

Julia: My favorite season is fall. In fall, you can go pumpkin picking, and I love to go trick-or-treating on Halloween. A fact about fall is that leaves change color and fall off the trees, and another name for fall is *autumn.*

Jason: My favorite season is summer. I like to go in the pool, go to the beach, and even go in the ocean. I learned that in summer, the days are longer and the nights are shorter. The temperature is higher than in the other seasons.

After all of the students have shared their work, Ms. Sano passes out copies of the class book. Then the students disperse through the crowd to proudly share their books with their guests. Throughout the classroom, parents and their children sit together, reading aloud the students' writing and chatting with family members about what it feels like to be a "real published author."

After students have had an opportunity to share their books, Ms. Sano uses a projector to display a slideshow she has created of the students working on creation of *Wild About Weather* in the classroom. This presentation gives parents a glimpse into the process students followed in writing and digitally publishing their stories. During the presentation, students enjoy ice-cream sundaes to celebrate the weeks of hard work that have gone into writing and publishing their class book.

Tips for the Teacher

THIS VIGNETTE MENTIONS ONE WEBSITE THAT teachers can use to assist students in digitally producing stories: StoryJumper. However, many additional storytelling websites can be used in the classroom to accomplish the goals of Standard 6:

StoryBird	www.storybird.com
Make Beliefs Comics	www.makebeliefscomix.com
My Story Maker	www.carnegielibrary.org/kids/storymaker/embed.cfm
KeKerpoof	www.kerpoof.com
ZooBurst	www.zooburst.com

Research to Build and Present Knowledge

Table 5.6 lists the first Writing standard for the category Research to Build and Present Knowledge, which has to do with shared research and writing projects for grades K–2.

TABLE 5.6 ● *Writing Standard 7 for Kindergarten–Grade 2:*
Research to Build and Present Knowledge

Kindergarten	Grade 1	Grade 2
Participate in shared research and writing projects (e.g., explore a number of books by a favorite author and express opinions about them).	Participate in shared research and writing projects (e.g., explore a number of "how-to" books on a given topic and use them to write a sequence of instructions).	Participate in shared research and writing projects (e.g., read a number of books on a single topic to produce a report; record science observations).

Source: NGA & CCSSO (2010).

Writing Standard 7   Participate in shared research and writing projects (e.g., explore a number of "how-to" books on a given topic and use them to write a sequence of instructions) (first grade).

In the Common Core Classroom
Research and Writing: First Grade

Doing research to find new information is a high priority in the CCSS, and children should begin researching topics as early as kindergarten. The following vignette portrays first-graders engaged in activities for a research-centered unit.

Springtime in Ms. Duino's class always includes a study of the plant life cycle during science. Small, black pots filled with soil line the classroom windowsill, and the beginnings of green buds are poking through. Every morning, after students toss their backpacks into their cubbies, they grab their plant observation notebooks and rush over to record any overnight changes.

The students have also been studying a variety of authentic examples of how-to writing, such as "How to Carve a Pumpkin," found in *The Pumpkin Book* (Gibbons, 1999), and "How to Plant a Seed," found in the text *From Seed to Plant* (Gibbons, 1991). Today, students have gathered on the classroom carpet and Ms. Duino sits in front of them, holding up *The Pumpkin Book* and displaying the section "How to Carve a Pumpkin." She asks students to turn and share with partners what they remember about the format of how-to writing. As she listens in, she hears students chatting.

Destiny: You have to put the steps in the right order. That's why they're numbered like that.

Eesha: Gail Gibbons put pictures next to each of the steps to show you what to do. See how she's showing how to carve each of the eyes? That helps you figure out the directions.

Sabrina: The author put some warnings in there. Like you should always have an adult help you.

Ms. Duino: You all remembered important parts of how-to writing. Let's record our ideas on this chart, titled "Features of How-To Writing."

Ms. Duino: *(After completing the chart)* Today, we're going to use what we've learned about how-to writing to complete our own how-to pieces—all about how to take care of a plant, which is something you all know quite a bit about!

The students work with partners around the room to discuss what they need to include in their writing and to began to sketch illustrations for the different steps. Then students work together to add the correct words, checking their plant observation notebooks to be sure they include all of the important information. As they work, Ms. Duino meets with a group of struggling writers and assists them in using transition words.

Ms. Duino: Last week, we talked about using transition words in our writing. Who can remember a good transition word for the first step?

Sophia: We could write *First of all.*

Ms. Duino: That's a great one! Let's add that to the beginning of our first step. How about for our second step?

Brandon: I remember one! *Next.*

Shawn: Or we could write *Second of all.*

Ms. Duino: Those are both great ideas. Pick one of those choices to write at the beginning of step 2. Then try adding a transition word for the last step on your own.

Ms. Duino supports students in the group who have difficulty finding a transition word for the last step.

As students complete their work, Ms. Duino asks them to add their writing to their science folders, as they will include these compositions in a unit-long book about plants. Here are samples of students' how-to writing:

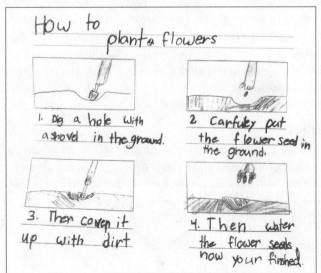

How to plant a flowers

1. Dig a hole with a shovel in the ground.

2. Carfuly put the flower seed in the ground.

3. Then cover it up with dirt

4. Then water the flower seeds. now your finshed.

Amy Monaco

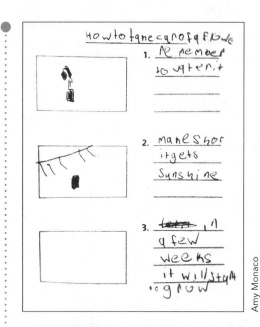

Amy Monaco

How to Plant Flowers

1. Dig a hole with a shovel in the ground.
2. Carefully put the flower seed in the ground.
3. Then cover it up with dirt.
4. Then water the flower seeds. Now you're finished.

How to Take Care of a Flower

1. Remember to water it.
2. Make sure it gets sunshine
3. In a few weeks, it will start to grow.

Plans for the Teacher

Materials Needed to Get Started

How-to mentor texts (examples can be found in *From Seed to Plant* and *The Pumpkin Book*, both by Gail Gibbons), how-to writing template, seeds and soil (for students to observe plant growth)

Content of Lesson

This lesson portrays activities in a science unit that corresponds with a writing unit. Students have been crafting how-to writing on self-selected topics during their Writer's Workshop block and are now applying their knowledge of this writing structure during a science unit on plants. To begin a similar unit, give students time to explore various how-to writing mentor texts to study the format of how-to writing. During the writing block, give students the opportunity to self-select topics. However, as this lesson demonstrates, students' knowledge of how-to writing can also be applied to a variety of content areas, such as science and social studies.

Differentiation

Ms. Duino supports struggling learners by working with them individually and in small groups during independent writing time. In addition, teachers can modify writing templates for struggling and more advanced students and arrange heterogeneous pairings to support students struggling with the concepts studied during the science unit.

Assessment

Develop a rubric or checklist to assess students' completed how-to writing.

Table 5.7 lists the final Writing standard for grades K–2, which is also under the category Research to Build and Present Knowledge.

TABLE 5.7 ● *Writing Standard 8 for Kindergarten–Grade 2: Research to Build and Present Knowledge*

Kindergarten	Grade 1	Grade 2
With guidance and support from adults, recall information from experiences or gather information from provided sources to answer a question.	With guidance and support from adults, recall information from experiences or gather information from provided sources to answer a question.	Recall information from experiences or gather information from provided sources to answer a question.

Source: NGA & CCSSO (2010).

Writing Standard 8   With guidance and support from adults, recall information from experiences or gather information from provided sources to answer a question (kindergarten).

In the Common Core Classroom

Answering Questions: Kindergarten

Answering questions helps children to recall information and learn to remember the most important parts. When children answer teacher-directed questions, they also learn how to form questions on their own. By knowing what questions to ask, children learn what to look for when they want to find out information.

Ms. McHugh is working on this skill in her kindergarten class. Today, she is sitting with a small group of students at a table near the back of the classroom. The class has been working on inferring the meanings of unknown words during interactive read-aloud time. Ms. McHugh has pulled together a small strategy group of students who seem to need additional practice with this skill.

Ms. McHugh: The title of the book we'll be reading today is *Move!* The author of this book is Robin Page, and the illustrator is Steve Jenkins. Let's take a picture walk through the book. *(Shows students each picture)* Do you predict that this will be a fiction book or a nonfiction book?

Siya: I think it will be nonfiction, because it doesn't look like a story. And it has pictures of lots of different animals.

Ms. McHugh: Good noticing! You're right that the words don't look like a story. There's a big word that tells an animal action, like *swim*, and then smaller words that tell information about each of the animals. As we read, I'm going to write down some interesting words from this book, and after we finish the whole book, we're going to talk about what they might mean.

Ms. McHugh reads the story aloud to the group without interruption. As she reads, she writes down various words from the text, such as gibbon, jacana, snag, prey, waddles, and so on.

Ms. McHugh: Now that we've finished the book, I'm going to ask you to infer, or figure out, what these words might mean, using clues from the book to help us.

She turns to the page on which the word gibbon appears and rereads the sentence that contains the word, in which a gibbon is described as an animal that swings through trees.

Ms. McHugh: *(Modeling her thinking out loud)* I'm noticing a picture of a monkey on this page, and a monkey is an animal that can swing through trees. So, I'm inferring that a gibbon must be a type of monkey. Did you notice how I used the pictures and the words to help me? Now, let's try one together.

Ms. McHugh turns to the page on which the word jacana appears and rereads aloud the sentence containing the word.

Ms. McHugh: *Jacana* is a tricky word. What do you think it might mean? Remember to use clues from the book to help you.

Ross: I think it's a type of bird. That's what it looks like in the picture.

Ms. McHugh: Did you all notice how Ross used a picture clue to help him figure out the meaning of this tricky word? That was smart work! Now that we've had some practice, I want you and your partner to work together to try the next one.

Ms. McHugh turns to the page with the picture of the crocodile and reads aloud the text. The sentence about the crocodile uses the word snag to describe how the animal eats. Ms. McHugh asks students to turn and talk to their classmates about what the word snag might mean. She listens in as students discuss this word.

Siya: I think it means to, like, "grab." Like the crocodile *grabbed* its meal.

Elizabeth: Maybe it means that he just took his meal quickly. I think *snag* means "take something really fast."

Ross: See how the crocodile has his mouth open like that in the picture? I think *snag* means that he *snatched* his food up.

Ms. McHugh: I heard some really smart thinking work as I was listening in on your conversations. You're absolutely right that the word *snag* means something very similar to the word *grab*. The crocodile *grabbed* his meal in a sneaky way.

The students continue this kind of discussion about the remaining words on the list.

Ms. McHugh: You did some very smart work today. We'll practice this again later in the week. Remember that a good way to figure out the meaning of a tricky word is to use clues from the words and the pictures in the book.

Tips for the Teacher

STANDARD 8 ASKS KINDERGARTNERS TO "RECALL information from experiences or gather information from provided sources to answer a question" (NGA & CCSSO, 2010, p. 19). Even though this vignette focuses on gathering information from the text to infer the meanings of unknown words, asking and answering questions is an integral part of the school day in every grade and subject area. Teachers may choose to meet the goals of this standard at various points in the day, such as interactive read-aloud, shared reading, guided reading, and Reader's Workshop.

Conventions of Standard English   The Language Standards of the CCSS address the conventions of reading and writing. We will review what students need to know about the conventions, or mechanics, of writing, which should be viewed as independent of writing content and the generation of writing ideas (see Table 5.8).

For kindergartners, the Language Standards focus primarily on encouraging children to write regardless of what conventions they may or may not use, but by the middle of first grade and certainly by second grade, children will be able to write more words and will have shown some progress and interest in punctuation and spelling. It is difficult to teach children, especially young children, to focus on the conventions of writing, because writing must be done in conjunction with the creation of ideas. Even some adult writers find it difficult to think about spelling, handwriting, and punctuation, as well as ideas—all at the same time.

Unfortunately, in some classrooms, children are not given as much time for writing as they are the other language arts, such as reading and listening, thus reducing opportunities to engage in writing skills. In addition, there are many irregularities in the English language, in which 26 letters represent 44 different sounds, and many irregularities in spelling words. There is less emphasis on penmanship than ever before, especially with very young children using computers. Some schools have eliminated teaching cursive writing altogether. Yet when a piece of writing is handed in to a teacher or goes home to a parent, what often attracts the attention of an adult are the neatness of the handwriting and the correctness of the spelling and punctuation (Collins Block, 1993).

Many educators have researched new ways of teaching mechanics, and a large body of research has demonstrated that out-of-context drilling is not beneficial for the majority of students. Teaching the conventions of writing within meaningful contexts has been proven the most effective way to help students internalize and utilize these skills (Hillerich, 1985; Hodges, 1981). For example, a teacher should instruct students on how to write a thank-you note by doing a whole-class lesson using interactive writing to write the letter to thank a firefighter for visiting the school. In doing so, the teacher should talk about where the salutation goes, what punctuation is involved, and what different closings can be used.

TABLE 5.8 ● *Language Standard 2 for Kindergarten–Grade 2:* Conventions of Standard English

Kindergarten	Grade 1	Grade 2
Demonstrate command of the conventions of standard English capitalization, punctuation, and spelling when writing.	Demonstrate command of the conventions of standard English capitalization, punctuation, and spelling when writing.	Demonstrate command of the conventions of standard English capitalization, punctuation, and spelling when writing.
a. Capitalize the first word in a sentence and the pronoun *I*. b. Recognize and name end punctuation. c. Write a letter or letters for most consonant and short-vowel sounds (phonemes). d. Spell simple words phonetically, drawing on knowledge of sound–letter relationships.	a. Capitalize dates and names of people. b. Use end punctuation for sentences. c. Use commas in dates and to separate single words in a series. d. Use conventional spelling for words with common spelling patterns and for frequently occurring irregular words. e. Spell untaught words phonetically, drawing on phonemic awareness and spelling conventions.	a. Capitalize holidays, product names, and geographic names. b. Use commas in greetings and closings of letters. c. Use an apostrophe to form contractions and frequently occurring possessives. d. Generalize learned spelling patterns when writing words (e.g., cage–badge; boy–boil). e. Consult reference materials, including beginning dictionaries, as needed to check and correct spellings.

Source: NGA & CCSSO (2010).

Language Standard 2   Demonstrate command of the conventions of standard English capitalization, punctuation, and spelling when writing (second grade).

In the Common Core Classroom

Punctuation: Second Grade

The second-graders in Ms. Richards's class have been working on writing informational texts to correspond with a social studies unit on American symbols. Students are at various stages of completing their texts, and during today's social studies block, several students sit with laptops and research information using the website BrainPOP Jr. (www.brainpopjr.com), while a small group sits at a round table and reads *O, Say Can You See?* (Keenan, 2004), a book Ms. Richards read aloud several days before. Other students work independently on their writing, while Ms. Richards meets with some students individually.

Ms. Levitt, the special education teacher in the classroom, works with a small group of students at a table near the literacy center. They have completed their writing and are ready to edit their informational texts.

Ms. Levitt: Last night, I took your books home with me to read, and wow! You really included lots of great information about the American symbols we've been studying. It seems like you're all ready to do some editing. Who can remember something we should check when we're editing our writing?

Luke: We need to have spaces between our words and make sure we've spelled the words on our word wall the right way.

Ms. Levitt: You're absolutely right! What else?

Kory: Um, we need capitals?

Anthony: Oh, and periods and question marks!

Ms. Levitt: You got it! We need to make sure our writing has capitals at the beginnings of our sentences and punctuation marks at the ends. Let's do some work with punctuation today. I'm going to read my writing aloud without punctuation. Your job is to listen carefully to help me decide where the punctuation marks should go. Listen to spots where my voice pauses, just like we've talked about.

Ms. Levitt begins to read aloud from a copy of her writing, which is also projected onto the interactive whiteboard.

Ms. Levitt: *(Reading from copy)* "The Statue of Liberty is an important American symbol it can be found in New York City the statue holds a torch in one hand." *(Pausing briefly)* It's hard to understand my writing without punctuation, isn't it? Did anyone notice a spot that needs some punctuation?

Anthony: I think after *symbol*. Before the part about it being in New York City.

Ms. Levitt: Great noticing. Don't forget that the first letter in the next word will need to be a capital for the beginning of a new sentence.

After taking the interactive whiteboard marker, Anthony adds the punctuation in the correct spot and changes the i in it to a capital letter. The group continues in this way until all of the missing punctuation and capitalization have been added.

Ms. Levitt: Great work, everyone. Now let's try the same thing with your writing. Please read it aloud to yourself and listen for spots where your voice pauses for the end of a sentence. That's the spot that you'll need to add punctuation. You'll need to work independently, but I'll be listening in to help you while you work.

At the end of the social studies block, the second-graders return their informational texts to their social studies folders to work on later in the week. They will soon create models or posters of the American symbol they select to present with their writing at the school Cultural Fair later this month.

Tips for the Teacher

IN THE CCSS LANGUAGE STANDARDS, STUDENTS' knowledge of the conventions of standard English is expected to increase through each grade level, so that they are able to master the skills noted in the standard for their current grade level, as well as all prior skills. Writing conventions can be addressed during Writer's Workshop, interactive writing, or a "word work" block, but it can also be reinforced during writing that takes place in the content areas, such as the social studies project described in this vignette.

Writing Throughout the Day

FOR STUDENTS TO BECOME LITERATE IN READING AND writing by the end of grade 3, they must engage in strategies to meet the goals of the CCSS. Teaching these strategies needs to be done consistently and systematically. Writing takes time for students to master, and teachers must set aside enough time each day for students to achieve success. Students also need multiple lessons on each topic to internalize the skills being taught. Focused mini-lessons should be provided to teach skills in writing, such as writing a description of the growth of a caterpillar to a butterfly.

To give children the time to write and the practice to become proficient, teachers must have them write often and in multiple genres. Teachers can accomplish this through the use of writing in content areas such as art, music, social studies, science, and math. In years past, mathematics for primary-grade students often involved only the completion of simple addition and subtraction problems, but now, it is customary for math problems to be written as word problems beginning in kindergarten or first grade. Working with these problems not only enhances students' reading and math, but it also provides them the opportunity to write their own math problems for others to solve.

Thematic units are the perfect vehicles for having student write in content areas. If the class is studying plants for example, mini-lessons can focus on writing the directions for planting seeds, writing a vivid description of a beautiful flower, or following the sequence of how a plant grows, from planting it, to watering it, to seeing the little green buds come up until it flowers. Students can write opinion pieces on favorite plants and flowers or letters to persuade family members to assist them in growing a garden. If children are given time and opportunities to write multiple times during the day, they can master the skills outlined in the CCSS.

Summary and Conclusions

LIKE LEARNING TO READ, LEARNING TO WRITE OCCURS when students are motivated to write about something that is of interest to them or serves a purpose in their lives. Functional writing is as important as narrative writing, if not more so.

The educators who created the CCSS were wise to focus on the writing component, because writing has not received as much attention in the past. Those educators were also prudent to separate the conventions and mechanics of writing from the creation of ideas when writing. In the past, parents and teachers have often evaluated writing more for its correct spelling, punctuation, grammar, and handwriting than for the merit of its ideas.

Effective writing instruction must be explicit and attended to on a regular basis, with teachers modeling types of writing, providing examples of different types of texts, and giving students time to write on their own. As previously mentioned, writing takes time, so a single piece of writing will rarely be completed in one sitting. Students' writing should be shared and distributed so students will come to view writing as relevant to their lives.

The CCSS provide the key skills that students should acquire. Teachers have the responsibility to be sure students have ample opportunities to develop proficiency with each skill.

ACTIVITIES

1. Ask three children of different ages to write about a favorite food, television show, storybook, or game. Take notes on each child's behavior during writing, and analyze each child's writing to determine his or her developmental writing level.

2. Think of several themes for dramatic play that you can develop in an early childhood classroom (such as a restaurant). For each theme, think of the writing materials you can provide for children to use as they engage in dramatic play.

3. Select three writing standards mentioned in this chapter, and describe activities that will satisfy each standard. Be sure that your activities reflect functional and meaningful writing tasks.

4. Think of a theme that can be developed in one of the content areas (such as science or social studies). Then describe three activities that will help students to learn content information related to the theme and that will engage them in one or more of the CCSS Writing standards.

5. Design a writing assignment or mini-lesson that will engage early childhood students in the use of digital literacies and satisfy one of the CCSS Writing standards.

REFERENCES

Bromley, K. (2007). Assessing student writing. In J. R. Paratore & R. L. McCormack (eds.), *Classroom literacy assessment: Making sense of what students know and do* (pp. 210–226). New York, NY: Guilford Press.

Bromley, K. (2011). Best practices in writing. In L. M. Morrow & L. B. Gambrell (eds.), *Best practices in literacy instruction* (4th ed.). New York, NY: Guilford Press.

Calkins, L. (1994). *The art of teaching writing.* Portsmouth, NH: Heinemann.

Calkins, L., Hartman, A., & White, Z. (2005). *One to one: The art of conferring with young writers.* Portsmouth, NH: Heinemann.

Collins Block, C. (1993). History of reading instruction. In C. Collins Block (ed.), *Teaching the language arts* (Annotated instructors ed.) Boston, MA: Allyn & Bacon.

Dyson, A. H. (1986). Children's early interpretations of writing: Expanding research perspectives. In D. Yoden & S. Templeton (eds.), *Metalingiustic awareness and beginning literacy.* Exeter, NH: Heinemann.

Graves, D. (1983) *Writing: Teachers and children at work.* Exeter: NH: Heinemann.

Graves, D. (1994). *A fresh look at writing.* Portsmouth, NH: Heinemann.

Gundlach, R., McLane, J., Scott, F., & McNamee, G. (1985). The social foundations of early writing development. In M. Farr (ed.), *Advances in writing research, Vol 1: Children's early writing development.* Norwood, NJ: Ablex.

Hansen, J. (1987). *When writers read.* Portsmouth, NH: Heinemann.

Hansen, J. (2012). Writing standards. In L. M. Morrow, T. Shanahan, and K. K. Wixson (eds.), *Teaching with the common core standards for English language arts, PreK–2.* New York: Guilford Press.

Hillerich, R. L. (1985). *Teaching children to write K–8: A complete guide to developing writing skills.* Englewood Cliffs, NJ: Prentice-Hall.

Hodges, R. (1991). *Learning to spell.* Urbana, IL: National Council of Teachers of English.

Jalongo, M. R. (2007). *Early childhood language arts* (4th ed.). Boston, MA: Allyn & Bacon.

McCarrier, A. (1999). *Interactive writing: How language and literacy come together, K–2.* Portsmouth, NH: Heinemann.

National Governors Association Center for Best Practices & Council of Chief State School Officers (NGA & CCSSO). (2010). *Common Core State Standards.* Washington, DC: Authors. Retrieved from www.corestandards.org/assets/CCSSI_ELA%20Standards.pdf

National Reading Panel (NRP). (2000). *Teaching children to read: Report of the subgroups.* Washington, DC: U.S. Department of Health and Human Services, National Institutes of Health.

Ritchie, S., James-Szanton, J., & Howes, C. (2003). Emergent literacy practices in early childhood classrooms. In C. Howes (ed.), *Teaching 4- to 8-year-olds* (pp. 71–92). Baltimore, MD: Paul H. Brookes.

Schickedanz, J., & Casbergue, R.M. (2004). *Writing in preschool: Learning to orchestrate meanings and marks.* Chicago, IL: International Reading Association.

Soderman, A., & Farrell, P. (2008). *Creating literacy-rich preschools and kindergartens.* Boston, MA: Pearson.

Spandel, V. (2008). *Creating young writers: Using six traits to enrich writing process in primary classrooms.* Boston, MA: Allyn & Bacon.

Spandel, V. (2001). *Creating writers through six-trait writing assessment and instruction.* New York, NY: Longman.

Taylor, S. P., & Calkins, L. (2008). *A quick guide to teaching persuasive writing, K–2.* Portsmouth, NH: Heinemann.

Temple, Nathan, Burris, & Temple. (1988). *The beginnings of writing* (4th ed.). Boston, MA: Allyn and Bacon

Tompkins, G. E. (2003). *Literacy for the 21st Century,* (3rd ed.). Upper Saddle River, NJ: Merrill Prentice-Hall.

Vygotsky, L.S. (1978). *Mind in society: The development of psychological processes.* Cambridge, MA: Harvard University Press.

CHILDREN'S LITERATURE CITED

Bauer, J. (2007). *Butterfly life cycle.* New York, NY: Scholastic.

Charlesworth, E. (2007) *Horse life cycle.* New York, NY: Scholastic.

Cronin, D. (2000). *Click, clack, moo: Cows that type.* New York, NY: Scholastic.

Evans, L. (2007). *Baby dolphin's tale.* New York, NY: Scholastic.

Frost, N. (2007). *Rescue dogs.* New York, NY: Scholastic.

Gibbons, G. (1991). *From seed to plant.* New York, NY: Holiday House.

Gibbons, G. (1999). *The pumpkin book.* New York, NY: Scholastic.

Heiligman, D. (1996). *From caterpillar to butterfly.* New York, NY: HarperCollins.

Keenan, S. (2004). *O, say can you see?* (A. Boyajian, illus.) New York, NY: Scholastic.

Page, R. (2009). *Move!* (S. Jenkins, illus.) Boston, MA: Houghton Mifflin.

Saunders-Smith, G. (1998). *Flowers.* Mankato, MN: Pebble Books/Capstone Press.

Integrating the Language Arts/Literacy Standards in the Content Areas

THE OVERARCHING PURPOSE THAT UNDERLIES THE ENGLISH LANGUAGE ARTS (ELA) Common Core State Standards (CCSS) is to coordinate students' education throughout the United States. Continuity is needed, especially in the teaching of reading. Today's families frequently move, and students should be assessed using the same grade-level standards from state to state and school to school.

Christian Schwier/Fotolia

The CCSS have several expectations of teachers. One is for teachers to provide students with equal amounts of informational texts and literature, having them read novels and poetry, as well as magazines and newspapers, and developing new literacies. Teachers are also expected to provide students with various sources and types of information and to build their vocabularies. Incorporating literacy strategies into the content areas, such as mathematics and science, can help teachers meet these expectations. However, integrated instruction should not replace small-group, differentiated, explicit literacy instruction. Instead, integrated instruction should be included within the whole-class, small-group, and individual instruction that teachers currently provide.

Teaching Language Arts and Literacy Throughout the Day

TEACHERS HAVE USED THEMES IN THE PAST BUT not necessarily with the intention of teaching and reinforcing literacy skills. According to the CCSS, literacy should be intentionally taught within the content areas. Doing so provides a way of teaching literacy throughout the entire school day. This reinforcement of the language arts will help to promote a child's abilities to read, write, listen, and speak.

Learning content provides a purpose for learning the language arts, and the language arts support content area learning (Akerson, 2001). In science, for example, students need to observe, discuss, hypothesize, and explain. These literacy skills should be taught in the science class (Lemlech, 2010). Reading and writing about a science topic is different from reading and writing about social studies or math topics. Therefore, for every content area, there are language arts skills to be learned. When engaging in reading and writing in science, for example, students develop specialized vocabulary, engage in writing expository text, and develop comprehension skills that ask them to predict outcomes, compare and contrast, and describe sequences of events. Guthrie, McRae, and Klauda (2007) found that when teachers integrated literacy instruction into the content areas, students showed gains in reading comprehension, conceptual knowledge, problem-solving skills, and motivation to read. Preparing and carrying out themes in content areas provides a venue for integrating the language arts.

Preparing the Classroom Environment for a Theme

For thematic instruction to be successful, teachers must prepare the classroom and prepare for instruction. For an integrated unit on nutrition, teachers can provide materials for activities and discussion across the content areas:

- **Science:** Provide seeds to plant and journals to track plants' development. Also provide "play" foods to sort and group.
- **Social studies:** Provide cookbooks and related resources from diverse cultures, so students can compare foods and customs.
- **Music:** Identify food-related songs and provide the lyrics for students to read (e.g., "Do You Know the Muffin Man?" and "On Top of Spaghetti").
- **Art:** Display magazines and newspapers that contain recipes and photos of food, as well as books with historical paintings of food (e.g., those of sixteenth-century Italian painter Giuseppe Arcimboldo).

- **Library corner:** Provide books from various genres about fitness, health, and nutrition, as well as cooking magazines and pamphlets about eating and living well.
- **Author's Spot:** Provide materials for students to write about topics related to nutrition and health, such as index cards for recipes and blank books for writing about food, listing new vocabulary words, tracking daily eating, recording types and durations of exercise, and charting plants' growth.

Applying the CCSS in a Thematic Science Unit

INTEGRATING THE LANGUAGE ARTS INTO CONTENT AREA LEARNING is an important recommendation of the CCSS, so the focus of this chapter is implementation of a content area theme. The following sections outline activities for a thematic unit in science called "Healthy Foods and Healthy Bodies." For each activity, both a science objective and a CCSS language arts and literacy objective are provided. The unit was created for primary-grade students, and literacy instruction has been purposely integrated throughout it. To help facilitate instruction and document progress, teachers should gather samples of the work students complete during the unit.

Healthy Foods and Healthy Bodies

GRADE LEVEL: Primary grades

DURATION: 3 to 4 weeks

ESSENTIAL UNDERSTANDINGS: The essential information children will learn in this science unit is that to remain healthy, they need to eat healthy foods and to participate in exercise.

GUIDING QUESTIONS:

Why should we eat healthy foods? Healthy foods provide our bodies with the nutrients needed to produce energy and strength, allowing us to work, play, and grow. Every day, we should eat approximately three servings of each of the following foods:

1. **Vegetables:** Broccoli, carrots, spinach, and squash all provide vitamins.
2. **Fruits:** Apples, oranges, pears, and bananas provide vitamins and other important nutrients.
3. **Grains/Cereals:** Bread, pasta, rice, and oat cereals contain carbohydrates and fiber, which provide us with energy.
4. **Proteins:** Meat, beans, poultry, fish, nuts, and eggs contain minerals and protein, which foster growth and build muscles.
5. **Milk, cheese, and yogurt:** Dairy foods provide protein and other nutrients, which build strong bones and teeth.

Why should we exercise? Exercise strengthens our muscles and gives us a healthy heart. Exercise also helps circulate our blood and makes us feel refreshed, and it relaxes us by relieving stress.

UNIT ACTIVITIES: The activities described in the following sections focus on the value of nutrition and exercise in promoting good health. At the beginning of each section, one or more of the CCSS is stated and described in terms of what skills students should exhibit to meet the standards.

Reading Informational Text

Introductory Lesson: Introduction to the thematic unit "Healthy Foods and Healthy Bodies"

RI 2.4   Determine the meaning of words and phrases in a text relevant to the theme.
- Read aloud these books to the class: *A Fruit Is a Suitcase of Seeds* (Richards, 2002) and *How a Seed Grows* (Jordan, 1992).
- Record the new words from *A Fruit Is a Suitcase of Seeds* and *How a Seed Grows* on a chart, and encourage students to use it as a reference. Discuss words that are related to seeds.

RI 2.6   Identify the main purpose of a text, including what the author wants to explain or describe.
- Ask the children to explain in their own words what the author means by the title *A Fruit Is a Suitcase of Seeds.*
- Ask the children to write four sentences about how the book *How a Seed Grows* explains the steps for growing a seed.

Writing and Reading Informational Text

RI 2.9   Compare and contrast the most important points presented by two texts on the same topic.
- We are learning about good foods to eat to stay healthy. Fruits, such as apples and bananas, are good for us because they have vitamins and nutrients. We learned this from the books we read.
- Show students an apple and a banana. Refer back to the books and then observe and describe the properties of these fruits. Cut them open, smell them, look at them, and touch and taste them.
- Discuss with students: How are the two texts similar? How are they different? Have students discuss and record the similarities and differences they identify.

L 2.4   Determine or clarify the meanings of unknown and multiple-meaning words and phrases based on grade-level reading and content.
- Ask students to write words about bananas on yellow sticky notes, one word per note, and words about apples on red or pink sticky notes, one word per note. Then have students put their sticky notes on a big Venn diagram that you have drawn on the board.
- Discuss how apples and bananas are alike and different, based on what students found in the books read earlier and learned on their own through observation.
- Discuss the words in the Venn diagram after students have completed the activity.

W 2.2   Write informative/explanatory text in which they introduce a topic, use facts and definitions to develop points, and provide a concluding statement or section.

- Provide each student with a sheet of paper that contains this sentence: *Apples and bananas are good for you because they have vitamins and nutrients.* Using this sentence as a main idea, have students write four paragraphs as follows:

  1. Write what you learned about apples from the books we read in class and from touching, smelling, tasting, and looking at them.

  2. Write what you learned about bananas from the books we read in class and from touching, smelling, tasting, and looking at them.

  3. Write how apples and bananas are the same based on what you have read and experienced.

  4. Write how apples and bananas are different based on what you have read and experienced.

Speaking and Listening

SL 2.1   Participate in collaborative conversations with diverse partners about grade-level topics and texts with peers and adults in small and large groups.

SL 2.4   Tell a story or recount an experience with appropriate facts and relevant, descriptive details, speaking audibly in coherent sentences.

SL 2.5   Create audio recordings of stories or poems; add drawings or other visual displays to stories or recounts of experiences when appropriate to clarify ideas, thoughts, and feelings.

- Read aloud the book *Mr. Rabbit and the Lovely Present* (Zolotow, 1962). Before reading, show students the pictures in the book and have a brief discussion about what students think the story is about.

- While reading the story, have a basket beside you. As the girl in the book selects apples, bananas, grapes, and pears for her mother's birthday present, have a student put each type of fruit in the basket. After reading, discuss whether students created a healthy present and why.

- Have children draw their own pictures of the little girl, the rabbit, and the basket of fruit.

Reading Informational and Narrative Texts

RL 2.7   Use information gained from the illustrations and words in a print or digital text to demonstrate understanding of its characters, setting, or plot.

- Read aloud *The Tiny Seed* (Carle, 1970), and ask students to retell the events of the story in chronological order. Discuss the book's introduction and its ending action.

- With the information from the book, demonstrate knowledge about planting seeds. Line the inside of a clear plastic cup with a wet paper towel. Put a bean seed between the wet paper towel and the wall of the cup so you can see the seed sprout and the plant grow. Fill the same cup with soil. Make a hole in the dirt to plant another bean seed, and sprinkle water on the dirt. Put your cup in a bright, warm place. Watch and chart the growth of the two beans.

RI 2.1   Ask and answer such questions as *who, what, where, when, why,* and *how* to demonstrate understanding of key details in a text.

RI 2.10   Read and comprehend informational texts in content areas at grade level or higher complexity, with scaffolding as needed at the high end of the range.

- Read aloud *Johnny Appleseed* (Demuth, 1996) to the class. Ask different children to listen for who is in the book, what is the most important thing that happens, when it happens, why it happens, and how it happens. After reading, have the children answer the questions.
- Hypothesize about what happens to apples when they are cooked. Then observe changes that occur to food while following directions for a recipe. For instance, make applesauce by following a recipe and discuss how and why the apples change.

Foundational Skills

RF 2.3   Know and apply grade-level phonics and word analysis skills in decoding words.

RF 2.3b   Know spelling-sound correspondences for additional common vowel teams.

- As a class, make a *Nutrition Alphabet Book* that includes many of the nutrition-related words learned in the unit. The pages should correspond to the letters of the alphabet in order, from A to Z. Each page should contain a word related to nutrition—for instance, A = *apple,* B = *bread,* C = *carrot,* D = *dairy,* E = *eggs,* F = *fish,* and so on—and a complete sentence using the word, such as *I like . . .* After completing the book, make photocopies to give to the students.
- Students will demonstrate knowledge of letters (both vowels and consonants) and words that are identified with specific letters and sounds. Students should discuss the letters, words, and sentences with the teacher and with each other.

RI 1.9   With prompting and support, identify basic similarities in and differences between two texts on the same topic.

- For an activity in the social studies, help students learn about healthy foods from different countries. Have students identify the similarities and differences between the foods they eat and foods from other countries. Each student should present an oral report about what he or she learned.
- Read aloud *Children Around the World* (Montanari, 2001), which discusses, among other things, the foods children eat. Compare and contrast foods from one country to another. Feature snacks from different countries. Have students write about what cultural food they like best.

Science

RI 2.6   Identify the main purpose of a text, including what the author wants to answer, explain, or describe.

- Create a K-W-L chart, labeling these three sections: "What We **K**now," "What We **W**ant to Know," and "What We **L**earned." Then begin a class discussion about exercise and how it affects the body. Ask students what they know about the importance of exercise. List their responses on the K-W-L chart under the heading "What We Know." Then ask students what they want to learn about the subject, and list those responses on the chart under the heading "What We Want to Know."

- Introduce and read several informational books, posters, pamphlets, and magazines about exercise and healthy bodies, such as *My Amazing Body: A First Look at Health and Fitness* (Thomas, 2002).
- After several days of discussion and activities done in conjunction with informational books, refer back to the lists the class made at the beginning of the lesson. Add items under the heading "What We Learned" by asking students to share what they have learned about exercise over the past several days. Compare this list to the list of what they wanted to know about exercise. Ask questions such as "How are the two lists different?" and "What can you do if you haven't learn something that you want to know?"
- Have students complete similar charts with partners before and after other lessons.

Social Studies

W 2.7   Participate in shared research and writing projects (e.g., read a number of books on a single topic to produce a report; record science observations).

- Learn about sports that children from other countries participate in to get their exercise.
- Working in small groups, students should use informational books and Internet sources to research sports from other countries. Compile all of the groups' findings in a class book about the topic.
- Have students play the different sports on the playground.

W 2.3   Write narratives in which they recount a well-elaborated event or short sequence of events, include details to describe actions, thoughts, and feelings, use temporal words to signal event order, and provide a sense of closure.

- As a class, discuss that books are written by authors and that pictures are drawn by illustrators.
- Provide an experience chart for use as a prewriting activity. Then read aloud the books *Mooncake* (Asch, 1983) and *Sleep Is for Everyone* (Showers, 1997). Create a story web on the experience chart as students talk about characteristics of sleep—for instance, why sleep is important, what happens when you sleep.
- Have each child write a story about sleep while teacher conferences take place. Their finished products will be written in books.
- Have children participate in brainstorming, drafting, conferencing, editing, and revising.
- Extend this activity to other topics related to the theme. For example, if the class reads a story about personal hygiene and create books.

Play

SL 2.1a   Follow agreed-upon rules for discussion (e.g., gaining the floor in respectful ways, listening to others with care, speaking one at a time about the topics and texts under discussion).

- Learn an exercise routine that the entire school will participate in three times a week.
- Set up an outdoor health club with different exercise stations, and provide a sign-in sheet at each numbered station. Have children choose roles and tasks, such as directing an exercise class, filling in membership cards, and writing receipts for payments. Encourage the children to name their club and hang posters as advertisements.
- Go online to find games, presentations, and materials for teachers about nutrition, including the food "plate" (www.choosemyplate.gov) and the food "pyramid" (www.facs.pppst.com/foodpyramid.html).
- Visit the website Kore Game Portal to find games about exercise (www.kidnetic.com/kore/).
- Go online to the Colgate Kids website to find games about dental care that are organized by children's ages (www.colgate.com/app/Kids-World/US/HomePage.cvsp).
- Activities about personal hygiene are available on several websites, including Livestrong (www.livestrong.com/article/227271-personal-hygiene-activities-for-children) and Personal Hygiene (www.mypersonalhygiene.com/personal-hygiene-worksheets-for-kids).

Art

SL 2.5   Add drawings or other visual displays or recounts of experiences when appropriate to clarify ideas, thoughts, and feelings.

- Based on what students have learned from their discussion and reading, plan a day of healthy foods and activities. Children should discuss their ideas in collaboration with partners.
- Provide a collection of magazines that feature food, and have children cut out images and create collages of the foods they eat for breakfast, lunch, dinner, and snacks during the day. As a class, review each collage and determine whether the foods included are healthy. For foods that are not healthy, have students write about what can be improved.

Music

RF 2.4   Read with accuracy and fluency to support comprehension.

- Discuss the importance of sleep for maintaining good health.
- Sing the song *Are You Sleeping?* in English and in French and then in a round. Post the lyrics so students can read them throughout the day.

Source of Standards: NGA & CCSSO (2010).

Culminating Activities

THE FOLLOWING ACTIVITIES HELP TO DEVELOP THE SKILLS identified in the CCSS for language, listening, and speaking. The conventions of both oral and written language are used in activities that involve a performance. Standards for listening and speaking are used in activities that have children summarize, present in diverse media, and be prepared to discuss (SL 2.4, SL 2.5, and SL 2.6).

Share the children's work created in the unit with their families, friends, and other classes in school.

- Prepare a nutritious food, such as fruit salad or applesauce, for a snack to share with guests.
- Sing the song *Are You Sleeping?*
- Display students' collages of healthy foods along with written pieces that identify students' healthy food items and healthy activities.
- Show and describe the plants grown by the class.
- As the teacher reads aloud the story *The Carrot Seed* (Krauss, 1945/2004), have five children chant the repeated phrase every time it appears and use American Sign Language as they speak.
- Have three children retell the story *Mr. Rabbit and the Lovely Present* (Zolotow, 1962). They should use props, as the teacher did in the earlier activity: a basket; an apple, a pear, grapes, and a banana; and a rabbit stuffed animal. One child should be the rabbit, one should be the girl, and one should be the narrator.
- Have two students present book talks that are intended to persuade adults to read them. One child should do a book talk on *Bread and Jam for Frances* (Hoban, 1976), and the other should do a book talk on *From Seed to Pumpkin* (Kottke, 2000).
- Have the class choral read poems from *Munching: Poems about Eating* (Hopkins, 1985).

REFERENCES

Akerson, V. (2001) Teaching science when your principal says: Teach language arts. *Science and Children, 38*(7), 42–47

Guthrie, J., McRae, A., & Klauda, S. L. (2007) Contributions of concept-oriented reading instruction to knowledge about interventions for motivations in reading. *Educational Psychologist, 42,* 237–250

Lemlech, J. K. (2010) *Curriculum and instructional methods for the elementary and middle school.* Boston, MA: Allyn & Bacon.

CHILDREN'S LITERATURE CITED

Narrative Literature

Asch, F. (1983). *Mooncake.* New York, NY: Simon & Schuster.

Carle, E. (1969). *The very hungry caterpillar.* New York, NY: Philomel

Carle, E. (1970). *The tiny seed.* New York, NY: Simon & Schuster.

De Brunhoff, L., & Weiss, E. (2002). *Babar's yoga for elephants*. New York, NY: Harry N. Abrams.

Demuth, P. (1996). *Johnny Appleseed*. New York, NY: Grosset & Dunlap.

Demuth, P. (1997). *Achoo!* New York, NY: Grosset & Dunlap.

dePaola, T. (1975). *Strega Nona: An old tale*. New York, NY: Simon & Schuster.

dePaola, T. (1978). *The popcorn book*. New York, NY: Holliday House.

Eberts, M. (1984). *Pancakes, crackers, and pizza*. Chicago, IL: Children's Press.

Hoban, R. (1976). *Bread and jam for Frances*. New York, NY: Harper & Row.

Izawa, T. (1968). *The little red hen*. New York, NY: Grosset & Dunlap.

Krauss, R. (2004). *The carrot seed* (C. Johnson, illus.) New York, NY: Harper & Brothers. (Original work published 1945)

McCloskey, R. (1948). *Blueberries for Sal*. New York, NY: Penguin.

Numeroff-Joffe, L. (1985). *If you give a mouse a cookie*. New York, NY: Scholastic.

Raffi. (1987). *Shake my sillies out*. New York, NY: Random House.

Shartmat, M. (1984). *Gregory, the terrible eater*. New York, NY: Macmillan.

Zolotow, C. (1962). *Mr. Rabbit and the lovely present*. New York, NY: Harper & Row.

Poetry

Hopkins, L. B. (1985). *Munching: Poems about eating*. Boston, MA: Little, Brown.

Silverstein, A., Silverstein, V. B., & Silverstein Nunn, L. (2000). *Eat your vegetables! Drink your milk!* New York, NY: Scholastic.

Informational Literature

Chambers, W. (1974). *The lip-smackin', joke-crackin' cookbook for kids*. New York, NY: Golden Press.

Cole, J. (1988). *The magic school bus inside the human body*. New York, NY: Scholastic.

Jordan, H. J. (1992) *How a seed grows*. New York, NY: HarperCollins.

Katzen, M., & Henderson, A. (1994). *Pretend soup and other real recipes: A cookbook for preschoolers and up*. Berkeley, CA: Ten Speed Press.

Montanari, D. (2001). *Children around the world*. New York, NY: Kids Can Press.

Reid, M. (1996). *Let's find out about ice cream*. New York, NY: Scholastic.

Richards, J. (2002). *Fruit is a suitcase for seeds*. Minneapolis, MN: Millbrook Press.

Ripley, C. (1997). *Why does popcorn pop? And other kitchen questions*. Toronto, ON: Firefly Books.

Rockwell, L. (1999). *Good enough to eat: A kid's guide to food and nutrition*. New York, NY: HarperCollins.

Showers, P. (1997). *Sleep is for everyone*. New York, NY: HarperCollins.

Thomas, P. (2002). *My amazing body: A first look at health and fitness*. Hauppauge, NY: Barron's Educational Series.

Using the CCSS Throughout the Day

IT IS IMPORTANT TO KNOW THAT THE ENGLISH Language Arts (ELA) Common Core State Standards (CCSS) are not a method of teaching or a curriculum. They are a series of objectives that outline knowledge and skills to be learned within the language arts. Even so, following the CCSS will cause some change in how we teach in early childhood classrooms.

Erin Kramer

Change is difficult. When we change, we need to learn new things, modify what we do now, and then evaluate whether what we are doing differently is better than what we did in the past. Change seems to be a constant in today's fast-paced world. Every year, a new program is added to the group of programs already in place. A new supervisor of curriculum is hired who has a vision of how things should happen and takes apart what teachers are just getting comfortable with since the last change occurred. Some teachers feel that we should refine what we are already doing before jumping into new territory.

The CCSS are changing the way we think about reading instruction in several ways. In some areas, things will remain the same. The CCSS include some excellent components but also some things that we question. Since this book is about the early childhood grades, this chapter will look at CCSS-related issues that have to do with that age group.

Using the CCSS in the Early Childhood Grades

ONE OF THE MOST POSITIVE CHANGES BROUGHT ABOUT by the CCSS is the emphasis on text—informational text, in particular. Reading informational texts provides the relevance being asked for across the curriculum, since these texts are about facts and details. As educators, we have to take inventory of our reading materials, because in the past, our libraries have included predominantly the narrative texts read in early childhood.

With the CCSS, we are changing how we ask children to comprehend text. Previewing a text prior to reading it now has a reduced function in the reading lesson, and more time is being given to reading and repeated reading. Also, rather than have students focus exclusively on text-to-life experiences, we want them to think about text-to-text similarities and differences, as well. The text has become the most important element. In the past, we talked about "learning to read" in the primary grades and "reading to learn" after second grade. Now, we recognize that reading is a skill, not a content area. If we do not give some meaning or purpose to reading from the start, children will not see the relevance of this skill.

Therefore in early childhood we need to learn to read but also to read to learn at the same time. The CCSS's recommends explicit teaching of foundational skills but also embedding them into a context. Skills taught in isolation do not always transfer for children when they are reading connected texts. Therefore, we need to think about teaching foundational skills concurrently with the reading comprehension, speaking, listening, and writing (Cunningham, Hall, & Sigmon, 1999).

In the early childhood grades, students are exposed to a plethora of children's literature—most of it, narrative stories. They read fables, folktales, fairytales, and picture storybooks that are designated as appropriate for this age group. We should not abandon these texts, but we must provide more time for informational books that deal with content areas, such as science and social studies. Students need to read about real topics that affect them, such as weather, good health, and safety. Other topics of importance are plants, animals, and the five senses. Students should also learn about other cultures, as well as occupations, families, communities, transportation, and so on. This information will come from sharing informational texts in the forms of books, pamphlets, newspapers, magazines, digital materials (such as videos), and virtual and real class trips. Children truly enjoy learning information, and once they have been exposed to it, they will want more. Research has shown that reading informational texts exposes children to more vocabulary; in addition, children find these books motivating and usually want to learn more (Duke, 2000).

Teachers should make sure that the informational texts that children read are quality texts that contain up-to-date information and follow a clear nonfiction structure. Good informational texts have definitive structures, such as sequence of events, description, compare and contrast, cause and effect, and problem/solution.

New elements to teach about informational texts include the integration of knowledge and ideas and the range of text complexity. In the Reading Informational Text category Craft and Structure, children learn about text features such as the table of contents, glossary, index, captions, headings, as well as diagrams and photographs of various text topics, rather than artistic illustrations. If all of these features are not covered in instruction, using the book will be more difficult and pertinent information will go unnoticed. Teaching about informational texts also requires an increase in teaching about complicated vocabulary and concepts. Teachers have a new responsibility to help students apply reading comprehension skills to informational texts in the content areas, such as science, social studies, and math. Teachers must guide students to notice the different text features in these content area book and then use what they have learned to gain information and extract the main idea.

The CCSS do not include a standard with the title *Vocabulary,* but emphasis on learning vocabulary can be found throughout the other ELA standards. Learning vocabulary is embedded in the Reading Literature and Reading Informational Text standards, and the Language standards include a category called *Acquisition of Vocabulary.* Therefore, learning vocabulary is not neglected but should instead be thought of as important and present throughout. If a student does not have the appropriate vocabulary, he or she may be able to decode words but will not understand what he or she reads. Teachers must make a point of preteaching important vocabulary and engaging students in complex discussions after reading a new informational text, especially if the topic is unfamiliar.

Reading complex texts is a major emphasis in the CCSS. The standards suggest exposing students to texts at grade level or even more difficult than that. The rationale is that if students deal with more sophisticated texts, they will learn more complex vocabulary and how to comprehend and think analytically about more difficult ideas. This is a focus in grades 2 and up and is not as important in pre-K, K, or first grade in terms of students' independent reading, because their ability to read at this age level may be limited. Asking beginning readers to read a complex text would be a very frustrating experience. However, teachers can read grade-level and above-grade-level texts aloud to these students, as long as the vocabulary and difficult concepts are discussed. Exposing students to complex texts helps them learn new ideas (Heibert, 1999; Morgan, Wilcox, & Eldredge, 2000).

One of the most powerful qualities of the CCSS is the spiraling of skills to be acquired across the grade levels. In the Reading Informational Text standards, for example, the first skill identified for kindergarten is the same skill identified for fifth grade. The difference is that for fifth grade, the expectations for mastering the skill are more complex. For example, under Reading Informational Text, the category Key Ideas and Details, note the progression in Standard 1 for kindergarten, grade 1, and grade 2 (NGA & CCSSO, 2010):

- **Kindergarten:** With prompting and support, ask and answer questions about key details in a text.
- **First grade:** Ask and answer questions about key details in a text.
- **Second grade:** Ask and answer such questions as *who, what where, when, why,* and *how* to demonstrate understanding of key details in a text.

Children need repeated practice with skills to acquire them, and this standard demonstrates how the CCSS repeat skills across multiple grades while increasing the degree of challenge. This approach is contrary to our current method of teaching, in which we can work on a skill that is identified as part of the first-grade curriculum with the possibility of never returning to it again.

Writing is also showcased in the CCSS—something that was not been done in the past, especially in early childhood. In the 2000 report of the National Reading Panel (NRP), writing was not discussed and therefore was neglected. In the CCSS, writing has been designated equally as important as reading. Writing should be based on students' experiences, as well as materials they have read. The CCSS recommend that children write about texts they have read or that have been read to them. Regardless of the types of texts students write, their writing should be backed up by facts.

Teachers should recognize that the CCSS are objectives for learning. They focus on some of the skills we may not have paid enough attention to and raise many new issues for our consideration. However, we need to keep doing what we know works with students and is good instruction. We already know a lot about reading instruction, and we have been using evidence-based practices. The CCSS do not prescribe a format for daily instruction, nor do they describe how to group students for instruction to meet individual needs.

Teachers are asking questions about these topics, which are not addressed in the CCSS. For instance, teachers want to know if following the CCSS means eliminating small-group instruction. Should all instruction be whole-class instruction? Teachers also wonder about the use of leveled books. Since the CCSS call for the use of quality literature and complex texts, are we allowed to use leveled books created for instruction? The use of theme-based units is another issue. Should thematic units be carried out all day long?

Of course there will still be small-group instruction to meet individual needs (Pinnell & Fountas, 1996). Small-group instruction is one of the best ways for teachers to get to know their students' needs, to provide targeted instruction at individual students' achievement levels, and to conduct formative assessment before instruction begins and summative at the end of a lesson or unit. In addition, teachers will use whole-class instruction for storybook reading and discussions, mini-lessons on comprehension, and writing and phonics on grade level to keep the complexity of work where it should be. Thematic units should be carried out all day long, but during explicit instruction for the whole class, teachers should concentrate on specific skills. Theme-based instruction will be most evident in science and social studies, but teachers should also be sure to embed the ELA CCSS when teaching in these content areas. The CCSS objectives should be embedded into all of the content areas, including art, music, and physical education. Under this approach, children will learn to read, write, and learn information from the content areas concurrently (Shanahan & Shanahan, 2011).

A Day in a First-Grade Classroom

IN THIS SECTION, WE WILL SPEND A DAY in a first-grade classroom. Our goal is to illustrate further what following the CCSS, along with successful evidence-based strategies, might look like in practice. The environment, class schedule, and daily activities are all considered to provide a complete picture of students' daily classroom experiences.

When the text describes something related to the CCSS, the relevant Anchor Standard will be referenced: (RL) for Reading Literature, (RI) for Reading Informational Text, (RF) for

Foundational Skills, (W) for Writing, (SL) for Speaking and Listening, and (L) for Language. The designation (CCSS) will be used for ideas, concepts, and practices that encompass the CCSS but do not align specifically with one of the Anchor Standards.

The Teacher and Students

Beth Miller has been teaching first grade for the past seven years. Recently, she completed a master's degree and is now eligible for a reading specialist certification. Ms. Miller teaches in a middle-income community. There are 22 students in her first-grade class: 9 are European American, 6 are Asian American, 5 are African American, and 2 are Latino. Twenty percent of Ms. Miller's students speak one of four languages other than English at home: Spanish, Japanese, Hindi, and Mandarin Chinese. Thirteen students are boys, and 9 are girls. There is a full-time aide in the room; she is assigned to one student who has physical disabilities and is in a wheelchair.

Ms. Miller's philosophy of teaching includes integrating the curriculum so that students can build connections between content areas. She purposefully integrates literacy skill development in reading, writing, listening, speaking, and viewing with her social studies and science themes as much as possible. Her small-group literacy instruction is explicit to emphasize specific skill development and uses the CCSS.

Ms. Miller has a special interest in using informational text with her first-grade readers and writers. She recognizes that background knowledge and vocabulary are enhanced by using expository material, and that adults read informational text in a variety of forms, such as how-to manuals, applications and instructions, and websites (RI). She has also found that many children seem drawn to informational texts, particularly boys, struggling readers, and children who are English language learners.

Ms. Miller teachers in a school that has been very engaged with the standards in shaping its literacy program. She is the chairperson of the CCSS professional development committee.

The Classroom Environment

Ms. Miller's classroom is friendly and engaging. A glance around the room reveals clearly defined and well-organized centers. On the walls, displays depict the theme being studied and provide examples of students' ongoing literacy development. For Ms. Miller, standard equipment includes these items: an easel to display the Morning Message, the day's schedule, a list of classroom rules, a calendar, a weather chart and temperature graph, a student helper chart, a chart for the centers, a pocket chart, and a word wall. Other equipment in the classroom includes several personal computers and a digital whiteboard.

The largest classroom center is the literacy center. A large rug creates an area for whole-class meetings and independent reading. Ample space is provided for storing books. On one set of shelves, books are organized in two different ways. Ms. Miller has created baskets of books at various levels of difficulty to correspond with her small-group reading instruction. She has also created baskets related to themes and authors—for example, dinosaurs, sports, and folktales plus Dr. Seuss and Eric Carle.

Every month, Ms. Miller changes many of the books in the baskets; she also changes the theme- and author-related books (CCSS). The theme-related books she has provided are not leveled (CCSS). For independent reading, students can choose books based on interest and difficulty. To guide students in returning books to the correct locations, Ms. Miller has put colored stickers on the books and baskets. Books and stories created by students are displayed in their own basket. Books about the current theme are on a special open-faced shelf. The books Ms. Miller provides are 50% informational text (RI) and 50% narrative literature (RL).

The literacy center is also equipped with a flannelboard and flannelboard characters, puppets, and props for storytelling. There is a rocking chair for the teacher and other adults to sit in when they read to the class. The children use the rocking chair to read independently and to read to each other. The listening area in the literacy center has a CD/tape player for listening to stories. There is a good selection of manipulative materials for learning about print, including magnetic letters, puzzle rhyme cards, and letter chunks for making words.

An extension of the literacy center is the writing center. Within this center is a round table, where Ms. Miller meets with small groups of students. Shelves along the walls hold various kinds of paper (lined and unlined), several dictionaries, a stapler, and a range of writing materials: markers, crayons, colored pencils, and stamps and ink pads. Ms. Miller assigns writing often, usually in response to books that she has read aloud to the class or that students have read themselves (W).

The writing center also includes a wall across which letters of the alphabet are taped horizontally. Each time students discover a new word, Ms. Miller writes it on a card and tapes it to the wall under the correct initial letter. Ms. Miller encourages her students to consult the word wall for both reading and writing. She also encourages students to come up with new words that start with the same letter or sound as one of the words on the wall or to think words that rhyme with one of the words on the wall. She has placed her students' names on the word wall, along with high-frequency words designated for first-graders. Each student has an alphabet strip on his or her desk (RF, L).

Ms. Miller's science center provides homes for the class guinea pig and hermit crab. Standard equipment in this center includes magnets, objects that sink and float, and plants. Materials are added to match each new theme being studied. Hands-on experiments are set up for the students to complete.

The dramatic play center includes typical kitchen furniture, such as a stove, refrigerator, and table and chairs, and empty food boxes are provided to display print. Changes are made to the area according to the themes being studied throughout the year. There is also a restaurant in the center, where children can take orders, read menus, and check their bills. The type of food in the restaurant changes about every six weeks, which helps students learn about multicultural foods and customs. So far, the class has had Italian, Chinese, Mexican, Portuguese, and Japanese restaurants and a Jewish deli.

The construction center has a variety of small blocks plus small cars, buses, people and animals. Labels designate where the different toys should be stored, and 5" × 8" cards and tape provide labels created by the children. Signs that read "Please Save" have been placed on several buildings under construction, and other signs name finished structures. Children sign their names on these signs.

Located near the sink is the art center, which contains an easel, table and chairs, and shelves for materials. The easels are set up and equipped with watercolor paints three times a week. On the shelves are scissors, markers, and crayons, as well as paper of many colors, types, and sizes. Collage materials are provided, too, such as cotton balls, doilies, foil paper, wallpaper samples, and paste.

The math center contains math manipulative materials for counting, adding, measuring, weighing, graphing, multiplying, subtracting, and distinguishing shapes. There are felt numbers for use on the feltboard, magnetic numbers for the magnetic boards, and numbers for sequencing in a pocket chart. There are also geometric shapes, such as squares, triangles, cylinders, and rectangles, in addition to Unifix cubes, counters, base-10 blocks, dice, and rulers.

All of the classroom centers contain books; topics include art, music, math, and many more. For each new theme the class studies, Ms. Miller adds books about it. To make sure students discover these new books, she displays them in centers around the classroom (RI, RL).

Ms. Miller has arranged students' desks in groups of four, which she calls *pods*. She conducts small-group instruction in the classroom's quiet corner, which features a half-circle-shaped table. Next to the table, shelves store materials for various small-group activities. Students have ready access to sentence strips, index cards, whiteboards and markers, leveled books, and word study games.

Managing Classroom Centers

Ms. Miller's students use the classroom centers every day. To meet the goal of having each student work in three centers a day, she created a contract on which she marks the centers in which each student is assigned to work. The name of each center and a symbol representing it are provided on the contract; the same name and symbol label the center in the classroom.

After a student finishes working in a center, he or she checks it off on the contract. The student also deposits the work he or she completed in the center in a basket labeled "Finished Work." Ms. Miller meets with students at the end of each day to review their work from the various centers. She also assigns the centers students will work in the following day.

If a student has incomplete work or his or her work demonstrates the need for assistance, he or she places it in the "Unfinished Work" basket. Students finish incomplete work at a designated time every day. Those who have time left after completing their work at the assigned centers can visit any other centers they choose.

Assessing Students' Needs

Ms. Miller's students have a range of needs, so she allows considerable time to conduct both formative and summative assessments using a range of formal and informal measures. Three times a year (in September, January, and June), she evaluates students' foundational skills and knowledge of reading and writing conventions: sound–symbol relationships, first-grade sight words, blending and segmenting, and identifying and writing the letters of the alphabet. (She makes more involved evaluations later in the year.) In addition, Ms. Miller evaluates students' speaking and listening skills (such as engaging in coherent conversations) and comprehension skills related to the facts of *who, what, where, when, how,* and *why*. Finally, she video records each child retelling a story. Ms. Miller collects students' writing on a regular and frequent basis. She creates lessons based on the expectations identified in her school's curriculum and in the CCSS.

Because most of Ms. Miller's students are reading, she also prepares monthly running records. She uses the information provided in these records to identify what kinds of errors students make, along with the reading strategies they apply and the improvements they make. She also writes down anecdotal information about students' progress and includes observations about their social, emotional, and physical development. Finally, she collects and dates performance samples and anecdotes and stores them in students' portfolios (CCSS).

Small-Group Reading Instruction

The schedule Ms. Miller has designed permits her to provide reading instruction to small groups of students. She uses the assessment information that she collects to group students with similar instructional needs. As Ms. Miller works with her students, she takes detailed notes about their literacy development and changes membership in the groups as necessary. When she meets with the small groups, she works with students to develop their skills in phonological awareness; identification of letters; sound–symbol relationships; listening comprehension; oral language; and knowledge about books, vocabulary, and writing (RL, RI, RF, W, SL, L).

Ms. Miller presently has four reading groups. She tires to see the children with the most needs 4 days a week. Those who are on grade level 2 to 3 times a week and those who are reading above grade level one to two times a week. Each Friday is the day to attend to any special needs that come up during the week. Ms. Miller finds that sometimes, she needs to meet with students who are struggling more often than with those who are doing well.

Schedule for a Literacy Day

8:30 **Do Now. Upon arriving at school children are to:**
- Partner read three times a week and write or draw one important item about what they read. Make entries in their journals about something they read or was read to them two days a week.
- Complete unfinished work.

8:45 **Word Work.**

9:10 **Vocabulary Morning Message.**
- Morning greetings are shared.
- The schedule for the day is reviewed.
- The Morning Message is read and additions are made.
- A vocabulary lesson is competed.

9:45 **Comprehension Reading Workshop.**
- A shared reading related to the theme of study. Includes a mini comprehension lesson and, after the story is complete, a discussion based on the skill.
- Children partner read a selected book of their choice. They read and reflect upon the story skill just taught. The teacher does mini conferences with some.
- At the end of the partner reading the children share what they discussed with the whole class.

10:30 **Guided Reading and Center Activities.**
- Children review center activities and go to work. They must hand in work accomplished at centers.
- Small groups meet with the teacher for explicit instruction of skills based on their needs.

11:20 **Snack and Play.**

11:35 **Writing Workshop.**
- A mini-lesson is included.
- Children engage in writing using the skill taught in the lesson.
- The teacher has short conferences with some children.
- The class shares what they have written.

12:20 **Play/Lunch.**

1:00 **Math.**

1:45 **Theme-related Language Arts (social studies or science).**

2:25 **Specials alternating with art, music, or gym (literacy is embedded).**

2:45 **WRAP Up.**
- Ask students what they learned in reading and writing and ask what was important to them.
- Plan for tomorrow.
- Read a poem, riddle, joke, a short story, or sing a song with words printed for the children to reference.

A Week in a First-Grade Classroom

MS. MILLER RUNS HER CLASSROOM in an orderly and businesslike manner. There is no time to waste! Children have opportunities to explore and experiment, and they also have explicit instruction. They have choices in selecting activities but are expected to complete designated work. The day is well organized and allows for some self-direction. Information is introduced, repeated, and reviewed. She uses the common core for first grade as her guide for skill development in the language arts.

We will spend five days in Ms. Miller's first-grade classroom. Throughout the week, there is an emphasis on explaining the literacy and theme-related activities. The observations of Ms. Miller's classroom were made in March of the school year, so the children were comfortable with the class routines. They were also very engaged in literacy activities throughout the course of the school day.

Each day, Ms. Miller reviews previously learned information and describes what things will be studied in the current thematic unit. Reading, writing, listening, speaking, and math activities are integrated throughout the unit. Ms. Miller focuses on meeting individual students' needs in small-group instruction.

Many details are presented in the description of Monday—the first day. Ms. Miller uses this day to organize activities for the week and to establish routines. Different activities are highlighted for the remaining days of the week and less detail is given to routines, since students are now familiar with them (McGee & Morrow, 2005).

Monday: Setting the Tone for the Week

8:30—Do Now   It is Monday morning. The students enter the room, unpack their bags, hang up their jackets, and immediately begin their "Do Now" work; it includes any jobs they have, such as feeding the fish, watering the plants, moving their nametags on the attendance board from the side marked "Not Present" to the side marked "Present," and putting their name sticks in the "Buy Lunch" or "Milk" can. Today is partner-reading day. Partners select books and begin reading. When the bell rings, students know that it is time to journal about something in their books that they want to remember. After writing, students return to their desks, and Ms. Miller calls on a few of them to share what they have written.

8:45—Word Work   Word Work is done with a district program the school has put into place. There are manipulatives and links to interactive materials on the computer. Ms. Miller has been doing explicit instruction about vowel rules with the school program. Since the theme they are studying is dinosaurs, however, and since the children are reviewing vowel rules, Ms. Miller takes the opportunity to present the words *dinosaurs, plant eaters,* and *meat eaters* to the children and ask them what vowel rules are evident. The children notice the words *eaters* and *meat* follow the rule, "when two vowels go walking the first one does the talking. They also notice that the word dinosaurs has an *"r"* controlled *a* and *u* in it. The *"r"* does not allow you to hear either the *a* or *u*.

9:10—Vocabulary Morning Meeting   The children sit on the rug in the library corner. Ms. Miller begins by greeting the children. "Good morning, Everyone." Children shake hands with each other and say good morning. Ms. Miller leads the class in reading the Morning Message, which is projected on a digital white board. Ms. Miller has the class choral read the message:

> Good morning first grade. We have been discussing dinosaurs. What new words
> have you learned about dinosaurs from our discussions? What new words have you

learned from the books you are reading and from songs and poems? Let's start with dinosaur names.

Ms. Miller puts up pictures of dinosaurs for the children to identify. Under "Dinosaur Names" the children identify Tyrannosaurs, Plateosaurs, Amargasaurs, and Stegosaurs. The children could not identify the Brachiosaurs and Centrosaurs so Ms. Miller names them for the children. The students, then, name and pass around dinosaur models and the names are added to the class thematic word wall.

The next activity is to list words under the category "Words We've Learned about Dinosaurs." Ms. Miller puts up a scene on the white board of dinosaurs in their environments and has the children indicate the words they had learned by pointing to the dinosaur scene. The children say: *meat eaters, plant eaters, fangs, fossils, Jurassic, migrated, beak camouflaged,* and *graze.* All of the words the children say were featured in the visual scene.

9:45—Comprehension Reading Workshop   During this time children participate in a comprehension lesson with a read aloud. When the read aloud ends, the children, each with a partner, practice the skills learned during the lesson with a self-selected book. As they read, the teacher moves around the room and offers help and conversation to the children. When this ends, the class discusses their readings based on the skill in the lesson.

Next, Ms. Miller selects to read an informational text entitled *Discovering Dinosaurs* (Sokoloff, 1997) This book enables the children to find information which discusses similarities and differences between meat eating and plant eating dinosaurs. Before Ms. Miller read the story, using the digital white board, she points out some of the book's features—pictures in the book, labels on figures picture captions, new topic headings, and bolded and larger vocabulary words—so that the children notice them as she reads. Once they discuss the features, they use a KWL chart to record what they know about meat eaters, plant eaters, and other dinosaur topics of which they want to know.

After reading *Discovering Dinosaurs,* the children select other informational books to learn more about meat eating and plant eating dinosaurs. Ms. Miller circulates amongst the partner readers, offering help, and discussing the children's research. At the end of this research time, the children read to the class what they learned about meat and plant eating dinosaurs and they add this information to their KWL chart. The list was long and said such things as:

Meat eaters have strong legs and jaws.	Long necked plant eaters were the largest dinosaurs.
Meat eaters were smaller than plant eaters.	They had long necks so they could eat from tree tops.
Meat eaters had crests or peaks on their for fighting.	Plant eaters without long necks ate plants from the ground.
Meat eater's teeth were very to tear skin and bones apart.	The large plant ate more and roamed to find food.
Meat eating dinosaurs ate plant eating dinosaurs.	Plant eaters had spoon- or pencil-shaped teeth and did not chew their food.
	Plant eaters had armor on their bodies for protection.

10:30—Centers Time   At this time of the day, Ms. Miller spends a few minutes telling students about the center activities for practicing learned skills, and then she explains the new activities and materials. The materials in the centers are provided for a certain time period, but new materials and activities have been added to relate to the theme of dinosaurs as follows:

- *Writing center:* dinosaur-bordered writing paper, dinosaur-shaped books, a dinosaur dictionary, and a dinosaur-shaped poster with words about dinosaurs (L)
- *Literacy center:* fiction and nonfiction dinosaur books, dinosaur books with accompanying CDs, a dinosaur vocabulary puzzle, a dinosaur Concentration memory game, a teacher-made dinosaur Lotto game (RI, RL)
- *Computer center:* the software Dinosaur Hunter (Eyewitness Virtual Reality Series, DK Multimedia) for printing dinosaur stationery, post cards, posters, and masks; a link for visiting a virtual museum exhibit about dinosaurs (CCSS)
- *Science center:* books for reference (RI, RL, W), small skulls and old animal bones, a magnifying glass and rubber gloves (to examine the skulls and bones), drawing materials (for capturing what the entire animal may have looked like, based on the skulls and bones), dinosaur pictures (for sorting into "Meat Eaters" versus "Plant Eaters" or "Walked on Two Feet" versus "Walked on Four Feet"), recording sheets for all activities
- *Math center:* measuring tools (in a basket), sheets to record measurements (of dinosaur skulls and bones), dinosaur counters, an estimation jar filled with little plastic dinosaurs, a basket containing 50 plastic dinosaurs numbered from 1–50 (for arranging in sequential order) (CCSS)
- *Block center:* toy dinosaurs, trees, and bushes; dinosaur books (CCSS)
- *Art center:* dinosaur books, dinosaur stencils and stamps, clay models of dinosaurs, pictures of dinosaurs (for students' use in making their own sculptures) (CCSS)
- *Dramatic play center* (re-created as a paleontologist's office): chicken bones embedded in plaster blocks, wood-carving tools and small hammers (for removing the bones from the blocks), safety goggles, paper and pencils (for labeling the bones), trays to display findings, dinosaur books, posters of fossils and dinosaurs (CCSS, RI)

In addition to practicing skills, centers occupy children in a productive manner which allows Ms. Miller to take small groups of children, who are similar in skill development, for explicit instruction. The children have center activities that are required and their names are displayed on the Center Work Board showing them where to work during center time. If the children finish their required centers then they can move on to a center of their choice once Ms. Miller rings a bell.

Small-Group Reading Instruction   The small group reading allows the teacher to work with a few students at a time for about 15 minutes to differentiate instruction and work on lessons that are created for their individual needs like writing, word work, vocabulary or comprehension. Ms. Miller meets 4 times a week with the struggling readers, 3 times with those on grade level, and twice a week with those who are working above level.

Ms. Miller designed the first small-group lesson to improve students' reading comprehension. She wants them to recall the sequence of events in a book they read earlier, *We Went to the Zoo* (Sloan & Sloan, 1996). This book—a patterned text with slight variations—is written at students' instructional level of reading. The group conducts a brief book walk, stopping to discuss a page or two, and then they identify the animals in the pictures.

As group members read, Ms. Miller observes that one student does not make any errors and finishes rapidly. She jots down a note to consider completing a running record; perhaps this student should be moved up a reading level. After students finish reading, they first discuss what animals they noticed, and then discuss the order in which the animals appeared. Ms. Miller has magnetic figures of animals, which the students arrange on the whiteboard.

Ms. Miller's next group will read the book *Who Can Run Fast?* (Stuart, 2001). The group has worked with this book before. To review it , they echo read the book with the teacher. Ms. Miller's next lesson will help her students to become more independent readers. She will teach them how to figure out unknown words by using the meaning of a sentence and looking at the letters in the words.

The lesson begins with a game called Guess the Covered Word, which they played while reading another book. The sentence with the covered word is "I can [blank] fast." The children are encouraged to select a word that makes sense in the sentence and then look at the letters in the word to see which is correct. Words generated for the missing word are *walk, eat, hop, sleep,* and *run*. After successfully determining the correct word, Ms. Miller reminds the children that when they read, the word must make sense and have the right letters. Ms. Miller explains that this is what good readers do when they and try to figure out words. The group repeats the activity throughout their book (RF).

The next group reads *Family Work and Fun* (Sloan & Sloan, 1996). In this group, Ms. Miller focuses on looking at ending sounds to figure out words. Ms. Miller has written this sentence on the chart: "I am **go** to the store." She reads the sentence and the children point out that it does not sound right. Ms. Miller writes a second sentence: "I am **going** to the store." Students identify the difference in the two sentences, pointing to the words *go* and *going*. Ms. Miller reminds students how they have to look at the ends of words, as well as the beginning of words, when reading. The group reads the book with special attention to the word endings. As Ms. Miller changes reading groups the children at centers change to their next center. All center work has some accountability item that is put in the finished work basket.

11:20—Snack and Play   At midmorning, everyone has dinosaur animal crackers for a snack When snack time is over, the children look at books.

11:35—Writing Workshop   The children gather for writing in the whole-class meeting area. The skill that is being reviewed is the format in writing a letter. The class has decided to ask the students in the school what their favorite dinosaurs are. Students will vote, choosing from several dinosaurs. Ms. Miller uses interactive writing to draft a letter asking the teachers and students in the school to participate. She begins by reviewing the format of a letter, which was introduced previously. The class discusses how to begin the letter with a salutation. Next, Ms. Miller helps the students to compose the text using the digital white board. Students are invited up to assist in writing the text. The class reads the finished letter together. The letter will be typed and distributed to each classroom and posted to the teacher's classroom websites.

In this week's writing activity, students will write informational stories about dinosaurs. Ms. Miller asks each student to select his or her favorite dinosaur and write a story that includes as many facts about it as possible. To decide on the dinosaurs they want to write about, students brainstorm. They also share what they already know from the books they have read and that have been read to them. As Ms. Miller moves around the room, seeing if anyone needs help, students conduct a quick Internet search to begin seeking facts. Tomorrow, they will learn more about the format of the story. After the activity has been completed at the end of the week, Ms. Miller will create a class book by combining the students' illustrated informational stories (W).

12:20—Lunch/Play/Independent Reading   If the weather allows it, students play outside and, if not, they play in the gym or the classroom. Fifteen minutes are left for independent reading and the students select from a number of books about dinosaurs like informational books, narrative pieces, a poetry book, craft book, and alphabet book.

Ms. Miller knows that it is good for children to explore with easy and difficult material and she is not concerned with the reading levels of the books. Each student has a weekly chart to fill in the book he or she is reading and to note what he or she does and does not like about it. Children put these charts on the bulletin board.

1:00—Math   A specific math curriculum is followed in Ms. Miller's class and she has embedded a language arts dinosaur activity into today's math lesson

The class refers back to their list of dinosaurs from the morning message and put up pictures of them they used earlier. After reviewing the list of dinosaurs, children vote for their favorites; one student records the votes using tally marks for counting. Six dinosaurs receive the most votes—Allosaurus, Iguanodon, Spinosaurus, Stegosaurus, Triceratops, and Tyrannosaurus—and Ms. Miller circles their names with a red marker.

1:45—Special Theme Activity   Ms. Miller has planned a themed art activity that the class will participate in during the week. The activity is to begin a mural that everyone will contribute to and that will act as a habitat or environment for the dinosaur sculptures the children will create. To introduce the activity, Ms. Miller explains the details while all of the students listen. They talk about the pieces of the mural they would like to work on, such as trees and vines, a cave a river, plants, and dinosaurs. Ms. Miller writes each child's name on a chart with the item he or she will draw on the mural.

One-third of the students remain on the carpet to work on the mural. The rest of the students use this time to complete unfinished journal writing, or center work. If they have completed all of their work, they can select any center activity they wish. This is a playful time of the day, when children use blocks, engage in dramatic play, and art, as well as explore in the science area, and look at books.

The students who are working on the mural search the internet and through books that depict plants, trees, and other elements from the time of the dinosaurs. Animated discussions take place as the children focus on drawing food, shelter, water, lakes, trees, bushes, caves, and other elements necessary to sustain dinosaur life (RI).

2:25—Art, Music, and Gym   At this time on different days, the class goes to a special teacher for art, music, or gym. Ms. Miller has coordinated with these teachers to address the theme being studied, so the art teacher has children making clay dinosaur sculptures, the music teacher has children sing some dinosaur songs (including one about habitats), and the gym teacher has students perform movement activities in which they walk and run like dinosaurs.

2:45—WRAP Up   At the end of the day students clean up the classroom and gather in the meeting area for WRAP Up time and a read-aloud. Today, Ms. Miller has chosen a poem called "I'm a Mean Old Dinosaur" (Pruett, 1991) and has displayed it on the digital white board. Ms. Miller reads the poem to the class and tracks the print with a pointer. First, the students echo read the poem and then do a choral read. Ms. Miller asks questions like "Why do you think the dinosaur may be sad?" One child said because he is hungry, another said because he is tired, another said maybe he hurt himself, and still another said, he can't find his family. Before they leave she asks them what the three most important things they read were and Ms. Miller writes the student answers on the "Important Things I Learned Today" Chart. Some of the answers include "facts about dinosaurs," "when I partner read I read better than when I read alone," "how to write a letter."

Tuesday

8:30—Do Now   The children come in and do their jobs and partner reading.

8:45—Word Work   Today the teacher follows the word work program.

9:10—Vocabulary Morning Message   Because today starts the new month of November, the Ms. Miller has the class echo read a poem called "November," from *Chicken Soup with Rice* (Sendak, 1962) (RL, RF). Ms. Miller has written the poem on chart paper. The children will illustrate personal copies of this poem and their work will be placed in their "Poem Books" along with other poems used throughout the year. Then, a vocabulary lesson takes place using tier 1 and tier 2 first grade words.

9:45—Comprehension Reading Workshop   The shared reading is an informational book called *Dinosaurs, Dinosaurs* (Barton, 1995). Together, Ms. Miller and the children talk about the title, author, and illustrations (RI). Ms. Miller shows the class a few of the pictures in the book, and they discuss what they think they will learn from the book. Ms. Miller tells the children that *Dinosaurs, Dinosaurs* has many difficult vocabulary words which makes the text complicated. This book is a bit above the first-grade level, but Ms. Miller has chosen to read it because one of her goals is to build vocabulary and enhance knowledge and teach the children that they can deal with complex text since she will do a lot of scaffolding to help them understand. (RI, L). During the reading, Ms. Miller stops to point out several new words, but she waits until finishing the book to discuss them. Some of the difficult words in the story include *armored plates, carnivore, habitat,* and *extinct.* Ms. Miller writes these words on the board and has also made copies from the book for each child in which these words appear. She then asks the children to partner read the paragraph and to circle words they didn't know. After reading, children ask questions which are answered by the teacher or another child. The teacher echo reads the paragraph with the children and then tells them to read it again with their partner. After the echo reading, it becomes clear that the children comprehend the text. There is one more reading and that is done chorally and almost every child can read the difficult passage and understands the new vocabulary.

10:30—Center Activities   The center activities are the same today as on Monday. Center assignments can be seen on the center board. Ms. Miller is ready to take her first reading group.

Small-Group Guided Reading   With her students engaged in center work, Ms. Miller calls her first group to the instruction table. This group is reviewing long and short vowels (RF). Each student is given a card that contains words with long and short vowels and asked to classify the words into two lists. In addition, the children write their own long and short vowel words on sticky notes and post them on the correct list. Ms. Miller asks the students if they can think of dinosaur words that have long and short vowels. One child says, "The *spikes* on their back, which is a long *i*." A second child adds, "Some are *big* and some are *huge*, and that is a short *i* in *big* and a long *u* in *huge*." Students are told to look in magazines and newspapers for words with long and short vowels and to cut out and paste the words in their word study notebooks.

Ms. Miller takes notes regarding individual students' progress with this task. Most of the students in this group are English language learners. Ms. Miller also works on students' oral language and vocabulary development in this small-group instruction session.

The second reading group has just begun studying patterns of short vowels at the ends of words (called *rimes*): -*ag*, -*at*, and -*an*. First, they work with word–picture card sorts. On the card, there is a guideword and picture at the top of each column and then words and pictures to sort into the columns. The guidewords are *bag* for the -*ag* rime, *pan* for the -*an* rime, and *hat* for the -*at* rime.

After the sorts, the children write one word for each rime, and then they do a word-building activity. Using cards, students build words using the three vowel rimes and several initial consonants. Ms. Miller models the activity: To create the word *bag*, she uses the initial consonant *b* card and the word-ending card -*ag*. She then leads students in changing the initial consonant card to create other -*ag* words. The children work on building -*ag*, -*at*, and -*an* words and then write them down.

The last activity for this group is to look in the book they are reading to find words with the same rimes. Students look for -*ag*, -*at*, and -*an* words and write them down.

The last group Ms. Miller will see today is working on reading color words by sight. The book Ms. Miller has selected for them is *Colors at the Zoo* (Henderson, 1988). Because three colors begin with the letter *b*—*blue*, *brown*, and *black*—Ms. Miller discusses with the children the need to look at the ends of the words carefully to distinguish among these colors.

The class takes a short picture walk through the book, identifying the colors that are named and discover there are eight. Ms. Miller asks the children to echo read the book with her one line at a time. When she comes to a color word, she pauses and lets the children fill it in.

After finishing the story, the class writes the color names on a chart. Then Ms. Miller gives each child eight cards containing color words. On one side of the card, the word is written in the color it represents, and on the other side of the card, the color name is written in black. The children read their cards to each other, first using the colored cards and then using the cards with the words written in black. To conclude the lesson, students write the words in their journals.

11: 20—Snack/Play/Writing Workshop   Yesterday, Ms. Miller introduced the writing activity for the week: Writing a factual story about a favorite dinosaur. Ms. Miller wants the children to each select a different dinosaur so the class reviews who is going to write about which dinosaur. After each child selects a dinosaur, Ms. Miller shares an example of a factual story she wrote. There are five pages to her story: a title page with the author's name, copyright date, and publisher with a small illustration; page two shows the name of the dinosaur with a student-drawn dinosaur picture; page 3 illustrates what the dinosaur eats; page 4 is another fact about the dinosaur; and page 5 is something that the child makes up about the dinosaur. On Ms. Miller's last page she wrote "I don't want to meet this dinosaur unless he is in a zoo since he is so dangerous." Ms. Miller also provides reference books to consult and the children have access to the Internet.

Today the children do the first page which is a picture of the dinosaur and a sentence that says his name, such as *this is a dinosaur and he is called a stegosaurus*. This project will take the rest of the week to complete (W, RI).

12:20—Play/Lunch/Independent Reading   Ms. Miller has collected enough tablets so that each student can select a book from the school's e-book collection.

1:00—Math   The children are interested in how tall and how short the different dinosaurs are. Ms. Miller finds these facts in the book *Visual Dictionary of Prehistoric Life* (Midgley, 1995). Children locate their dinosaur in the book and write down their height Ms. Miller makes a bar graph for the class to see the dinosaurs in order of height—from tallest to the shortest. She continues with the regular math curriculum.

1:45—Theme-Related Center Time   Ms. Miller calls her second mural group to help with this activity and with building the dinosaur habitat. Other students, complete unfinished center activities from the morning and go to other centers when they are done. Ms. Miller takes a quick look at centers in the room and sees children in the themed restaurant, now called The Dinosaur Den. Children are taking orders for dinosaur pizza, dinosaur burgers, and dinosaur drinks. In the block center, a group continues to work on a dinosaur zoo. They are using different-sized blocks to create spaces for the plastic dinosaurs. Students role-play a fight between a Stegosaurus and a Triceratops. The children decide that these two dinosaurs must be housed in two separate spaces in the zoo.

2:25—Art   Ms. Miller accompanies the children to art to see their progress in making their clay dinosaurs. The art teacher discusses painting their dinosaurs. The first coat of paint is to cover the entire sculpture. Next time they would decorate them.

2:45—WRAP Up   For today's shared reading, Ms. Miller has selected *Mary Anning and the Sea Dragon* (Atkins, 1999), a biography about a young girl who is one of the first female paleontologists. This is difficult but Ms. Miller's students like hearing new words and remember them well.

After Ms. Miller reads the book, the students talk about all of the different kinds of work that Mary Anning did as a paleontologist and if any of the students would like her job when they grow up. The discussion continues for a few minutes with the children taking turns listening and speaking Before leaving for the day, they write down three reading or writing activities they liked the most and put them on the chart.

Wednesday: The Dinosaur Unit Is in Full Swing

8:30—Do Now   Journal writing about their favorite dinosaur book so far.

8:45—Word Work

9:10—Vocabulary Morning Message   Since lots of new vocabulary has been introduced this week during Vocabulary Morning Message, the children make up a message using several of the new words that are on the word wall.

9:45—Comprehension Reading Workshop   Ms. Miller reads a poem called "I'm a Mean Old Dinosaur" (Pruett, 1991). The poem is at beginning-second-grade level in terms of difficulty. Ms. Miller has written the poem on chart paper, and as the children echo read it with her. Ms. Miller She uses a pointer to help the children follow the words from left to right across the page. Repeating difficult text, with echo, choral reading, and repeated reading provides the support children need to meet the challenge posed by this poem.

Reading a poem is a good opportunity to look at the punctuation at the ends of sentences and discuss how it is different than in a story. The children use highlighter tape to identify the periods and questions marks in the poem and converse:.

> *Ms. Miller:*   Let's put magic tape on the end marks, or punctuation at the ends of the sentences, so we can see them really well."
>
> *Student 1:*   There shouldn't be a period here and there is.
>
> *Ms. Miller:*   No period? Isn't there supposed to be a period at the end of a sentence?
>
> *Student 2:*   That's not the end of the sentence.
>
> *Ms. Miller:*   It's not? Where does it end?
>
> *Student 3:*   Maybe the next page?

When Ms. Miller turns the next page, the class discovers that the period is there. After putting highlighter tape on the end-of-sentence marks for the entire poem, the class comes to the consensus that one line of words is not necessarily a sentence. Ms. Miller models how a reader drops his or her tone of voice and stops at a period. Now the class choral reads the poem and uses the punctuation to determine their expression The books for partner reading are all poetry books. After reading the class discusses how poetry is different from prose.

10:30—Center Work   Ms. Miller reviews children's assignments for center activities before they go to work. The centers have not changed. Ms. Miller has students' family members help in class on a regular basis. Today, a grandfather will help students with ideas, spelling and punctuation in their informational stories about dinosaurs.

Small-Group Guided Reading   Ms. Miller has noticed that most of the children in one of her reading groups have not participated in the shared reading of "I'm a Mean Old Dinosaur" (Pruett, 1991). Therefore, she repeats the activity in their small-group meeting. First, she uses the word chart, and echo reads the text with them, pointing to the words as they read. After echo reading, the group choral reads the poem.

Evidence from the running records Ms. Miller has done over the past week indicates that the children in the second reading group are ready for longer and more difficult books. Ms. Miller begins by introducing the new book she has selected. Then she reads it aloud to the children as they follow along, and then she has them whisper read together. This type of scaffolding provides children with the confidence and support they need to read alone.

Ms. Miller's next group to enhance reading comprehension retell the story. One of the children begins the retelling, another child continues it, and another finishes the story. Then Ms. Miller asks each child to write a summary of the story. She tells them that the first sentence is to begin the story; the second sentence is to tell about the characters; the third sentence it to be about the character's problem; and the last sentence is to tell how the problem is solved.

11:20—Snack and Play

11:35—Writing Workshop   Ms. Miller's students have written the first page of their factual stories, now they will draft the rest. To help her writers, Ms. Miller has chosen three topics to focus on in today's lesson. The topics include (1) beginning a story, (2) presenting facts, and (3) illustrating the text. Ms. Miller distributes a guide to help the children with this mini-lesson. The guide has three spaces, each of which corresponds to one of the topics related to writing. Space 1 is for beginning the story, space 2 is for presenting facts about dinosaurs, and space 3 is for an illustration. Children are asked to take what they have already written and fit it into these three spaces. The children begin to draft their facts for their story. The teacher conferences with those she knows need some help and, at the end of this time, they report out on their progress.

12:20—Play/Lunch/Independent Reading   Today, children select narrative literature to read since they have been reading a lot of informational text.

1:00—Math   Ms. Miller made a bar graph to illustrate the heights of favorite dinosaurs: Allosaurus, Iguanodon, Spinosaurus, Stegosaurus, Triceratops, and Tyrannosaurus. Today, she distributes copies of the graph and asks the children to color the six bars six different colors so they can see the differences in height clearly. Looking at the different-colored bars, children compare their favorite dinosaurs. Ms. Miller encourages conversation, which results in a good exchange of ideas. Then, the regular math curriculum continues.

1:45—Theme-Related Centers   The children work in different centers. The third group works on the dinosaur mural and habitat.

2:25—Art   Children go to art to decorate their clay dinosaurs and the teacher will put them in the kiln to bake.

2:45—WRAP Up   The read-aloud book that Ms. Miller has selected for Wednesday is *Patrick's Dinosaurs* (Carrick, 1985). In this story a boy imagines that he sees dinosaurs everywhere after a visit to the zoo. It is a nice change to have a narrative book about dinosaurs that isn't factual.

After Ms. Miller reads to the students, she asks them to make connections between themselves and the story. Many of them recall times when they imagined that they saw something that was not really there. Ms. Miller guides the conversation, comparing this book to others they have heard or read that weren't about dinosaurs. Students made many connections, and Ms. Miller asks them to provide evidence from the text.

Thursday

8:30—Do Now   Children partner read whatever they would like.

8:45—Word Work   Ms. Miller uses the word work program.

9:10—Vocabulary Morning Message   Tiered words are worked on today.

9:45—Comprehension Reading Workshop   The read aloud for today is *Dinosaurs, Dinosaurs* (Barton, 1989). The class focuses on finding facts in this informational text, and the characteristics of the text. She tells the children that the types of books they have been reading are called *nonfiction and informational books.* They are books about real people, animals, and things that happen.

After reading to the class, Ms. Miller asks, "How can you tell that *Dinosaurs, Dinosaurs* is an informational book?"

Student 1: There aren't characters that have a story to tell.

Student 2: It is about real things.

Student 3: It teaches us things.

Student 4: It has a table of contents and a glossary and an index.

After the discussion, Ms. Miller makes a web that includes the facts students found in the text. She draws a circle on a piece of chartpaper and writes the word *Dinosaurs* in the center. She draws lines radiating out from the larger circle and adds smaller circles at the ends of the lines. As each new fact is identified, Ms. Miller records it in one of the small circles. When students are finished, they review new dinosaur facts on their web: "baby dinosaurs come from eggs laid by their mothers," "baby dinosaurs are very little for animals that grow so big," "spikes on the backs and tails of some dinosaurs were used as weapons."

The children look up dinosaur facts and report on their findings.

10:30—Centwer Activities   Centers are the same. Children go to their designated places.

Small-Group Guided Reading   Ms. Miller meets with her first group, which continues to work on ending word chunks that rhyme. Ms. Miller selects the word *cat* and asks the children to think of words that have the same *-a* chunk. The children suggest the words *mat, fat, rat, pat, hat, bat, nat, sat,* and *cat,* and she writes them down on the chart.

Next, Ms. Miller writes these two sentences on a sheet of chartpaper:

I like Pat.   He is a nice cat.

She asks the children to think of another sentence that can follow *I like Pat* and that end with a word using the same *at* chunk. The children think of two more sentences, which Ms. Miller adds to the chartpaper:

I like Pat.   He is a nice cat.

I like Pat.   He has a bat.

I like Pat.   He has a rat.

The book this group is reading has words with the *-at* pattern throughout. The children use cards to build words with consonant onsets and ending chunks. They build words with the consonants and the *-at, -an,* and *-ag* endings, and then they find words with these endings in their reading book (RF).

Next, Ms. Miller meets with her second group. They are reading *Things That Go* (Mayes, 2002). Ms. Miller is still working with this group on figuring out unknown words by looking at the letters in the word and the meaning of the sentence. The class reads through the book again, playing the game Guess the Covered Word. Ms. Miller had recorded the sentences in the book on a chart during the first reading. She tracks the print from left to right and covers up a word for students to figure out. The students read the sentence together and then go back to identify the covered word. They predict by using the context of the sentence, and then they look closely at the word to see if the letters in it match their prediction. By now, the children are quite good with this strategy, which is helping them become independent readers.

With the next group, Ms. Miller reads the story *Dinosaur's Day* (Thomson, 2000) for the second time. After her reading, the children collaborate to find facts about dinosaurs. They put a sticky note next to every fact they find about Triceratops and Tyrannosaurs, and then each student copies the facts on a sheet of paper. After writing, the children share their facts with each other. They are finding it hard to find new facts since they have found so many already.

11:20—Snack and Play

11:35—*Writing Workshop*   The children have worked on their dinosaur stories throughout the week. Ms. Miller has discussed adding enough space between words; the right amount is two finger spaces between each pair of words. She has also discussed how using the word wall can help with children's spelling. Ms. Miller circulates assisting children as they put the finishing touches on their stories.

Ms. Miller provides time for children to share their stories. Here is one typical story, which includes four facts about the dinosaur (W, L):

> My dinosaur is a T-Rex
> T-Rex is 35 feet tall and he was grey.
> He was a meat eater.
> He was mean and very scary.

Because of the modeling that Ms. Miller has provided, students comment about each other's work: "I noticed that you have a lot of detail in your sentences" and "You did such a good job in getting a lot of facts to write down."

Students spend most of Writing Workshop illustrating their completed informational stories. The children refer to their dinosaur book collection to help them with their pictures (W). A copy of all of the dinosaur books is made into a big bound book using a computer program. The book is also put on to the class website. Each child keeps his/her original copy.

12:20—*Play-Lunch-Independent Reading*   The children read poems about dinosaurs.

1:00—*Math*   The regular math curriculum continues.

1:45—*Theme-Related Activities*   Many of the projects that Ms. Miller's students are working on were started earlier in the week, and now, they are putting the finishing touches on these projects. Some children are counting votes to figure out the favorite dinosaurs for the entire student body another group of children are adding details such as vines, plants, and trees on the mural habitat, where they will display their dinosaur sculptures.

2:25—*Music*   The children had learned some songs about dinosaurs in their classroom and the music teacher practices with them for the dinosaur celebration they will have.

2:45—*WRAP Up*   For today's shared book reading, Ms. Miller has selected the informational book *How Big Were the Dinosaurs?* (Most, 1994). After reading the book, she asks the children whether the book is informational or fiction. Here are some responses:

Student 1: I think it was make-believe, because the pictures are drawings. If it was an informational book, there would be photographs that we take with cameras.

Student 2: But they can't have real pictures, because dinosaurs are extinct, they are all dead.

Student 3: Every page taught us about a different dinosaur.

Student 4: Yeah. There was no story. It was all things about dinosaur information.

The children agree it was an informational book. Before they left their classroom they write down the three most important things they did that included reading and writing.

Friday

8:30—Do Now   The children write about their favorite things they have read or written during journal writing. If students have unfinished work, then they do this instead of journaling.

8:45—Word Work   Ms. Miller makes a list of the dinosaur words discussed during the week and the children look for words that demonstrate the vowel rules on which they had been working. They found the short vowel rule in the word fossil twice, *when a vowel is surrounded by two consonants the vowel is short, fos and sill.* They find that the word *spike* had the silent *e rule,* that is, when there are two vowels in a word and one is an e at the end, the first vowel is long and the e is silent. They also find that *meat* used the rule *when two vowels go walking the first one does the talking.*

9:10—Vocabulary Morning Message   At today's morning meeting, Ms. Miller spends time reviewing the activities done during the week. The class choral read "I'm a Mean Old Dinosaur" (Pruett, 1991), and students identify the words that rhyme.

Ms. Miller brings back the book *Dinosaurs, Dinosaurs* (Barton, 1989) and, after reviewing the facts, the class echo reads a small portion of this informational text.

Next, they revisit the words on the word wall. They count 17 new words related to dinosaurs like *spikes, extinct, horn, crest, Jurassic, beak, armor, graze, migrate, camouflage,* and *habitat.* The children select words to create and share a sentence.

9:45—Comprehension Reading Workshop   Ms. Miller brought several narrative and illustrated books by Jane Yolan and Mark Teagues from their series about dinosaurs to use in class today. An example title is *How do dinosaurs say goodnight?* She starts the lesson by introducing one of the books to the children and asking the students to think about how these books are different from other books *Discovering Dinosaurs,* and *Dinosaur Days.*

After the story there was a discussion:

Student 1: This was silly and our other books had facts.

Student 2: They both have drawings of dinosaurs but his is kind of a cartoon of a dinosaur and in the other books they look like the real animals.

Student 3: This book rhymes. We read poems that rhyme but not books.

Student 4: I liked it. It was fun and it seems like it is easy to read.

Ms. Miller agrees that all their answers were correct and now they could partner read their books and come back remembering one thing about the main idea of the story. By the end of the lesson, they are all laughing and wanting to borrow the other dinosaur books.

10:30—Center Activities   Same centers activities as previously discussed.

Small-Group Guided Reading   Ms. Miller assesses her students' progress and reviews the work each group has completed.

Her first group reviews the initial consonant digraphs *ch, sh,* and *ph* this week. She asks each student to make a simple three-column chart with *ch, sh,* and *ph* in one of each of the columns. As Ms. Miller shows the class the picture cards, each student writes a word that begins with sh such as *shell.* This continues for each letter. Some students are still having trouble with the digraphs so Ms. Miller records that more work will be needed in this area.

With the next group of students, Ms. Miller checks on their ability to use the cloze procedure. With this procedure, the teacher covers some words in a few sentences and asks each child to predict the covered words based on the meanings of the sentences and the initial letter.

When Ms. Miller meets with the third group, she works on comprehension. She asks the children to retell the story they were reading.

11:20—Snack and Play

11:35—Writing Workshop   Before binding the students' factual stories into a class book, they all discuss a book title. Ms. Miller tells the children that a good title helps readers predict what the book will be about and she shows the class a book about dinosaurs and asks if *The Elephants Went Walking* is a good title. After the children stop giggling, they agree that, because the book is about dinosaurs, the title has to be about dinosaurs. Students mention three titles for the book and Ms. Miller writes them down. A vote is held and the title with the most votes is *Dinosaur Information Stories.* Ms. Miller adds this title to the cover and binds the class book.

12:20—Lunch/Play/Independent Reading

1:00—Math   So that other students and teachers can see the results of the "Favorite Dinosaur" contest, Ms. Miller's students display the bar graphs they colored around the school.

1:45—Theme Related Language Arts   The children choose centers on which to work and, during this time, each one comes to the habitat mural they made to place their clay dinosaurs. This display is on the windowsill, and the mural students painted is hanging over the window. Now that the habitat is complete, the students discuss and admire their work (SL).

> **Student 1:** I really like the dinosaurs. Everyone's is so different from the others.
>
> **Student 2:** I like how the carnivores are where they can find their food, and the vegetarians are by the plants. It's good we did this together! It couldn't be done alone! (L).

2:25—Gym   Since the special teachers work with the classroom teachers, the physical education teacher had the students play dinosaur dodge ball.

2:45—WRAP Up   Instead of having a new read-aloud on Friday afternoons, Ms. Miller's class choral read poems they have collected in a three-ring binder. Today, students chant poems from the past week and from other weeks, as well.

Today is the end of a busy week. Before the children leave, Ms. Miller takes time to reflect on what they have accomplished in the morning meetings, small-group reading instruction, Writing Workshop, math, art, play, and themed center time. In the week ahead, the students will continue working on dinosaurs and will invite other classes to see their dinosaur display and hear stories and poems.

Ms. Miller's first-graders receive intentional, explicit instruction and also have opportunities to explore and experiment. They have some choices in selecting activities but are also expected to complete designated work. Because Ms. Miller is well organized, the day is carefully planned out but allows for some self-direction with little or no time wasted (McGee & Morrow, 2005).

In Ms. Miller's classroom, large amounts of information are introduced, repeated, and reviewed. Attending to individual needs is an important part of her instruction, as well as integrating literacy development into the content area subjects. Using this approach, Ms. Miller is teaching reading, writing, listening, and speaking all day using the CCSS.

REFERENCES

Cunningham, P. M., Hall, D. P., & Sigmon, C. M. (1999). *The teacher's guide to the four blocks, grades 1–3: A multimethod, multilevel framework for grades 1–3.* Greensboro, NC: Carson-Dellosa.

Duke, N. K. (2000). 3.6 minutes per day: The scarcity of informational texts in first grade. *Reading Research Quarterly, 35,* 202–224.

Hiebert, E. H. (1999). Text matters in learning to read (Distinguished Educators Series). *The Reading Teacher, 52,* 552–568.

McGee, L., & Morrow, L. M. (2005) *Teaching literacy in kindergarten.* New York, NY: Guilford Press.

Morgan, A., Wilcox, B. R., & Eldredge, J. L. (2000). Effect of difficulty levels on second-grade delayed readers using dyad reading. *Journal of Educational Research, 94,* 113–119.

National Governors Association Center for Best Practices & Council of Chief State School Officers (NGA & CCSSO). (2010). *Common Core State Standards.* Washington, DC: Authors. Retrieved from www.corestandards.org/assets/CCSSI_ELA%20Standards.pdf,

National Reading Panel (NRP). (2000). *Teaching children to read: Report of the subgroups.* Washington, DC: U.S. Department of Health and Human Services, National Institutes of Health.

Pinnell, G. S., & Fountas, I. C. (1996). *Guided reading: Good first teaching for all children.* Portsmouth, NH: Heinemann.

Shanahan, T., & Shanahan, C. (2012). What is disciplinary literacy and why does it matter? *Topics in Language Disorders, 32,* 1–12.

CHILDREN'S LITERATURE CITED

Atkins, J. (1999). *Mary Anning and the sea dragon.* Madeira Park, BC: Douglas & McIntyre.

Barton, B. (1989). *Dinosaurs, dinosaurs.* New York, NY: Scott, Foresman.

Carrick, C. (1983). *Patrick's dinosaurs.* New York, NY: Clarion Books.

Dixon, Dougal. (2000) *Amazing Dinosaurs the fiercest, the tallest, the toughest, the smallest.* Honesdayle, PA: Boyds Mills Press.

Henderson, P. (1998). *Colors at the zoo.* New York, NY: Sadlier-Oxford.

Mayes, K. (2002). *Things that go.* Boston, MA: Sundance.

Midgley, E. R. (1995). *Visual dictionary of prehistoric life.* New York, NY: Dorling Kindersley.

Most, B. (1994). *How big were the dinosaurs?* New York, NY: Harcourt Brace.

Pruett, D. (1991). "I'm a mean old dinosaur." In *Dinosaurs.* Monterey, CA: Evan-Moor.

Sendak, M. (1962). *Chicken soup with rice.* New York, NY: Scholastic.

Sloan, P., & Sloan, S. (1994). *We went to the zoo.* Boston, MA: Sundance.

Sloan, P., & Sloan, S. (1996). *Family work and fun.* Boston, MA: Sundance.

Sokoloff, M. (1997). *Discovering dinosaurs.* New York, NY: Sadlier-Oxford.

Stuart, M. (2001). *Who can run fast?* New York, NY: Sadlier-Oxford.

Thomson, R. (2000). *Dinosaur's day.* New York, NY: Dorling Kindersley.

AUDIOBOOKS AND SOFTWARE

Osborne, M. P. (2000). *Dinosaurs before dark* [CD-ROM]. Random House Audio Listening Library. New York, NY: Random House.

DK Publishing. (1996). Dinosaur hunter [CD-ROM]. Eyewitness Virtual Reality Series. New York, NY: DK Multimedia.

ADDITIONAL BOOKS FOR UNIT ON DINOSAURS

Aliki. (1985). *Dinosaurs are different.* New York, NY: HarperCollins.

Barton, B. (1990). *Bones, bones, dinosaur bones.* New York, NY: HarperCollins.

Branley, F. M. (1989). *What happened to the dinosaurs?* New York, NY: HarperCollins.

Brown, D. (2003). *Rare treasure: Mary Anning and her remarkable discoveries.* New York, NY: Houghton Mifflin.

Carrick, C. (1986) *What happened to Patrick's dinosaurs*? New York, NY: Clarion.

Cohen, D. (n.d.). Discovering Dinosaurs Series. Bridgestone Science Library. North Mankato, MN: Capstone Press.

Cole, J. (1995). *The magic school bus in the time of the dinosaurs.* New York, NY: Scholastic.

Dussling, J. (2000). *Dinosaur eggs.* New York, NY: Scholastic.

Hennessy, B. G. (1990). *The dinosaur who lived in my backyard* (S. Davis, illus.). New York, NY: Puffin.

Joyce, W. (1995). *Dinosaur Bob and his adventures with the family Lazardoro.* New York, NY: Laura Geringer.

Lindsay, W. (1988). *On the trail of incredible dinosaurs.* New York, NY: Dorling Kindersley.

MacLeod, E. (2001). *What did dinosaurs eat? And other things you want to know about dinosaurs.* Toronto, ON: Kids Can Press.

Matthews, R. (n.d.). Heinemann First Library Series. North Mankato, MN: Captone Press.

Moss, J. (1997). *Bone poems.* New York, NY: Workman.

Most, B. (1978). *If the dinosaurs came back.* New York, NY: Harcourt Brace.

Most, B. (1984). *Whatever happened to the dinosaurs*? New York, NY: Harcourt Brace.

Most, B. (1991). *Dinosaur named after me.* New York, NY: Harcourt Brace.

Simpson, J. (1996). *Mighty dinosaurs.* New York, NY: Time-Life.

Taylor, P. (1990). *Fossil.* New York, NY: Dorling Kindersley.

Yolen, J. (2000). *How do dinosaurs say goodnight?* New York, NY: Scholastic.

Wahl, J. (2000). *The field mouse and the dinosaur named Sue.* New York, NY: Cartwheel Books.

Whitfield, P. (1992). *Children's guide to dinosaurs and other prehistoric animals.* New York, NY: Simon & Schuster.

Wilkes, A. (1994). *Big book of dinosaurs: First book for young children.* New York, NY: Dorling Kindersley.

Index

Note: Page numbers with *t* indicate tables; those with *f* indicate figures.

Interior Credits: **Introduction Chapter:** Pearson Education; p. 6 (quote), p. 7 (Standard), p. 8 (TI.1), p. 10 (FI.1 Standards), p. 17 (T1.1), p. 18 (T1.2, **Standard), p. 20 (T1.3, Standard), p. 22 (T1.4, Standard), p. 24 (T1.5, Standard), p. 25 (T1.6, Standard), p. 28 (T1.7) p. 29 (Standard), p. 31 (T1.8, Standard), p. 34 (T1.9, Standard), p. 37 (T1.10, Standard), p. 40 (T1.11, Standard), p. 48 (T2.1, Standard), p. 49 (Standard), p. 51 (Standard), p. 53 (T2.2), p. 54 (Standard), p. 56 (T2.3), p. 58 (Standard), p. 60 (Standard), p. 63 (T2.4, Standard), p. 73 (T3.1, Standard), p. 75 (T3.2), p. 78 (Standard), p. 80 (T3.3, Standard), p. 82 (T3.4), p. 84 (Standard), p. 86 (T3.5, Standard), p. 87 (T3.6), p. 88 (Standard), p. 89 (T3.7), p. 90 (Standard), p. 91 (T3.8, Standard), p. 93 (T9.3), p. 94 (Standard), p. 104 (T4.1, Standard), p. 107 (T4.2, Standard), p. 109 (T4.3, Standard), p. 112 (T4.4, Standard), p. 114 (T4.5, Standard), p. 116 (T4.6, Standard), p. 119 (T4.7, Standard), p. 121 (T4.8, Standard), p. 123 (T4.9, Standard), p. 126 (T4.10, Standard), p. 136 (T5.1, Standard), p. 140 (T5.2, Standard), p. 144 (T5.3, Standard), p. 146 (T5.4, Standard), p. 148 (T5.5, Standard), p. 150 (T5.6, Standard), p. 153 (T5.7, Standard), p. 156 (T5.8, Standard), p. 164–168 (Standards), p. 173 (bullet list)** © Copyright 2010. National Governors Association Center for Best Practices and Council of Chief State School Officers All rights reserved; **p. 13 (URL)** Partnership for Assessment of Readiness for College and Careers (PARCC). © Achieve, Inc; **p. 13 (URL)** Smarter Balanced Consortium; **p. 19 (lyrics)** Reprinted by permission from John Farrell, Rock 'n Roll for Mother Earth. Published by Hope River Music. Copyright © 2010 by Hope River Music; **p. 128 (bullet list)** Based on Brophy, Jere. (1987). On Motivating Students. East Lansing, MI: Institute for Research on Teaching, Michigan State University. **All material not credited is courtesy of Lesley Mandel Morrow.**